CW00767069

Sentenced to

Sentenced to Everyday Life
Feminism and the Housewife

Lesley Johnson and Justine Lloyd

Oxford • New York

First published in 2004 by
Berg
Editorial offices:
1st Floor, Angel Court, 81 St Clements Street, Oxford, OX4 1AW, UK
175 Fifth Avenue, New York, NY 10010, USA

Berg is the imprint of Oxford International Publishers Ltd.

Library of Congress Cataloguing-in-Publication Data
A catalogue record for this book is available from the Library of Congress.

British Library Cataloguing-in-Publication Data
A catalogue record for this book is available from the British Library.

ISBN 1 84520 031 4 (Cloth)
1 84520 032 2 (Paper)

Typeset by Avocet Typeset, Chilton, Aylesbury, Bucks
Printed in the United Kingdom by Biddles Ltd, King's Lynn

www.bergpublishers.com

Contents

List of Figures

Preface and Acknowledgements

This study is part of an increasingly important cross-generational dialogue within feminism. This discussion has revolved around exactly what the domains of work and home might mean to and offer us as women. We contribute to this debate by building on the observation made by many feminist scholars that as feminine as well as feminist subjects, we are 'made up' in different ways depending on our historical and social situations. Our personal desires for and aversions to domesticity have been shaped by moments in feminist activism as much as they have been influenced by the ways in which feminine gender roles changed for Western women in the twentieth century.

While such personal differences can be extrapolated in historical terms, they also reflect the practical considerations of how we might organise our lives taking into account our needs and those of others. For feminists of the baby-boomer generation, denigration of the housewife role in the 1960s and 1970s represented an affirmation of women's role in the workplace and their equality with men. For women born after the feminism of this period, the housewife's role and new interpretations of its meaning offer a different space for the self, one that is not 'sentenced' to everyday life, but actively chosen because it provides for the possibility of a different relationship to work and a work-based identity. Many women are now insisting on the recognition of caring and affective relationships within an identity that goes beyond who they are at work. Whether they are doing so through what some are calling 'third wave feminism' or by apparently turning their back on feminism, women are increasingly wishing to assert the importance of domesticity and child rearing at the same time as they are insisting on their equality with men. Drawing on a mix of cultural studies, sociology, social theory and feminist thought, this book seeks to contribute to this debate in a way that we hope will assist in the revitalisation of feminism and particularly in making it again relevant to the everyday lives of a broad range of women.

We are both daughters and granddaughters of women who spent at least some of their lives defined as 'housewives'. These women created the context for this project to take place, as did so many of their contemporaries. The variety of experience of women in the post-war generation cannot be adequately documented here, and this is not the focus of our book. But this study goes some of the way to accounting for the ways they transformed the notion of home and shaped public awareness of its demands. The claim for a better redistribution of the economy of care made by women in the post-second world war era, which we outline in this book, started, but will not necessarily finish, at home.

The research for this project was funded initially by the Australian Research Council and then subsequently by the University of Technology, Sydney (UTS). We are most grateful for this assistance, and in particular to the University for providing us with the opportunity to undertake this work together. Several people have contributed to the research. We want to pay tribute to Maureen Bark, who very sadly died during the course of the project, but who left behind a detailed and meticulously organised set of materials. Terri McCormack provided valuable assistance along the way, and Margaret Park undertook what turned out to be a far more difficult task than we expected of obtaining permissions for the visual images used in this book. She also assisted with final preparation of the manuscript. The staff of the UTS library, the State Libraries of Victoria and New South Wales and the Australian Archives were enormously helpful in tracking down films, magazines, radio transcripts and other materials. With their great assistance we have collected a wealth of material, only a small proportion of which have we been able to use in the book itself. Craig Archer has been a great help too in various ways during the course of this project with his usual high level of professionalism and good humour. Justine would also like to thank her colleagues at the Department of British and Commonwealth Studies, University of Łódź, for their support during her move there in 2003. Special mention must be made of the efforts of Elżbieta H. Oleksy, as Director of the University's Women's Studies Centre and Dean of the Faculty of International Relations and Politology, and Wieslaw Oleksy of the same Faculty, to provide office space and a computer in order to make the final changes to the manuscript.

Various people have read bits and pieces of the manuscript along the way, and Lesley would particularly like to thank Pauline Johnson and Paula Hamilton. Justine would like to acknowledge comments from and discussions with Wanning Sun, Kirsty McKenzie, Shane Homan, Anna Cole, Fiona Allon and Sylvie Haisman. We are grateful for all their insights and support. Anonymous reviewers for the journals *Feminist Media Studies* and *Environment and Planning D: Society and Space* also provided generous and useful critiques on our arguments and approach. The Ian Potter Foundation and UTS Vice-Chancellor's Travel Fund provided a travel grant in 2001 which enabled Justine to make contact with scholars in Finland, Canada and the USA through conferences and seminars. Her gratitude is extended to Liz Milward and Caitlin Fisher of York University, Toronto, James Hay of University of Illinois, Urbana-Champaign, and Susanna Paasonnen of Turku University, Finland, for their hospitality and intellectual engagement during that trip.

We pay thanks to the various companies who have granted us permission to use the visual images in this book. They are acknowledged separately at appropriate points in the book. We were disappointed that we could only gain approval to use images from two of the Hollywood films we discuss in Chapter 4. We hope our readers will follow up on our analysis to look at all three of the films we discuss in detail, as well as images from some of the others we refer to at other times in the book.

The project commenced in 1996 but we have become increasingly excited by the growing relevance of its concerns in the last few years and are hence keen to have our work out there and read by others. As we came towards the end, Justine's appointment to teach Australian Studies in Poland has meant our collaboration has had to adapt to the demands and possibilities of the globalisation of the academic world. But we both have very much enjoyed and benefited from the partnership and the unique possibilities of such joint authorship. We hope that the readers of this book are able to share in this sense of an open-ended dialogue about the effects and goals of the feminist project that has emerged in our collaboration.

November 2003

–1–

'Only a Housewife'

Once a figure of considerable interest to the popular media in the 1950s, the housewife has received renewed attention in the daily press in recent years, but for very different reasons. In 1996 a debate that began in a major sociology journal between British feminists spilled over into the popular media. Claimed by the press to be a disagreement over whether women can be 'happy housewives', newspaper articles in both Britain and Australia reported on the controversy with a certain amount of relish as a 'falling out' among feminists after British sociologist Catherine Hakim published her controversial article in the *British Journal of Sociology* the previous year.[1] In 2000, an article from *The New York Times*, reprinted in the *Sydney Morning Herald*, reported on a feature article in *Cosmopolitan* which announced that young women were the 'New Housewife Wanna-bes'.[2] In 2002, articles appeared prompted by a new book by British academic James Tooley discussing whether 'thirty-something' women have been misled by feminists into thinking incorrectly that they could 'have a career and an independent life without forgoing motherhood'.[3] And in 2003, feature articles appeared in the Australian press comparing the housewife of 1953 with 'busy mums' of 2003 in the context of a visit to Australia by Hakim.[4] Such newspaper articles explore the extent to which women today prefer full-time employment to 'domesticity' – staying at home to look after their children – as does Hakim's original article and subsequent work.

Other articles have appeared in the Australian press exploring related issues concerned with gender relations and the worlds of home and work. Some have proposed that professional women are achieving success at the expense of their children.[5] Similarly articles discuss reports on whether children are disadvantaged by spending too much time in child care.[6] And talk-back radio explodes whenever the issue is mentioned as women respond justifying their decisions to stay home or go to work when their children are young. In 2002, Virginia Hausseger, an Australian journalist, created a furore in the press when she wrote an article about being failed by 'our feminist mothers'. She blamed her mother's generation for telling 'us we could have it all and carve out brilliant careers without warning young women to listen to their biological clocks'. Rather than questioning the pressures of a workplace culture which makes increasing demands on employees' emotions, as well as their time, she was now angry at her own foolishness in listening to her feminist mothers. She had 'ended up childless', she lamented, because she had failed to take sufficient time to nurture her relationships and partnerships.[7] Meanwhile other reports have emerged, seeming to represent a quite different sense of the *zeitgeist*, that give accounts of how all aspects of one's personal life, for men and women alike, can now be managed with the assistance of professional agencies. These articles suggest that it is now possible to have a nanny to look after your children, a person to clean your house or do your garden, as well as an agency to arrange your social life, your holidays, someone to let the washing-machine repair person to come into the house when you are at work, buy presents for your children and your spouse, and so on.[8] Indeed, lifestyle managers and consultants from companies such as the London-based TimeEnergyNetwork will run your household, co-ordinating all these sub-contractors to undertake your domestic chores.[9] The housewife in this context, with all her caring and household management skills, would appear quite redundant if you have enough money to outsource these tasks.[10]

Underlying these popular representations of the housewife is the question of what it means to be a woman in the modern world. In this book, we are interested in the way feminism since the second world war appears to have had a troubled relationship with the figure of the housewife. We will discuss how feminists today, but more particularly in the early years of second wave feminism, have represented the housewife. This analysis will demonstrate the way in which feminists during the first few decades of second wave feminism constituted 'the housewife' as 'Other' to themselves as they sought to elaborate a speaking position for feminists and the feminist intellectual in particular. We will suggest that the way in which the figure of the housewife was used in these contexts can still be seen today to limit the extent to which feminists of different generations understand each other. And we will argue that such problematic representations continue to curtail feminists' ability to participate effectively in contemporary debates about how modern families can balance family and work life.

In the following chapters we will explore how the figure of the housewife emerged in a number of different contexts in the 1940s and 1950s primarily in Australia. It has long been recognised that histories of modernity need to be sensitive to the particularities of different historical moments as well as specific national trajectories.[11] This does not mean, however, that we will be presenting the Australian experience as insular and unique. On the contrary, much of the materials that we look at are from syndicated magazines and the movies that we look at are American because of their centrality to the Australian cultural experience at the time. As Nava and O'Shea commented in their important study of English modernity, transcultural processes are crucial to the formation of the distinctive histories of modernity in any one country.[12] In tracing the history of the figure of the housewife in the 1940s and 1950s we will be seeking to understand the particular nuances of this history in Australia as a way of providing a more subtle and complex analysis of the pre-history of second wave feminism as a global phenomenon than has been provided to date.

This is no simple history of clear shifts in how the housewife is represented over a period of time; nor does it clearly delineate the subject positions that were made available for women in this period. Instead we look at a range of possible and emergent meanings that can be traced in various settings. Our interest, as we indicated above, is in providing a different history of the housewife than second wave feminism has provided for her to date, and thus to enable a different history to be told of the relationship between feminism and the housewife in the 1960s and 1970s. We argue that the history of the housewife, dominant to date in accounts of the emergence of second wave feminism, has been productive of a particular form of feminist subjectivity. It is that subjectivity which has been in trouble for some time now as the conversation for women between race, generations and classes flounders and the question arises of whether we are in a 'post-feminist age'.[13] We wish to contribute to the continuing conversation about the question of what it means to be a woman in the modern world, but in a way that is more reflective about how these bodies and selves are produced. Feminist subject positions are produced in the very act of writing 'as a feminist' rather than simply existing 'out there' to be represented in writing. At the same time we want to contribute to a clearer understanding of the apparent backlash against feminism in the 1990s, and more recently, both in Australia and internationally.

In this chapter we will look at how contemporary as well as early second wave feminists in Australia, the UK and the USA conceptualise the relationship between work and family life in women's lives. We will then go on to argue for a new history of the figure of the housewife in the 1940s and 1950s which will enable a different understanding of the roots of contemporary feminism, as well as a rethinking of the issues at stake when discussing work and family life. In doing so we will explore the major historical issues that need to be addressed in revising the history of the housewife; in particular, the issues of how we understand modernity, everyday life and boredom. The subsequent chapters will look at a range of different material to explore how the figure of the housewife was understood in the 1940s and 1950s in order to provide the beginnings of such a history. The histories to be developed in different countries will have important variations on the history we provide here of the figure of the housewife in Australia, but we suggest that the implications will be similar to those that we draw from our analysis in terms of the significance of this new understanding of the housewife for contemporary debates about domestic labour and gender roles.

Defining the Housewife: Contemporary Feminism

A major debate, ostensibly concerned with women's participation in the labour market, was initiated by the article mentioned above by Catherine Hakim, titled 'Five Feminist Myths about Women's Employment', published in the *British Journal of Sociology* 1995.[14] A number of feminists replied to her article in the following issue of the same journal. The press in Britain and Australia, as we have seen, reported the controversy as a 'falling out' among feminists and covered it under headlines such as: 'Women at war as feminists rail at happy housewives theory'.[15] Hakim made a number of further interventions, replying to her critics in the same academic journal and in the media.[16] She insisted that the issue rested on the question of whether or not all women 'reject the role of full-time homemaker; that they seek to participate in the labour market on exactly the same basis as men'. She claimed that she had once thought that women would 'flood into wage work on a full-time basis if at all possible' if all the barriers to women's full participation in the workforce were removed, but now she realised that her own research had 'proved me wrong'. She argued that feminists needed to recognise that not all women want to work full-time and, indeed, many do want to stay home. In Australia, *Sydney Morning Herald* columnist and family therapist Bettina Arndt took up the issue with relish, claiming to have talked to a number of Australian feminist scholars who had suffered considerable antagonism from other feminists for similarly arguing that significant numbers of women would prefer to stay at home with their children and be full-time housewives.[17]

Many issues underlie this and subsequent discussion in the media about women and the full-time role of the housewife: women's ambivalence about the 'superwoman' myth, the continuing paucity of adequate and reasonably priced child-care services and the anxieties provoked by contemporary research about the extent to which children need full-time mothering – at least in the first few years of their lives. What these debates do not acknowledge is the extent to which women, particularly in the 1960s and 1970s, were fighting for access to part-time and more flexible working hours rather than simply access to the labour market 'on exactly the same basis as men', to which Hakim refers. But what interests us is the way references to the 'happy housewife myth' were deployed in this argument and how such a heated debate could be provoked by the question of whether women want to be full-time home-makers. The figure of the housewife, whether in these arguments about the contemporary condition of women, or, as we will show, in feminist histories, incites considerable anxiety. Furthermore, the entrance of this figure appears to create difficulties among feminists in sorting out just what issues are at stake in the formation of a gendered self.

Hakim published a book in 2000, *Work–Lifestyle Choices in the 21st Century*, which has contributed to her controversial status among feminists in the UK, the

US and Australia. But what ensured that she would be vilified by feminists in Australia was her selection by the conservative Prime Minister, John Howard, as a favoured expert in his discussions of family policies for the country. Howard is reported by the Australian press as being most impressed by Hakim's work and as adopting her argument that women can be divided into three groups – 'home-centred', 'adaptive' and 'work-centred' – in discussions with his Ministers.[18] Making over-inflated claims to be developing something she calls 'preference theory', Hakim argues that a number of historical changes, common to all developed societies since the 1960s, have made it possible for women to make lifestyle choices about how they wish to handle the demands and opportunities of family and work life. And women, she says, are heterogeneous in how they make these choices. But she then goes on to claim that women can be divided into just three groups according to how they make their choices – those groupings that John Howard has so eagerly latched onto. The largest group, she argues, are those who are 'adaptive'. They want to combine work and family but are not totally committed to a working career and wish to move in and out of the workforce at different times in their lives. Government policy, she argues, favours 'work-centred' women to the detriment of this larger group as well as to the concerns of 'home-centred' women who prefer not to work at all because they make family life and children their main priorities throughout life.

Australian feminists have not necessarily disputed her claim about the groupings of women, but they have been vehement in their dismissal of her claim that government policies systematically favour 'work-centred' women. Anne Summers, for example, argues that research shows that women in Australia at least are united in the belief that government policy should provide better and cheaper child care. She also argues that under the Howard government, family and work-related policies have consistently favoured 'home-centred' mothers, introducing a 'persistent anti-working woman bias into welfare, childcare and taxation policies'.[19]

While some feminists like Summers have challenged Hakim on the accuracy of her generalising claims about government policies, others have disputed her thesis of choice. Joan Williams in the USA context argues that choice is about making decisions within constraints. She argues for a 'reconstructive feminism' that will challenge the way work is organised around an 'ideal of a worker who works full-time and overtime and takes little or no time off for childbearing or child rearing'.[20] She accuses 1970s feminists of making the mistake of pursuing a commodification strategy to deal with the demands of family work, delegating child care to the market. They attacked housework and child caring responsibilities as making women sick and in doing so devalued family work and underestimated the structural changes needed in the world of work for women to gain true equality.[21] Williams suggests that the continuing importance of the ideology and practice of domesticity makes it difficult for feminists to promote the need for changes to the structure of paid work and to the assumptions on which it is based about who the ideal worker is. This ideology arose in the late eighteenth and early nineteenth centuries with the separation of market and family work, particularly among the middle classes as they sought to differentiate themselves as a class.[22] This domesticity did not die; it mutated, she argues. Women as caregivers remain marginalised in the market economy, even though they may have re-entered it, and are cut off from the social roles that offer responsibility and authority in contemporary society. But Williams wants to resist the glorification of paid work that stems from the arguments of 1970s feminists and the associated devaluation of family work. This stance of feminists of the past leads to the defensiveness provoked and articulated by the self-description 'just a housewife' and to an antagonism towards feminism. The alternative to this impasse lies in her notion, mentioned above, of a 'reconstructive feminism' which will focus on changing the conditions under which both men and women work.

Belinda Probert in Australia has also challenged Hakim's arguments about choice and confirms a commitment to the goal of gender equality in the workplace. This agenda has stalled, she argues, not because women have exercised their choices in ways which should require us to question the agenda itself, but because an ideology of domesticity has combined with an unwillingness to focus on the family as a serious object of social policy. Drawing on Williams' work, Probert suggests that this ideology of domesticity 'identifies issues related to care-giving simultaneously as women's issues and as matters that "naturally" belong to the private sphere'. It is an ideology, she suggests, that 'requires women to become mothers and requires mothers to be selfless'. Probert finds evidence of this ideology and its centrality to what she refers to as the gender culture of the 1990s in popular culture as well as in the interviews she and her colleagues have undertaken with contemporary men and women.[23] She argues for a coherent family policy across the traditionally separate portfolios of industrial relations and social security if the pursuit of gender equity in the workplace is to be revitalised. It is policy that is shaping the choices that women make, and, she insists, 'These are not the choices that women want.'[24]

In her concern to promote gender equality in the workplace, Probert asserts that self-actualisation for women is to be found in paid work. Her focus is very much on shifting the role of the state to play a more active role in the care of children so that all women can become full and equal participants in the world of paid work. Williams is more circumspect about placing such an importance on work, speaking instead of women being excluded from the roles in our society which currently offer responsibility and authority and warning of the dangers of provoking an antagonism towards feminism by devaluing family work. But what they both reveal is an ambivalence about or discomfort with the notion of a full-time home-maker or housewife. It is this unease which Hakim's arguments stir and provoke. We are not suggesting that Hakim is right; on the contrary. But we believe that reviewing the history of this ambivalence will help feminists participate in arguments about how to better understand and organise the relationship between family life and work life. In pursuing this understanding, we wish to move beyond existing arguments that propose that women (and men) continue to be led astray by an ideology of domesticity.

Defining the Housewife: Early Second Wave Feminism

Ambivalence, if not antagonism, towards the figure of the housewife can be seen to have a crucial role in the history of second wave feminism. Simone de Beauvoir used the figure of the housewife to encapsulate all that she saw wrong with women's lives. Conjuring up an image of 'the manic housekeeper', she claimed that the housewife wears herself out marking time in the endless repetition of her work and in waging a furious war against dirt and life itself for the rubbish and mess it creates.[25] 'Woman', she declared in *The Second Sex* (1949), 'is doomed to the continuation of the species and the care of the home – that is to say, immanence.'[26] De Beauvoir believed that their engagement in these activities prevents women from achieving or pursuing self-actualisation or self-realisation. The sexual division of labour dooms the 'wife servant' to immanence, whereas marriage for the husband enables a happy synthesis of immanence and transcendence. For man, marriage means a balanced existence in which productive work – through which he is involved in making a future – is combined with activities concerned with the maintenance of existence. Woman, according to de Beauvoir, does not have control over the meaning of her life in her hands; she can only seek to create some sort of dignity out of her vassalage.[27]

Germaine Greer's solution in *The Female Eunuch* (1970) involved women rupturing the circle – defying the compulsion involved in activities like housework and embracing the risk and insecurity implicit in refusing the polarity of masculine–feminine: 'Abandonment of slavery is also banishment of the chimera of security.'[28] She condemned the life of the full-time housewife by characterising her life as one of absolute servitude. Women, she said, 'represent the most oppressed class of life-contracted unpaid workers, for whom slaves is not too melodramatic a description'. Equal pay for equal work, equality of opportunity: these claims are not enough, she predicted, for women will want to revolutionise completely the conditions of work and the opportunities available along the female road to freedom.

In a rather different style of analysis, Ann Oakley in the early 1970s undertook what still probably remains one of the largest scale investigations of housewives. Three books resulted, focusing on different features of what was mostly a sociological project on British housewives. In *Housewife* (1974), she discussed what she referred to as historical and ideological material as well as providing case studies of four contemporary housewives. Thanking her family for the experience of her own oppression as a housewife in the preface to this book, Oakley claimed that most women in modern industrialised societies shared the experience of being a housewife. The primacy of the housewife role in women's lives today, she argued, plays a major part in hampering progress towards sex equality. By the end of her book, she had concluded that the housewife role must be abolished. This, she said, 'follows directly from the kind of work role it is, and would stand whatever the sex of the worker'. 'Housework', she announced, 'is work directly opposed to the possibility of human self-actualization.'[29] But to abolish the housewife role, she added, we will have to abolish the family too as the site in which young girls are prepared for the housewife role and gender roles more generally. Oakley's discussion of the housewife role reflected and made a major contribution to feminist theorising in the 1970s, in which sex role theory and the social division of labour were major preoccupations. Her work was less polemical than de Beauvoir's or Greer's but her conclusions were nonetheless forthright and just as dismissive of the figure of the housewife.

Anne Summers, writing about Australia in *Damned Whores and God's Police* (1975), similarly argued that equality was not enough. The liberation of women, she insisted, entailed the elimination of social and economic differences between people as a means of decentralising power and making self-management possible. Between the two world wars, she claimed, women had accepted the housewife role and their primary definition as mothers and wives. Their lives had been very demanding and a certain social status had been given to their role, in large part due to the campaigns of first wave feminists. After the second world war, women were no longer so prepared to accept this role. The war, Summers suggested, had opened up new opportunities to them, but the housewife's role had also become less demanding with the assistance of new technologies. Many women in the 1950s manifested psychiatric problems such as depression and drug addiction, showing their dissatisfaction with this role and 'the ravaged self' produced by the contradictions and constraints of their lives. But some women had begun to speak out against the ways in which their lives had been so confined; others had simply started to go out to work, and hence in practice, at least, begun to defy the ideological prescriptions about their lives. What was needed, Summers concluded, was a radical renovation not of women themselves, but of the structure of sexism and its supportive institution, the family.[30]

But it is Betty Friedan who is best known as a critic of the figure of the housewife as she emerged after the second world war. Friedan took a less revolutionary stance than some of the early second wave feminists whose arguments we have referred to briefly here, but the impact of her work was profound. It was she who claimed to expose 'the happy housewife myth'. In *The Feminine Mystique* (1963),

Friedan argued that there had been a major shift in the popular media between the 1930s and 1950s. In the 1930s, the heroines of women's magazines at this time were creating a life and identity of their own: the 'new woman' received considerable attention. Mostly such women were career women with 'spirit, courage, independence and determination'. By the 1950s, Friedan claimed, 'career woman' had become a dirty word and 'Occupation housewife' celebrated. The new, happy-housewife heroines were young and content to have their identities defined for them by their husbands' lives.[31]

Women were prepared to accept this depiction of their lives and 'go back home', according to Friedan, because of a crisis in women's identity. Women growing up had no image of their future, of themselves as women. As the solution to this crisis, she proposed that all women should develop life plans, plans which were about their whole life as women, not just one part of it. They should refuse the housewife image and see housework for what it is: work to be done and got out of the way speedily and efficiently, not a career. De Beauvoir had spoken of the need for women to be self-actualising, drawing on existential philosophy. Friedan too spoke in these terms but within the framework of the humanistic psychology of the period and, in particular, the work of identity theorists like Erik Erikson.

Reviewing the 1950s

Accounts of their early involvement in the women's liberation movement of the 1970s by contemporary feminists frequently refer to the importance of Betty Friedan. The stories typically told are of a revelation, of reading *The Feminine Mystique* and realising that they 'were not alone':

> [I] read Betty Friedan's *The Feminine Mystique*, so discovering 'the problem which has no name', and that I had it! I still recall the sense of excitement and revelation I felt, shared by millions of women before and after, when I found myself reading about myself, my own life, discovering that I wasn't alone, there wasn't something wrong with me.[32]

Friedan had written her book 'as a housewife', claiming herself to have also been trapped within the feminine mystique. She deployed this rhetorical strategy as a way of creating an audience for herself – an audience who would recognise themselves in the call to 'we women', women who were now beginning to experience 'the problem that has no name', the stirring of dissatisfaction that she was giving voice to in this book. Contemporary narratives of feminists, writing about the emergence of second wave feminism, frequently take a similar form. These stories speak of Friedan's text as articulating a slow dawning among women of a need to leave behind the housewife's role, to create a new life for themselves as women.

Friedan provided a sense of connection to a wider, shared community and identity, giving women a position from which to speak and act as 'we women' who all share the same problem and needs.

But recent revisionist historiography in the United States has raised a number of new and interesting questions about both Friedan's analysis of the feminine mystique and her own self-representations in this text. Daniel Horowitz, for example, asks why it is that Betty Friedan, a labour journalist and union activist, re-invented herself as a suburban housewife in writing and promoting *The Feminine Mystique*. Her involvement in left politics before she wrote this book, contrary to her own claims, he argues, points to strong connections between the struggle for justice for working women in the 1940s and 1950s and the feminism of the 1960s.[33] Horowitz explains Friedan's apparent wish to repress her past in constituting herself as the frustrated housewife for this book as, at least in part, an understandable desire to avoid the anti-communist attacks of the period in which she was writing. It may, too, he suggests, have arisen from some sort of recognition that the political rhetoric of the old left 'shed little light on the realities of millions of American women'.[34] He draws connections between Friedan's text and the works of William Whyte, Vance Packard and David Riesman, and notes that, 'With them, she assumed that the problem resulted from the struggle to enhance identity',[35] intimating a possible ambition on Friedan's part to produce a book with as much selling power as Packard's *The Hidden Persuaders* by applying to middle-class women the ideas of these authors about middle-class men. Horowitz asks why a woman who had so much experience with political movements turned away from her former persona and focused on what he identifies as adult education and self-realisation strategies, turning a social and political problem into a psychological one. But he is unable to provide a satisfactory answer. This is a question to which we will return. The final and most important point that Horowitz does not acknowledge, however, is that in speaking 'as a housewife' Friedan, as we have noted above, was deploying a powerful rhetorical strategy to constitute an audience for herself.

Joanne Meyerowitz, on the other hand, concentrates on reassessing Friedan's claims that a repressive image of women dominated American mass circulation magazines in the 1950s. The impact of Friedan's book, Meyerowitz argues, can be seen not just in the way in which so many women have testified to the book changing their lives, but more negatively in the way many American historians have adopted her version of post-war ideology. Until recently, Meyerowitz suggests, American historians have represented the 1950s for women as dominated by the conservative promotion of domesticity. Through a careful analysis of a wide selection of American women's magazines between 1946 and 1958, however, Meyerowitz tests Friedan's generalisations and concludes that domestic ideals did not exist in isolation. On the contrary, 'domestic ideals coexisted in ongoing tension with an ethos of individual achievement that celebrated nondomestic activity, individual striving, public service, and public success'.[36] Indeed, these magazines were just as likely to portray domesticity as exhausting and isolating, depicting the discontent of housewives rather than necessarily glorifying their lives. A recent major study of Australian women's magazines in the post-war period supports Meyerowitz's arguments by showing how contested and tension-ridden the dominant images of women were in this period.[37] As Meyerowitz concludes, mass-circulation magazines were depicting domesticity as a problem for women and indicating a tension between public achievement and domesticity in terms not unlike those identified by Friedan herself in *The Feminine Mystique*. The success of this book, Meyerowitz suggests, may have been as much to do with the way it reworked themes already rooted in mass culture as it was to do with the way Friedan countered them with what she claimed to be an oppositional discourse.[38]

On the basis of Meyerowitz's argument and the Australian material referred to briefly above, we want to suggest that, rather than simply articulating the suppressed voice of women, Friedan was constituting what has become a central shibboleth of the feminist past in reinterpreting the women's magazines of the post-war period. The 'happy housewife myth' was not a product of popular culture but itself a myth – a myth of a myth – conjured up by feminism in the attempt to construct a narrative that would make sense of and dispel the sense of contradiction and tension women felt between public achievement and femininity.

In their accounts of the emergence of second wave feminism in the country to date, Australian feminists have certainly frequently reproduced this social myth of the dominance of the housewife ideal in the 1950s, for which Meyerowitz holds Friedan at least in part accountable. Gisela Kaplan, in her history of the Australian women's movement, *The Meagre Harvest* (1996), paints a picture of the experience of growing up, which she, in post-war Berlin, shared with friends born in Australia, in which the 1950s were constrained and prescriptive years for girls and women. But she suggests, 'notwithstanding the mythology of women homemakers', many women who later entered the women's movement also had examples from their childhood from their immediate or extended family of women with working lives that contradicted this mythology.[39] While providing important examples of the prescriptions surrounding women's lives in this period in educational, medical and legal discourses as well as popular culture, Kaplan thus continues to construct the story of the emergence of second wave feminism as a linear narrative of women 'breaking out' or 'leaving home' – of the emergence of an oppositional discourse rejecting the dominant myth of the 'happy housewife', which Meyerowitz's analysis so effectively questions.[40]

The issue, however, is more than one of simply developing a revisionist history of the place of the 1950s in the emergence of contemporary feminism. Such histories as those by Meyerowitz are certainly valuable and interesting for this purpose. But we are more concerned with feminism's continuing attachment to the shibboleth of a feminist prehistory in which women were trapped in a 'happy housewives' myth and with feminism's continuing attachment to a narrative of escape from this myth. We want to analyse the investment of feminism in this narrative of oppression-then-liberation, as it was established by early second wave feminists in accounts of the formation of the contemporary feminist subject.

Feminism and the Subject of Modernity

Betty Friedan's solution to women's entrapment in domesticity, as we have seen, advocated that they develop life plans through which they could define themselves, their identities and their futures. The self-realisation or actualisation she advocated for women involved them making projects out of their lives and their selves. In drawing on identity theorists like Erikson, Friedan presented these claims as if they were necessary to women having a sense of identity at no matter what point in history. Tamara Hareven, in her book *Family Time and Industrial Time* (1982), however, demonstrates that the extent to which people develop life plans or make projects of their lives is an historical phenomenon. Focusing on the nineteenth century, she discusses life plans as 'a wide range of goals and aspirations around which an individual or family organizes its life'.[41] The changes brought about by large-scale industrialisation in the nineteenth century increasingly required families and individuals to plan their lives, to project themselves into the future and to take action. Migration, as Hareven points out, is an obvious example of a long-range life plan in which individuals and families make decisions to migrate as an act of deliberate planning of their lives and futures. In other words, Friedan was advocating a set of practices of the self for women that were historical in nature and, indeed, were relatively recent technologies of the self at least for the population as a whole.

But Friedan wanted women to do more than devise life plans for themselves. She advocated women undertaking a project of re-making themselves. Recent social theory provides a means of understanding both the context and the impetus behind her claims in this instance. Anthony Giddens, in his work on modernity and identity, has suggested that new requirements are being imposed on modern individuals in their shaping of a sense of selfhood. He argues that in settings of what he calls 'high' or 'late' modernity – 'our present-day world' – 'the self, like the broader institutional contexts in which it exists, has to be reflexively made'.[42] Our selves as well as our lives have now become projects. The reflexive project of the self becomes a feature of modernity as individuals can rely less and less on tradition or authority in the organisation of their everyday lives. Individuals are forced to negotiate life choices among a diversity of options.

Giddens is vague on the historical periodisation of his claims. However, Frank Mort's work on masculinity in Britain in the 1940s and 1950s, using Gidden's analysis, suggests that the project of the reflexive self has been democratised in the post-second world war period. In discussing the life of his father, Mort talks about the way people were increasingly required to take on responsibility for their lives and identities.[43] The self became something to be actively made rather than simply determined by one's life circumstances and status. Indeed the works of D.W. Winnicott and Erik Erikson, on whom Giddens draws to theorise how the reflexive self develops, were precisely contributing to this process. These writers were analysing the formation of this self from a psychological point of view. The popularity of their work in the 1950s ensured that their ideas had a profound impact on child-rearing, educational and social welfare practices in Britain, Australia and other Western countries. Through radio broadcasts and lectures, Winnicott became a household name as he spoke to women in particular about how to ensure their children (and, by implication, themselves) took on this project of self-identity in ways that he saw as appropriate to the modern world.

The reflexive self of late modernity, as defined by Giddens and others, has its historical roots in Enlightenment ideas of the project of modernity. Central to these ideas is the belief in the 'self-determining' individual – the individual who, freed of the bonds of tradition and authority, will readily take responsibility for making 'his' own self and life. Analyses by Foucault and others have drawn attention to the way taking responsibility for one's own self and understanding oneself as self-choosing are cultural acquisitions. The capacities to choose and to seek to govern one's own life are not characteristics of an individual who will spontaneously emerge once freed of the bonds of tradition, but are produced in the individual through a range of institutional practices and associated forms of expertise.[44]

Giddens discusses one form of cultural institution that has precisely functioned to shape or produce the reflexive self in this way. He draws attention to how conduct books have become increasingly popular in the period of late modernity as 'practical "guides to living"' as people increasingly take on the responsibility of making their lives and selves a project. Giddens suggests conduct books are 'not just works "about" social processes, but materials that in some part constitute them'.[45] In providing guidance to readers about how to construct a coherent sense of self and a life plan, texts about self-therapy, for instance, not only assist in shaping a reflexive self but also incite the desire to have such a sense of self. Conduct books are not necessarily clearly prescriptive in their advice to readers but offer themselves as providing ways in which individuals can become self-forming.

We want to suggest that the key texts of second wave feminists in the 1960s and 1970s similarly could be seen as conduct books of a kind. These works, such as those analysed briefly in the first part of this chapter, were not just constituting 'woman' as a political and social identity, but also reflecting and contributing to the increasing democratisation of the reflexive self in western societies.[46] Thus instead of understanding the claims that women make of finding Friedan's book 'a revelation' within a linear narrative of liberation, we suggest that she provided 'a guide to living'. Her text appeared to resolve the tensions that women experienced between public achievement and domesticity and it provided an apparent solution in suggesting there was a straightforward journey in which all women should participate. In this narrative, the housewife represented the past self – the quintessentially prescribed self – who was to be left behind as bowed down by tradition and authority. This argument provided a sense of the self as having a trajectory of development from the past to an anticipated future in which the individual can and must make choices and take control of her life. Friedan, like others, was arguing for a feminist subject who was a reflexive self, and therefore was providing practical guides for women about how they should and could become such a self.

The texts of early second wave feminists, as conduct books of a kind, thus provided forms of training through which women could learn to understand themselves as self-choosing and acquire the desire to be self-determining, able to order their lives and the world around themselves by planning and making their own selves. Understood in this way, it becomes clearer why Friedan's book sought to make the issues of feminism psychological and primarily personal. While the work of Simone de Beauvoir and Germaine Greer also functioned as conduct books, providing women with guidance about how to think about their lives and selves, Friedan set out to be a populist writer and to speak to women more explicitly about how to change their lives and become autonomous selves. In this context, she devised a linear narrative in which women could see themselves as having been oppressed or manipulated by the media to believe themselves fulfilled as housewives. In reading her book, they would find a new, more coherent sense of self through which they became autonomous, self-defining – no longer trapped in a limited world in which they were defined by others. The housewife represented all that such modern selves would want to leave behind.

As we have seen, Joanne Meyerowitz has queried whether women were confronted with a dominating, oppressive ideology of domesticity in the 1950s from which Friedan helped them to escape. We will be building on this argument to show how popular and governmental discourses in the 1940s and 1950s were far more complex than Friedan claimed. The reason why Friedan's argument had such a powerful effect for many women was more likely to do with the way her linear narrative resolved a set of tensions and uncertainties about how modern women should live their lives in this period – how they should think about the responsibilities and opportunities represented by work life and family life. Her story appeared to make sense of the contradictions and conflicts in women's lives in a way that provided a biographical solution to what in fact were structural problems, a point we will return to in the conclusion to this book. In doing so, she drew on a familiar trope of modernity in which the modern self leaves behind the banality or everydayness of home life to become such a self. As Rita Felski argues, 'The vocabulary of modernity is a vocabulary of anti-home.'[47]

Charlotte Brunsdon has provided a similar perspective on the way in which feminist scholarship has constituted the figure of the housewife, although focusing on a slightly later set of developments. Investigating the emergence of feminist cultural studies of the soap opera, she argues that the figures of the television viewer, 'the housewife' and 'the ordinary woman' constitute a shadowy collective presence in this scholarship. In the 1970s and early 1980s the figure of the housewife or a non- or pre-feminist female served as the 'Other' of conventional femininity against which the feminist intellectual could define herself. In creating the study of soap opera as a legitimate field of scholarship, one which feminist intellectuals were clearly ambivalent about, 'the labour of "writing as a feminist"', says Brunsdon, 'was being elaborated'.[48] Brunsdon explains the emergence of the feminist intellectual in this context as reflecting the contradictory positioning of women in the academy. By the 1970s a certain population of young women now had access to the predominantly masculine academy, but the discrimination and gendered culture they met in this context endlessly returned them to the culture they had abandoned or disavowed to gain such an entry: the 'pleasures, concerns and accoutrements of femininity'.[49] One way of dealing with these painful contradictions, Brunsdon suggests, was 'through a classic splitting in which the feminist academic investigates her abandoned or fictional other – the female consumer of popular culture'.[50]

This 1970s feminism, Brunsdon argues, was a particular attempt to 'compete in the field of the feminine'[51] at a time when there was considerable public negotiations going on about what it meant to be a woman. Attempting to speak 'as women', they pitted themselves against conventional femininity and claimed a unified identity for themselves. Such a split between feminist/non-feminist can no longer be assumed. Gender is recognised as just one determinant of identity and feminists have many different affiliations. But it is also clear that the tensions for women between achievement and domesticity have not been resolved by a story that calls on women to leave their 'home selves' behind. As a biographical solution to what are fundamental systematic contradictions and tensions between the way home life and work life are organised in contemporary society, this narrative no longer works and we need to find other ways to understand and face the dilemmas involved.

'Good-Enough Feminists?'

Developments in the 1980s may initially have appeared to have resolved this tension between public achievement and domesticity for feminists. Carol Gilligan, in her highly influential book *In a Different Voice* (1982), elaborated a feminist framework that appeared far more woman-centred, rejecting ideas of the autonomous, self-determining individual as the value framework for feminism. She argued that, rather than seeing relationships of dependence as impediments to the need to define an autonomous self, women had developed a different framework. An image of the self-in-relationship, Gilligan claims, is characteristic of how women define themselves and their orientation to the world. Women seek to juggle loyalties to other people's needs and demands as well as their own. In undertaking the work of caring for the family and organising family life, women have developed an ethic of care, she argues, that is based on a vision of the importance of respect for others' needs and of a self that is immersed in relationships with others.[52] Joan Williams, in her essay 'Domesticity as the Dangerous Supplement of Liberalism', argues that what made Gilligan's work so popular and influential was precisely that it appeared to resolve the conflict between domesticity and public achievement. Williams criticises Gilligan's work for what she believes was a thin empirical base on which to build its thesis, but goes on to suggest that these problems were irrelevant, at the time at least, because this account resonated deeply with women, providing, in essence, a status report on how many women were thinking about their lives in the late twentieth century.[53]

Whether or not it is appropriate to criticise Gilligan's work for a thin empirical base, it was soon recognised that she had failed to solve the tension between public achievement and domesticity. Her claim that women have a particular way of operating in the world and of producing the self was too normative to provide a satisfying solution for long. Other influences also continue to ensure the persisting and troubling character of this tension within feminism. Contemporary histories of feminism, for example, with their attachment to linear narratives of women leaving behind domesticity, in the housewife role, and finding liberation reactivate and signal continuing anxieties around this issue. Similarly, histories of the 1950s that set out to understand what is represented as 'the problem of the return to domesticity' both appeal to and incite such anxieties.[54] They can be seen to operate powerfully too in the debate around Catherine Hakim's article in the *British Journal of Sociology*.

Anne Summers in the 1990s re-invoked the unease around this issue with her 'Letter to the Next Generation'.[55] Published as a new concluding chapter to the second edition of her *Damned Whores and God's Police* (1994), she explains the letter as a response to young women who she claims reject 1960s and 1970s feminism as remote from them and their lives and ambitions. She quotes an article by a young American woman in 1991 as supposedly encapsulating this view. Feminism for this young woman poses an impossible choice between 'heart and mind', 'our attractiveness or our independence'. Feminism means 'becoming unfeminine, anti-men and ultimately alone'.[56] The painful choice she posits between independence and femininity echoes once again the conflict at the heart of contemporary feminism between public achievement and domesticity. This is a conflict which has been picked up, at least in part, by discussions of what now is being depicted by some as 'third wave feminism' as young women in their 20s and 30s explore what they see as a new understanding of the project of feminism. They argue for a feminism which they see as being about 'the lives of *real women* who juggle jobs, kids, money and personal freedom in a frenzied world'.[57]

Instead of confronting this issue, however, Summers sets out to provide a history lesson to her projected audience of younger women. They are the 'daughters of the feminist revolution', she insists, who must recognise that they are custodians of the future.[58] 'Our story' of the 1970s, as she tells it, is an exuberant one in which she speaks of women beginning to recognise the restrictions on their lives in the decade leading up to the emergence of the women's movement. They realised that they could go to university, but ended up studying arts because no one suggested they consider law, medicine or engineering. They now felt that they could expect a companionate marriage, but had to face the reality that the responsibility of children would be entirely theirs, even if this meant setting aside career aspirations. Second wave feminism accomplished wide-ranging reforms in terms of challenging these restrictions, but this came at immense personal cost for some women at least, Summers acknowledges, as they 'opted for independence at whatever price'. And this is a choice, she concludes, that will have to continue to be made until 'the human species completes its evolution towards true equality'.[59] Young women will have to face the challenge of finding new ways of reconciling the desire for love and the need for independence.

In setting out to provide a history lesson to the 'next generation', and in the form of the history she provides, Summers reinstates, in unproblematic form, an account of feminism as an (unfinished) story of oppression-to-liberation. A history is invoked in which women have supposedly to move from being prescribed to autonomous selves. Issues of the needs of everyday life, of relationships of care and human interdependence, are swept aside as having to be left behind with such an earlier form of selfhood. The figure of the housewife and all that she represents can only be rescued, liberated, abandoned or left behind in this form of history.

But perhaps it is more the narrative – the use of history – that should be seen as a problem for contemporary feminism than the figure of the housewife. Certainly, this narrative was productive of the feminist subject of the 1960s and 1970s. In this story the feminist resolves the tension between domesticity and public achievement by leaving the former at home for the latter. It is a story too which allows for only one form of feminist subject. Yet, as we have argued, this is a tale that echoes the gendered account of the formation of the modern self and hence all the ambivalences and anxieties that underlie it. It requires of women that they pursue a fantasy of the feminist subject as fully unified and coherent, able to define herself and her world un-ambiguously. It is this figure, we suggest, that is a problem for young women today, not the housewife. This particular fantasy of the feminist subject sets up ordinary women (of the 'new' generation and 'the old') for failure. 'New generation' women, discussed by Summers, solve this dilemma by rejecting feminism as inappropriate or irrelevant to their lives.

In the histories that follow, we look at various ways in which the figure of the housewife emerged in the 1940s and 1950s. In public policy, in the writings of community organisations and social movements, in the popular press, in films, in radio programmes and popular magazines, a range of tensions were explored about what it meant to be a woman and how the housewife might satisfactorily represent feminine aspirations and understandings of the role of women in modern society. These histories will re-tell the history of the emergence of second wave feminism and with this seek to re-cast the relationship today between feminist scholars and the needs of everyday life.

Notes

1. *Sydney Morning Herald*, 4 April 1996, p. 13.
2. *Sydney Morning Herald*, 20 June 2000, p. 17.
3. *Sydney Morning Herald*, 23 May 2002, p. 15. James Tooley, *The Mis-education of Women*, London, Continuum International Publishing Group, 2002.
4. *Sun-Herald*, 2 March 2003, pp. 22–3.
5. *Sydney Morning Herald*, 3 June 2000, Spectrum, p. 1.
6. *Sydney Morning Herald*, 23 May 2002, p. 15.
7. Virginia Hausseger, 'The Sins of Our Feminist Mothers', *The Age*, 23 July 2002.
8. *Australian*, 25 October 1997, p. 2; 3 May 2001, p. 11.
9. *www.tenuk.com*.
10. Barbara Ehrenreich discusses this trend in the article discussed in the conclusion of this book: 'Maid to Order: The Politics of Other Women's Work', *Harper's Magazine*, April 2000, pp. 59–70. See also Barbara Ehrenreich, *Nickel and Dimed: On (Not) Getting By in America*, New York, Metropolitan Books, 2001, and Barbara Ehrenreich and Arlie Russell Hochschild (eds), *Global Woman: Nannies, Maids, and Sex Workers in the New Economy*, New York, Metropolitan Books, 2003.
11. Mica Nava and Alan O'Shea, 'Introduction', in Mica Nava and Alan Shea (eds), *Modern Times: Reflections on a Century of English Modernity*, London, Routledge, 1996, p. 1.
12. Ibid., p. 5.
13. See, for example, Elisabeth Bronfen and Misha Kavka (eds), *Feminist Consequences: Theory for the New Century*, New York, Columbia University Press, 2001.

14. Catherine Hakim, 'Five Feminist Myths about Women's Employment', *British Journal of Sociology*, vol. 46 (3), 1995, pp. 429–55.
15. *Sydney Morning Herald*, 4 April 1996, p. 13; article reprinted from *Guardian*, 2 April 1996, p. 7.
16. Catherine Hakim, 'The Sexual Division of Labour and Women's Heterogeneity', *British Journal of Sociology*, 47 (1), 1996, pp. 178–88.
17. *Sydney Morning Herald*, 9 April 1996, p. 9.
18. *Sun-Herald*, 2 March 2003, pp. 22–3; *Sydney Morning Herald*, 3 March 2003, p. 15. Catherine Hakim's arguments have also been favourably mentioned in British parliamentary debates by Andrew Selous, Conservative Party Member for South-West Bedfordshire, who 'commends' her work to the House for showing that governments should 'not impose choices on women. British Parliamentary debates, 14 March 2002, Column 1107.
19. *Sydney Morning Herald*, 3 March 2003, p. 15.
20. Joan Williams, *Unbending Gender: Why Family and Work Conflict and What to Do About It*, Oxford, Oxford University Press, 2000, p. 1.
21. Ibid., pp. 45–7.
22. Her argument here is similar to the one developed by Leonore Davidoff and Catherine Hall in their important book *Family Fortunes: Men and Women of the English Middle Class 1780–1850*, London, Hutchinson, 1987.
23. Belinda Probert, '"Grateful Slaves" or "Self-made Women": A Matter of Choice or Policy?', Clare Burton Memorial Lecture 2001. The reference in the title of this lecture is to a 1991 article by Catherine Hakim.
24. Ibid.
25. Simone de Beauvoir, *The Second Sex*, H.M. Parshley (trans.), Harmondsworth, Penguin, 1981, p. 449.
26. Ibid., p. 471.
27. Ibid., pp. 468–77.
28. Germaine Greer, *The Female Eunuch*, London, Granada, 1970, p. 328.
29. Ann Oakley, *Housewife*, London, Penguin, 1974, p. 222.
30. Anne Summers, *Damned Whores and God's Police: The Colonization of Women in Australia*, Harmondsworth, Penguin, 1983, pp. 30f.
31. Betty Friedan, *The Feminine Mystique*, Harmondsworth, Penguin, 1983.
32. Jocelynne Scutt (ed.), *Different: Reflections on the Women's Movement and Visions for Its Future*, Ringwood, Penguin, 1987, p. 111. This entry is by Lisa Newby; scc also entry by Vera Levin, p. 119.
33. Daniel Horowitz, 'Rethinking Betty Friedan and *The Feminine Mystique*': Labor Union Radicalism and Feminism in Cold War America', *American Quarterly*, 48 (1), 1996, p. 2.
34. Ibid., p. 28.
35. Ibid., p. 24.

36. Joanne Meyerowitz, 'Beyond *The Feminine Mystique*: A Reassessment of Postwar Mass culture, 1946–1958', in Joanne Meyerowitz (ed.), *Not June Cleaver: Women and Gender in Postwar America, 1945–1960*, Philadelphia, Temple University Press, 1994, p. 231.

37. Helena Studdert, '"You're 100% Feminine if . . .": Gender Constructions in Australian Women's Magazines, 1920–1969', unpublished PhD thesis, Kensington, University of New South Wales, 1997.

38. Meyerowitz, 'Beyond *The Feminine Mystique*', p. 252.

39. Gisela Kaplan, *The Meagre Harvest: The Australian Women's Movement, 1950s–1990s*, Sydney, Allen and Unwin, 1996, p. 8.

40. Kaplan does point to some contradictory messages in the examples of women who lead more complex lives, but she nevertheless reproduces Friedan's very one-sided interpretation of the dominant culture as represented in the media of the time. For another example of this feminist narrative of women having to break away from the 'happy housewife myth', see Kristen Henry and Marlene Derlet, *Talking Up a Storm: Nine Women and Consciousness Raising*, Sydney, Hale and Iremonger, 1993, pp. x, 23.

41. Tamara Hareven, *Family Time and Industrial Time: The Relationship between the Family and Work in a New England Industrial Community*, Cambridge, Cambridge University Press, 1982, p. 339.

42. Anthony Giddens, *Modernity and Self-identity: Self and Society in the Late Modern Age*, Cambridge, Polity Press, 1991, p. 3.

43. Frank Mort, 'Social and Symbolic Fathers and Sons: A Cultural History', paper delivered at the University of Technology, Sydney, Sydney, Ultimo Series, 2 April 1997. Nikolas Rose also discusses these changes in the 1950s and 1960s as requiring individuals to construe their lives in terms of choices. See Nikolas Rose, *Governing the Soul: The Shaping of the Private Self*, London, Routledge, 1989, pp. 224–8.

44. This issue is discussed in Lesley Johnson, *The Modern Girl: Girlhood and Growing Up*, Buckingham, Open University Press, 1993, p. 17.

45. Giddens, *Modernity and Self-identity*, p. 2.

46. Giddens (ibid., pp. 216–17) refers to interest in Friedan's text in life planning, but he accepts her self-representation as a frustrated housewife and does not make the connection being proposed here between such feminist texts and his interest in conduct books.

47. Rita Felski, *Doing Time: Feminist Theory and Postmodern Culture*, New York, New York University Press, 2000, p. 86.

48. Charlotte Brunsdon, *The Feminist, the Housewife, and the Soap Opera*, Oxford, Clarendon Press, 2000, p. 3.

49. Ibid., p. 5.

50. Ibid.

51. Ibid., p. 14.

52. Carol Gilligan, *In a Different Voice*, Cambridge, MA, Harvard University Press, 1982.

53. Joan Williams, 'Domesticity as the Dangerous Supplement of Liberalism', *Journal of Women's History*, 2 (3), Winter 1991, pp. 69–88.

54. See, for example, Stephen Garton, 'The War-Damaged Citizen', in Paul Patton and Diane Austin-Broos (eds), *Transformations in Australian Society*, Sydney, University of Sydney, Research Institute for Humanities and Social Sciences, 1997.

55. An issue of *Australian Feminist Studies* devoted a major section to responses to this 'letter' and other interventions in the so-called 'generation gap' debate within feminism – 12 (26), October 1997. These articles on the whole were critical of Summers, but nevertheless the vigour of the responses suggest that the issue continues to be a fraught one within feminism.

56. Summers, *Damned Whores and God's Police*, 2nd edn, 1994, p. 506.

57. Quote from website of 'The 3rd WWWave', *www.io.com/~wwave*. As would be expected, much of the writings and discussions of third wave feminism are being conducted on the web. A key text in this movement, however, is: Jennifer Baumgardner and Amy Richards, *Manifesta: Young Women, Feminism and the Future*, New York, Farrar, Straus and Giroux, 2000.

58. Summers, *Damned Whores and God's Police*, 2nd edn, p. 507.

59. Ibid., pp. 521–5.

–2–

Whom Does She Represent?

In 1947, the Town Clerk for Ryde Council, an outer north-western region of Sydney, proposed a number of strategies designed to improve home and social life in the area. The Council was sponsoring housing developments in the area, previously consisting of market gardens and considerable pockets of vacant land, which they hoped would create high-quality living environments for young families. Included in the Town Clerk's proposal was the suggestion of establishing 'civic restaurants' and a central kitchen. Central to his concerns was a desire to 'lessen the monotony and strain on the housewife', to reduce her 'drudgery'. Partly based on the British Civic Restaurants scheme, his proposal envisaged 'a central kitchen where food will be cooked for the proposed civic restaurant or restaurants and for sale and distribution to private homes by means of "hot-boxes"'.[1]

The 'drudgery of the housewife' had become a topic of some concern in the political arena during the 1940s and 1950s, although the terminology changed over this period. This chapter explores why the housewife became such a focus of public attention at this time and how the nature of that focus evolved during the 1950s. We begin with a brief consideration of the housewife's conditions as detailed in Kate Darian-Smith's account of the 'home front' during the second world war. We then turn to look at how the housewife's cause was taken up in the 1940s, at some of the ways in which women themselves sought to speak of their lives in these terms, and then at the changes that began to appear in the 1950s. Finally, we discuss some of the feminist literature of the 1950s and early 1960s that begins to address the issue of the housewife's lot in rather different ways.

'The Future in Her Hands'

Appalling domestic conditions for women, particularly during the second world war, were a reality for many. Kate Darian-Smith paints a vivid picture of the difficult conditions under which working-class women laboured to create a home life for their families. They were expected and needed to undertake both paid employment and home duties, but 'housework in the 1940s was unmechanized drudgery'.[2] Kitchens were often primitive, food preservation difficult, the weekly laundry a strenuous manual operation and vacuum cleaners rare. Making it even more difficult, many low-income households lived in appalling surroundings with dampness and inadequate drainage a common problem. Sewerage in inner-city houses was often faulty and in outer suburbs, it was non-existent. But some middle-class and working-class housewives shared a problem of not being able to find any accommodation at all. They had to rely on relatives, sleeping and living in a spare bedroom or 'sleep-out' verandah because of the shortage of housing stock during and after the war.

Also increasing the similarities between the lives of middle-class and working-class housewives, in form if not substance, was the absence of domestic help. This had been a growing problem for middle-class women in the early decades of the twentieth century, but, according to Darian-Smith and other Australian historians such as Saunders and Evans,[3] the second world war 'brought to a close an era where middle-class families employed one or more domestic servants'.[4] Servants left private homes for better-paid employment in the many jobs now available in industry. Indeed so acute were the manpower needs at this time that John Dedman, the Director-General of the Department of War Organisation of Industry, sought to prohibit the employment of domestic servants. But the outcry from the middle and upper classes was effective and Dedman was forced to modify the Domestic Servants Order. A key argument given was that middle- and upper-class women were making a major contribution to the war effort through their voluntary work for war-time charities, such as the Red Cross, and needed domestic help to release them from home duties. But the point that we are interested in is that the difficulties of finding domestic help made the life of middle-class housewives more like that of the working class. While the whole notion of the housewife was a middle-class ideal, it was not until this period that middle-class women had prime responsibility for not just the management but the actual work of domesticity. Of course, fundamental differences remained, with working-class women continuing to be more likely to be both in the paid workforce and responsible for the domestic life of their families, but the changes that, at least on the surface, made their lives increasingly similar also made it easier to talk about the housewife as a general category of women in this period in the media and in political discourses.

The similar as well as rather different problems of women during the second world war were summarised in frequent references to 'the burdens of the housewife' or the 'harassed housewife'. Though the quality of women's material conditions might differ markedly, this terminology constituted for them all as a common problem the difficulty of managing a home under wartime conditions and the prospect that this might not improve significantly once peace was restored. In 1944 Mrs Quirk, the Member for Balmain in the New South Wales parliament, for instance, made a passionate speech about improving family conditions during the war and in particular addressing the issue of adequate housing. Married women who had reared a family should be appointed to housing, health and social services committees, she argued, as they knew the deprivation that families had had to suffer during the war:

> In the main, a man eats, sleeps and rests in the home, but the woman lives day after day between four walls, providing for her family, cooking, laundering, cleaning, mending, scrubbing, nursing, going from shop to shop to make the money spin out, being exploited at every turn and sometimes being compelled to buy on the black market. She makes the sacrifices and she makes them with a smile. She sees to it that the father and children have sufficient to eat even though she may have none. She needs fresh air and light, space and playing areas for her children, modern equipment to save her poor tired limbs and above all a kitchen where work will be a pleasure rather than drudgery.[5]

Adding a sense of urgency to claims such as these was a concern about the decline of the birth-rate during the war. The National Health and Medical Research Council (NHMRC) provided a report to the Commonwealth Government in November 1944 on a problem that it saw as causing the 'gravest anxiety about the future of the Australian people': the decline in the birth-rate that had been occurring for the past couple of decades and which seemed projected to continue.[6]

The NHMRC report sought to identify the reasons for women's 'failure' to have children in reasonable numbers. It outlined three main factors as influencing the birth-rate: the decreasing dependence of women; increasing economic insecurity due to wars and economic depression; and the 'desire of the parents to ensure appropriate educational and other justifiable advantages to the children already born to them'.[7] Summarising the statements women themselves made to the Council, the Director-General for Health outlined his impressions of how they defined the issue in more pithy terms than the report itself. Women limit their families for the following reasons, he concluded: 'no home; no help; no security – national or economic; and no hope for any change for the better in any of these things'.[8] Some of the women quoted in his summary made forthright statements about what the problem was in their view, declaring that women were 'on strike' and wanted 'a fair deal', whereas others wrote in detail of the problems of their everyday lives, of how tired they were, of their work being 'unpaid drudgery', of the need for adequate housing, and so on. One woman warned of the dangers of educating girls as they would now, like her, all want a full life rather than being tied down by 'having baby after baby'. Others argued for the necessity of raising the status of mothering, as well as improving hospital and other social services.[9]

Women in this context became responsible for the future of the nation. '[I]f we want women to have children,' said Mrs Quirk in the same speech to the New South Wales parliament, 'we must look after them.'[10] Similarly, the media sought to promote this sense of women's centrality to the future of the nation. A broadcast by the ABC in 1947 on the *Women's Session* programme, concluded that:

If only women realise it, they have the future of the world in the hollow of their hands. We have spoken about the past and the present – of yesterday and today. There is still tomorrow – the world of tomorrow grows from the children of today, and who creates the children of today, but the women of today? I use the word create because it is the correct word to use. It signifies more than the mere bringing into life of a physical being. Woman not only bears the child – she guides and influences him through his most impressionable years – hers is the power to create him as a personality. Hers is the power to mould his *outlook*, and it is the outlook of the individual that shapes the destiny of nations.[11]

Denise Riley, in the British context, looks at reports and investigations similar to the one undertaken by the NHMRC in Australia during the latter years of the second world war. She argues that the 'pronatalism' that emerged with these reports and various reforms introduced during and after the war created a conservative account of motherhood, a legacy that women's liberation in the 1970s had to vigorously contest. We do not wish to deny the problems that Riley and others have outlined in these discourses of motherhood that emerged after the second world war. In an immensely challenging book, Riley provides a subtle and nuanced analysis of the governmental and psychological discourses of the 1940s to unsettle any notion of collusion between psychology and the state. She suggests, however, that invocations of motherhood in this period 'effectively rendered invisible the needs of working women with children'.[12] Walkerdine and Lucey have similarly made a very powerful case that the construction of women during and after the second world war as 'responsible for democracy' served to oppress women. In requiring women to be deeply involved in the education of their children, women's lives after the second world war became increasingly regulated by the fantasy of liberal democracy. And women were to be involved in the oppression of each other through the teachings of the psychological texts which promoted this fantasy. Middle-class women as nurses, teachers and social workers were positioned as the guardians of democracy and made alert to the failure of working-class women to adopt appropriate child-rearing practices, to be 'sensitive mothers' like themselves.[13]

While not disputing the importance and ground-breaking character of these analyses, we want to suggest that we also need to recognise the productive nature of these discussions about the drudgery of the housewife and the emergence of pronatalist discourses signalled in contexts like the NHMRC report. Riley sees a conservative ideology of motherhood emerging in the latter years of the second world war that second wave feminists would then have to combat in the 1960s and 1970s. We want to suggest, however, that it is precisely the focus on housewives and mothers in these years and immediately after the war that also creates the conditions of possibility for the emergence of second wave feminism. While being told about one's responsibility for the democratic future of the nation might place a considerable burden on women, and a constraint on how they are to understand themselves at one level, such statements also speak of a considerable entitlement. The popular media in the years immediately after the second world war, as we will see in the following chapters, began to talk about women as the moral core and authority of the family and the controller of man's environment. As the agents of the future in these political discourses, women were being given a powerful sense of the possibilities for argument and action in a world in which the divisions between the public and private established in the nineteenth century were being destabilised. In suffering drudgery and deprivation, they might be damaged selves, but the injured self of the housewife was nevertheless precisely a self, a modern identity with responsibilities, entitlements, a sphere of importance in which to act and hence also the potential to move beyond this sphere, and to begin to define her own responsibilities.

'As Housewives, We Are Worms'

The fact that women spoke 'as housewives' in the 1940s and 1950s suggests the emergence of a consciousness of this modern identity of the housewife. They spoke 'as housewives' in the popular media in various contexts but they did so also in more organised form through housewives' associations. These were not new organisations at this time. Historians such as Judith Smart have provided detailed histories of the housewives' associations in Australia and their complex internal politics. But it is interesting that they have failed to gain a place in accounts of feminism's *own* history of itself in Australia, such as in the otherwise excellent and detailed history provided by Marilyn Lake.[14] Their absence from these histories cannot be attributed to their characterisation as 'conservative', as they were diverse in terms of their political stances. The problem seems more to be a question of what is seen as feminist. Women arguing for and promoting their needs as managers of domesticity and consumers would appear to fail to register as such. They bring with them the whiff of a world that is still perhaps to be denied by feminism, or at least one with which we remain uncomfortable.

As Smart has remarked, there was an 'efflorescence' of such associations from the beginning of the first world war until the 1960s.[15] She suggests that in the 1950s they became a symptom of the 'last flowering of the suburban domestic and maternal ideal' preceding 'its fracturing and diverse reconstitution in the 1960s and 1970s'.[16] Smart describes one of the most powerful of these organisations, the Federated Housewives' Association under the leadership of Cecilia Downing, as a women's organisation that – like those active in the USA during the same period – posited women as 'moral beings', responsible for applying the principles of the 'well-run Christian home' to the community.[17] This understanding, Smart argues, makes such appellations as 'radical', liberal' and 'conservative' inappropriate and the public/private dichotomy meaningless. Just as Downing herself argued that government and society were simply an extension of the household and family, the Federated Housewives' Association employed a 'philosophy of citizenship [modelled on] the home and church congregation rather than the competitive business model so frequently employed by men'.[18] This concept was explicated in term of service, moral responsibility and collective endeavour.

The oldest of these organisations, the Australian Housewives' Association (AHA), was formed from a consumer co-operative in Victoria (Housewives' Co-operative Association) in 1915. During the first world war, projects of this Association included encouraging housewives to take up growing herbs and flowers as cottage industries; a campaign against rising prices; and a Housewives' Tea Room.[19] Following the war, a major project was the Municipal Kerb Markets, but these ultimately had to be abandoned due to 'interested pressure'.

Fuelled by post-war discontent in the late 1940s over the failure of governments to address the management of the modern household, further interventions by the Australian Housewives' Association reflected broad-scale economic change felt at the level of daily life and the organisation of family. Inflation and price rises in the post-war economy were the battlegrounds over which the housewives waged their war, each offering a solution to the problem of domestic management. The election campaign of 1948 saw the opposition Liberal Party target women voters via the readership of the *Australian Women's Weekly* through the image of the housewife beset by 'Government interference' in her daily shopping, and in 1954 the Australian Labor Party, now itself in opposition, took out paid advertisements in the *Housewife* magazine to show how prices had soared under the free market policies of Robert Gordon Menzies' Liberal Government (figures 2.1 and 2.2). While Ben Chifley's price control referendum of March 1948 was rejected and his Labor government defeated, so was Menzies' anti-communist referendum of 1951 narrowly turned down by Australian voters. The powers of the Commonwealth Prices Commissioner, responsible for rationing and price control during the war years, were rescinded by 1950 and inflation and profiteering abounded during the transition from command to market economy.

Under their motto 'For the Good That We Can Do', the Federated Housewives' Association presented a 'Bill of Rights for the Home' to the Premier of Victoria, Mr Holloway, in 1948. Echoing policies established by the Beveridge report of the early 1940s in the UK, which recognised the housewife's role as 'vital though unpaid',[20] the Associations asked 'that any expenditure involved shall be borne by a grant from the Social Service taxation now collected by the Federal Government':

Following the lead of English-speaking nations in preceding centuries, when human rights have been demanded by these nations, and later by the Human Rights

Figure 2.1 Liberal Party of Australia, 'The War Is Over – but She Still Carries a Pack', *Australian Women's Weekly*, 22 June 1948, p. 36. By permission of the Liberal Party of Australia.

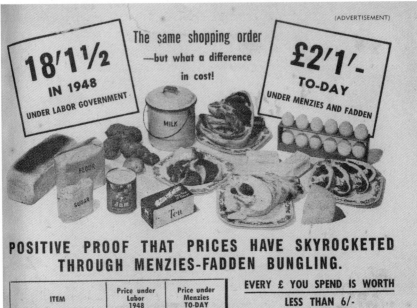

The same shopping order —but what a difference in cost!

18/1½ IN 1948 UNDER LABOR GOVERNMENT

£2'1'- TO-DAY UNDER MENZIES AND FADDEN

POSITIVE PROOF THAT PRICES HAVE SKYROCKETED THROUGH MENZIES-FADDEN BUNGLING.

ITEM	Price under Labor 1948	Price under Menzies TO-DAY
BREAD (2-lb. loaf) · · ·	6½	1 0½
FLOUR (2 lb.) · · · · ·	5½	1 7½
TEA (1 lb.) · · · · ·	2 9	4 8
SUGAR (1 lb.) · · · · ·	4½	9
JAM, PLUM (1½ lb.) · · ·	1 5	2 5½
POTATOES (7 lb.) · · · ·	10½	3 6
BUTTER (1 lb.) · · · ·	1 11½	4 1½
CHEESE (1 lb.) · · · ·	1 6	3 9
EGGS (1 doz.) · · · · ·	2 10½	6 0
MILK, FRESH (1 qt.) · · ·	8	1 9
BEEF, RIB (1 lb.) · · · ·	8	2 2
STEAK, RUMP (1 lb.) · · ·	2 0	5 0
MUTTON, LEG (1 lb.) · · ·	10½	1 10
MUTTON CHOPS, LOIN (1 lb.)	1 2	2 4
TOTAL · · · · ·	**18 1½**	**£2 1 0**

Average retail prices shown are based on Sydney (March quarter). A number of these food items have since soared still higher in price.

EVERY £ YOU SPEND IS WORTH LESS THAN 6/-

simply because the Menzies-Fadden Government has run away from the problem of inflation and has completely dishonoured Menzies' solemn election pledge to "put value back in the £."

ONLY A FEDERAL LABOR GOVERNMENT WILL GIVE YOU A BETTER DEAL

The housewife is always better off under Federal Labor Government

ON MAY 29th VOTE FOR THE LABOR CANDIDATE ' YOUR ELECTORATE

Authorised by C. W. Anderson, 4 Goulburn Street, Sydney.

THE HOUSEWIFE, April, 1954   7

Figure 2.2 Australian Labor Party, 'Positive Proof That Prices Have Skyrocketed Through Menzies–Fadden Bungling', *The Housewife*, April 1954, p. 7. By permission of the Australian Labor Party.

Commission of the United Nations Organisation, it is felt that the time is ripe for a Victorian Bill of Rights for the Home, since the maintenance of the British Empire depends on the happiness and solvency of the homes of its citizens. Further, the home should be maintained at a high moral and spiritual level. It should be entitled to the assurance of economic stability, with the consequent provision of good and convenient housing, adequate and nutritious food, clothing and medical attention.[21]

The Bill asked for various state-sponsored institutions to be established which would be supportive of family life, including marriage clinics, parents' education centres (to train in financial and other matters) and a Court of Conciliation and Domestic Relations. The Bill also demanded a set of employment rights for women at home, such as the ability of the

> wife to retain savings from housekeeping allowance; To be insured against accident; To have a rights to share in deceased husband's estate; Child endowment; and Comfortable and convenient homes with labour-saving appliances. Better preparation for marriage was called for in compulsory home-craft training for one year at least for all girls; Instruction classes for making children's clothes; Boys to learn in primary school how to sew, knit, help in the home and garden.[22]

They sought the formal recognition of mothering tasks in schemes proposed for: rest rooms for mothers and crèches in every municipal shopping centre; municipal home help bureaux, including an emergency housekeeper scheme; holiday homes and boarding houses for children with or without mothers; free holiday homes for tired or sick mothers (without children); and King's Honours for mothers who had brought up large families well. A series of additional demands were appended to the original Bill, which interestingly distinguished the Federated Housewives' Association from its more radical socialist rivals, with a call for existing marketing boards to be abolished in favour of producer and consumer management.

By 1954 the aims of most housewives' associations were being substantially reformulated to become more purely consumer-oriented. *The Housewife*, the publication of the Housewives' Association of NSW, for example, asked its readers 'Are you just a HOUSEWIFE or are you a good CONSCIENTIOUS HOUSEWIFE and a member of the Housewives' Association?':

> In order to be truly effective in all the aims we hope to accomplish, we need the support and co-operation of every housewife.
> This is our slogan: "YOUR PROBLEM IS OURS."
> The aims and objects of the Association are:-
> TO maintain and safeguard the interests of the housewife.
> TO help the housewife in all her difficulties whenever possible.
> TO give advice and expose all existing evils that cause the housewife worry and discomfort.

IF any problem is not in our province, we can direct you to the right quarter.

TO compel hygienic handling and wrapping of all foodstuffs.

WHERE we consider it essential, we advise boycotting.

This Association is a representative body that can speak and fight for you where you cannot do so yourself, and will watch your interests the same as Unions watch over the interests of their members.

There is no compulsion to join the Association; every housewife in Sydney should do so for her own advantage.[23]

Another group, however, abandoned their focus specifically on the housewife in the 1950s. The Progressive Housewives' Association was formed in Sydney in June 1946 by a group of women linked to the Australian Communist Party who had marched as 'housewives' alongside trade unionists in the 1946 May Day March. In order to prevent confusion with another group, the name was changed in October to the New Housewives' Association. This association drew on the official Communist Party platform, arguing for both a rise in the basic wage and strong price control to combat inflation.[24] According to a leaflet distributed by the New Housewives' Association in the late 1940s: 'Before the last war a man with a wife and two children could feed, clothe, and shelter them for 6 pounds a week. He cannot possibly maintain them on the same standard today for less than 12 pounds a week, and yet the basic wage is only 7 pounds 2 shillings.'[25]

A National Conference of Communist Women challenged the Communist Party's blind spot regarding women's role at home.[26] While working-class men organised for their rights in the workplace under the banner of their respective trade unions, New Housewives' Association spokeswomen like Ella Schroeder urged working-class women to organise for their rights in the home.

The aims of the organisation at this time included organising 'housewives in order that they may exercise their influence in the interests of the community, in a non-sectarian and non-party manner', as well as a focus on price controls, free kindergartens and nursery schools. By 1948 it had expanded its focus, with a constitution now headed by the slogan 'FOR PROGRESS', to campaign for free medical and dental services, children's libraries, play centres and clubs; 'to encourage and extend the use of wholesome and nutritious food'; and to 'prevent the manufacture and false advertising of shoddy clothing, furniture and other essential goods'.[27]

But by 1950 the New Housewives' Association abandoned its former focus explicitly on the housewife to become the Union of Australian Women. In a letter to suburban branches, the New South Wales secretary, Elwyn Cunningham, speaking as the outgoing official, explained the reasons behind the change of name:

We have lost many members, who, through economic circumstances have been forced to enter industry either casually or permanently. No longer regarding themselves as housewives, but because of their position as wife and mother, they have little time to spare for union activities. They still believe in our principles, but cannot see how they can fit into an Association of Housewives. [It is necessary] to open our ranks to all women who wish to join us in our work.[28]

While the New Housewives' Association had always included a focus on issues of international peace and worker solidarity, in its new incarnation as the Union of Australian Women, the organisation spoke to a diverse set of interests now centring on peace and human rights, including indigenous people's rights, and built links with international women's organisations. In this form, its activities linked up with the focus of other women's groups, whose preoccupations in this period, as we will discuss later in this chapter, were more on equal pay for women. Their abandonment of the term 'housewife' signalled a recognition of the complexities of women's lives and the many forms of identification that might be appropriate to their understanding of themselves. But the identification 'housewife' continued during the 1950s to play a significant role in enabling some women at least to speak about the conditions of their everyday lives.

A newspaper article entitled 'As Housewives, We Are Worms' appeared in 1945 in a newspaper column typical of the period. On a page that usually gave the weather forecasts and shipping news, the *Sydney Morning Herald* ran a series of columns for women. Some covered social events, others provided pictures of women in uniform during the war, some were entitled 'The Women's View', and there was usually a column such as this one written 'by one of them'. This particular article appeared in May 1945 and declared a housewives' strike to be long overdue. The writer complained vehemently of electricity, gas, water and food shortages and of railway, tram and bus strikes. As housewives, she said: 'We women have been worms for too long. All those pretty phases about the hand that carries the string-bag being the hand that rules the world or something are as empty as the butchers' shops.'[29]

Her proposed 'sit down strike', she announced, would bring 'the life of the home' to a standstill for men – 'these great tough creatures' – while she would be found 'preferably in a nice comfortable chair with a picnic basket beside me'. This text is clearly about the struggle for power and agency. The article is about the housewife as a form of agency, a form of personhood, which has a sphere of activity, a world to act upon, capacities, responsibilities and powers. And the popular media encouraged women to find a collective voice in these forms.

Women spoke 'as housewives' in a variety of contexts during the war and in the years immediately following, through bodies like the housewives' associations, as we have seen, in individual letters to the editors of newspapers, as representatives on the bodies of planning agencies like the Commonwealth Housing Commission and through the words of publications like the *Australian Women's Weekly*. These statements made 'as housewives' mobilised and shaped a form of identification that took on more than private significance as women protested about how the shortages of food and other amenities were being handled during and after the war. Women found a voice 'as housewives' as they developed and pressed their claims for the proper organisation and recognition of the space of everyday life.

The Meanings of Home

A central preoccupation in the articulation of these concerns was the problem of housing, of adequate accommodation. But what were the meanings given to this issue by women at this time? During the war, Australians were spoken about as 'home-hungry' and ex-servicemen were reported as holding protest marches to demand that higher government priority be given to housing.[30] The problem of the 'housing shortage' continued for some time after the war. W.J. McKell, the leader of the New South Wales Labor government, announced in 1946 that there was a shortage of 90,000 homes in Sydney and its suburbs.[31] But such calculations did not acknowledge that not only the numbers of domestic buildings but also the types of accommodation and housing tenure represented matters of considerable political significance.

Clearly the political rhetoric of the period as well as the growing significance of consumer culture played a powerful part in shaping the meanings given to the kinds of choices the Australian population was seeking to exert at this time. Allan and Crow argue in the British context that, after the second world war, 'a home of one's own' came to mean something which is not fully achieved without ownership of a dwelling.[32] Successive government policies since the 1950s, they point out, have promoted the idea that home ownership is a 'natural' aspiration. Similarly, it is clear that government policy in Australia not only encouraged home ownership, but also shaped the desires of its citizens in this way. Carolyn Allport points, for instance, to low interest rates, war service loans, lump sum cash for ex-service personnel and the expansion of the lending policies of banks and co-operative building societies as producing a rapid rise in rates of home ownership from 52.7 per cent in 1947 to 63 per cent in 1954 and 70 per cent in 1961.[33] 'Home' was defined as a suburban house that the nuclear family either owned or was buying with assistance of such financial institutions.

Policy makers fervently believed in the national importance of ensuring that every family lived in a home of their own. J.T. Purcell, the Chairman of the Housing Commission of New South Wales, for instance, wrote a passionate account of the 'housing shortage' in 1954, in which he spoke of the horror of the man who must return each night to his family when they are not adequately housed in a home of their own. The 'vain and unsuccessful striving for the modest home . . . is disheartening and soul destroying', he said. But more than this, he went on, the 'social value' of home ownership cannot be over-emphasised: 'It is justly claimed that it encourages and develops initiative, self-reliance, thrift, responsible citizenship and other good qualities which strengthen the moral fibre of the nation . . . To a community it gives stability, and to the owner it gives a constant sense of security, pride and well-being.'[34]

Such sentiments were reiterated in the popular press. The *Australian Women's Weekly*, for instance, declared that 'homes and hearts are still being broken for the lack of a place to live'.[35] Home ownership, this editorial insisted, was a necessity in providing such places, for it would safeguard 'the backbone of national stability'. 'A home of one's own' guaranteed a solid and loyal citizenry.

But it also meant a population that would embrace and participate in the making of the new, post-war world. Despite the shortage of building materials and the struggle of a significant section of the population simply to find any sort of accommodation during the war and in the years following, advertisements abounded in newspapers and magazines about the pleasures of owning a modern house, a new home. Similarly, advertisements for commodities to fill that house and make it a 'home' evoked the comforts and delights of a 'home of your own'. This publicity material spoke of dreams that were modern not only in their desire for newness, the latest designs or technological developments or the efficient and rational organization of everyday life.[36] The very forms of dreams themselves were modern: they involved rational planning and thinking about the future and they involved adventure, a commitment to progress and the making of a new world. 'Designing the home in which you will live so many years of your life' was 'a great adventure', said an advertisement for Masonite, a cheap, mass-produced wood-fibre building material, termed 'the wonder board with 1000 uses'.[37]

In her social realist novel set in the 1950s, *Bobbin Up*, Dorothy Hewett (1959) interweaves the stories of a group of women whose lives are brought together by their work at a clothing mill in Sydney. As a text of the period, it demonstrates how these dreams of a 'home of one's own' in the form of the suburban house with a garden promoted by both policy makers and consumer culture had taken a powerful grip on the cultural imaginary of the nation. But it also indicates how 'home' defined in these terms played a powerful role in women's lives. Though the situations of the central characters are very different outside the workplace, they all share the desire for a home of their own. Alice longs for the 'business girl's dream in *House and Garden*', but shares a bed-sitting room in a lodging house with her sister.[38] Jean's dream of a 'house with the bright garden, shining from the kitchen to the bedrooms with its compact newness', enables her to cope with grinding factory work and the struggle to pay the rent on the decaying house in Five Dock.[39] But Jessie has already achieved her dream in the form of a suburban home in Tempe where she is greeted by the smell of new-mown grass and the companionship of her husband and son when she returns from the mill on a hot summer's afternoon.[40] These women struggle to create an everyday life for themselves and their families at the same time as the publicity images of dream homes sustain them with a belief in a future of a bright and comfortable modernity.

A bright, new home of one's own in advertisements and articles of the popular press frequently appeared to be the means by which the individual could express themselves as individuals. Though this publicity material sometimes seemed to be addressing a male readership, more frequently it was women as housewives who were being called on to express themselves through their choice of modern home decorations or through the very design of the home itself. An article in *Australian House and Garden*,[41] for instance, told the story of how a course on 'Marriage and the Home' had awakened the writer to the possibilities of designing her own modern house in terms of what she wanted or imagined her future to be rather than what she was used to in the past. She rejected the house designs of her childhood, which she described as intimidating, with their Gothic façades, dark colours and high ceilings. She decided instead that she wanted light, friendly rooms with a modern, compact V-shaped kitchen, a workroom for her husband-to-be and a living room where her children could play. By drawing the 'plan and elevations of the perfect house', the writer explained, she went through a process of self-realisation, coming to know herself (in the future) as wife and mother.

But most of all, the modern suburban home represented for women a proper place to bring up children, just as it had in this story of a woman discovering a clear sense of herself and her future. As Carolyn Steedman notes in the British context, the 1950s was a 'watershed in the historical process by which children have come to be thought of as repositories of hope, and objects of desire'.[42] Children (and the reproductive capacities of women) became central to governmental programmes in Australia for building a 'modern nation', just as they became central to the life plans of individual women as they sought to establish a sense of a future for themselves. A letter to the *Australian Women's Weekly*, entitled 'Flats Can Never Be Real Homes', exemplifies the connections being made between owning your own home, having children and being part of the future of the nation. Flats, the author writes, are 'spurious, counterfeit homes', and she calls for the plea for homes from 'flat-dwellers and others less fortunate' to be heard:

> Our children don't know what it is to build a cubby house – to have a sandpit – to own a dog.
>
> We all want to be home-owners and citizens in the fullest sense. When we give our addresses we want to be able to quote a house number . . . not Flat 1, or 3, or 18. We want our children to grow up in safety in their own gardens.[43]

Steedman makes the point that the desire to have children is historically determined. Why women have children, and the meanings they give to that expectation (or its refusal), is shaped by a range of discourses and social practices in any historical period.[44] Children as the repositories of hope, for whom safe places – homes with particular characteristics – were needed, represented the focus of a set of gendered desires in the 1950s, not for the past, for tradition, but for a commitment to and an expectation that 'as housewives' women were part of the nation – citizens in the fullest sense – and part of its future.

But these understandings of the desires of women, articulated by publicity material in the popular press as well as in the letters and stories of women themselves, were to be destabilised or at least contested in the 1950s. The conservative politician Robert Gordon Menzies, who was to become Prime Minister in 1949, both enlisted and sought to reshape these desires in his political crusades of the 1940s and 1950s. Judith Brett examines the way Menzies elaborated a set of political values focused on an image of the home. In seeking to mobilise and recruit the Australian population in his campaign to regain (and then to retain) power, Menzies set out to establish a new form of unifying political and social identification through developing a particular understanding of the nature of 'the middle class'. His famous 1942 speech 'The Forgotten People' claimed the home to be the central and defining value commitment of this class: a commitment, he insisted, that upheld the fundamental importance of 'homes material, homes human, and homes spiritual'. This, he said, was where the life of the nation was to be found and this was where people were to find true expression of their individuality.[45]

Women were a particular target of Menzies' campaign, argues Brett.[46] He addressed them indirectly in 'The Forgotten People' when he spoke of 'the real life of the nation [that] is to be found in the homes of people who are nameless and unadvertised, and who . . . see in their children their greatest contribution to the immortality of the race'. He also addressed them directly, as in a speech in 1946, when he spoke of their hardships during the war and claimed that 'it is the women of Australia who most eagerly seek those policies which will build homes, will banish the fear of depression, will hold out the hope of advancement for husband or son or daughter'.[47] Menzies' appeal to women as 'housewives' built on and sought to formulate that social identification as the major form of political identity available to them. He took what had been a middle-class ideal and translated it into an identification for all women. But he also transformed this identity into one in which they would be spoken for rather than one on the basis of which they would seek to establish their own voice, to take action on their own behalf. This political rhetoric reworked the image of the home for women as a site in which they would be valued but silent. It was a place of traditional values, Menzies claimed, where women would exist in a safe, secure, bounded existence, waiting for their husbands to return from work each day.

For men, on the other hand, home ownership meant independence and the manly virtues of self-reliance; owning your own home – 'one little piece of earth with a house and a garden which is ours' – guaranteed their manhood, in terms of a sense both of individual agency and of citizenship.[48] In challenging the Labor Party's hold over Australian politics in the 1940s, Menzies set out to destabilise its capacity to mobilise the population politically as 'workers'. In the 1950s, communism became a crucial target in this campaign as he exploited the themes of individual independence versus an overweening state – a state, he declared, that by continuing to nurse its citizens throughout their lives would reduce all men to children. Brett points to the way Menzies set up an opposition between the world of work and the economy – aspects of modern life which he represented as diminishing the individual's agency – and the home as a place to which a man could withdraw, a bounded space where these processes of modernisation could be excluded, just as could all strangers and unwanted intruders.[49] Here, too, for men, the home signified tradition, security, a place to withdraw into – to come back to. Menzies translated a fortress view of the self into a political platform.

Menzies' recruitment of notions of tradition, modernity and home in his mobilisation of a powerful political platform demonstrates the instability of notions of home and modernity in the lives of women in the 1940s and 1950s. In this sense, the desire for home women articulated 'as housewives' in this period cannot be seen as an existential longing. Such is the claim now made for the desire for home by some recent post-colonialist writings.[50] As Jenny Bourne Taylor points out, some kind of 'native experience', an experience of home, community or locality, functions as a type of cultural imaginary of a past form of social existence for these writers, to which exile – claimed to be the characteristic experience of the (post)modern age – is opposed.[51] Similarly, we are rejecting claims such as those made by David Harvey that the private home in modernity represents the focus of a desire for escape where material objects are collected in the form of a 'private museum to guard against the ravages of time-space compression'.[52] Such theorists, in spite of their overt commitment to historical and political analysis, nevertheless in practice maintain a nostalgic and universalistic concept of home that retains its gendered subtext.

We are suggesting that in certain contexts in the 1940s and 1950s, home represented, for women, the site of their agency. Defined as the suburban house with its modern appliances, planned spaces, garden and comfortable domestic existence, it constituted the sphere of everyday life which they were actively involved in making. Home was not a place separate from the contingencies of the modern world to withdraw into, but a place to be created – and if necessary, to go on strike for – if the future was to be possible. Women were involved, in de Certeau's terms, in an 'active practising of place'.[53] Their capacities and responsibilities in this sphere gave women a stake, as they saw it, in the life of the nation and in building modern life. In this scenario, women were active participants in modern social existence; they were central to what they believed to be the project of this new world – ensuring people could be in control of their own lives, to define their futures. The modern for them did not mean undertaking heroic voyages or making great scientific discoveries in a world from which the traveller could then return to existing security, to home as tradition. No such place existed for them. Home was not a bounded space, a fortress into which the individual could withdraw and from which all others could be excluded. Their modernity was about actively creating a place called home, securing a future for their children and an everyday life in which personal and intimate bodily relations could be properly looked after.

In this sense we agree with Iris Marion Young, who argues against the views of a number of feminists who say that we should give up on the longing for home. De Beauvoir is surely right, she claims, that 'much of what we call housework is drudgery, necessary but tedious, and also right that a life confined to such activity is slavery'.[54] But neither she nor more contemporary feminists like Irigaray or de Lauretis, Young points out, have recognised that preserving the meaningful identity of oneself and one's family by means of the loving care of the mementos of the home and of its very space is 'simply a different order of activity':

> [H]ome carries a core positive meaning as the material anchor for a sense of agency and a shifting and fluid identity. The concept of home does not oppose the personal and the political but instead describes conditions that make the political possible. The identity supporting material of home can be sources of resistance as well as privilege.[55]

But home has only had the potential to function in this way in modern times; it is not guaranteed as the site for this sort of meaningful human project. The arguments of women speaking as housewives in the 1940s and 1950s in Australia often sought to ensure that the home functioned in this way. At the same time other discourses of the period were also working to persuade women to operate precisely in the way that Irigaray finds so alarming – to 'pour their soul into the house because they have no other envelope for the self'.[56]

Certainly the political rhetoric of Robert Gordon Menzies sought to rework the sense of home to entice women into operating in this way. He employed the image of home as the suburban house and garden, but the role of women in this space was transformed. Menzies represented the social identification of housewife not as a form of agency but as a defensive solidarity into which women should withdraw to be 'spoken for', rather than to 'speak as'. He defined women in the home as constituting a sustaining world of tradition for men that could enable them to go out into the public sphere – fortified, strengthened against the terrors and risks of a society in which the individual was battered by forces beyond 'his' control. The 'modern housewife' became traditional in Menzies' terms. Modernity was the world of men, a world in which no one felt comfortable, but nevertheless a world that had to be. Oppositions between home/voyage, tradition/modernity, dependence/independence were employed in ways that were irrelevant in the arguments made by housewives in the 1940s and 1950s about how the nation should understand its political priorities.

At Home and at Work

At the same time as women were uneasily testing their voices as housewives, organised feminism was pursuing a quite different way of understanding women's agency. As Marilyn Lake argues, the feminist platform had been reformulated in the 1930s 'to accommodate the new emphasis on women's right to work'. 'In a major discursive shift,' she says, 'the woman as worker began to replace the woman as mother as the ideal feminist subject.'[57] Feminism began to focus less on the difference of women than on their equality with men. In the 1940s and 1950s, feminists like Jessie Street worked within this equal rights framework in which women's rights to equal pay were central to their political platform, but she retained an interest in women as mothers and housewives. Women's domestic responsibilities became mostly an issue of adequate financial remuneration or financial independence. She argued for wages for mothers, as had Muriel Heagney in her presentation to the Royal Commission established in 1927 by the Nationalist Prime Minister Stanley Bruce to inquire into the feasibility of introducing a federal scheme of motherhood or childhood endowment.[58]

But in the Women's Charter of 1943, which Jessie Street played a major part in developing, only one section specifically mentions 'women as mother and/or homemaker'. The Charter declared a strong commitment to the 'indispensable service rendered to the community by mothers, accompanied as it is by inevitable and specific handicaps, and responsibilities'. It focused on ensuring economic independence for the woman at home through an adequate child endowment and a personal endowment for the mother and/or home-maker.[59] But the Charter did also call for adequate day nurseries, a casual nursing service, community centres and child-care centres. As Marilyn Lake argues, the latter proposal indicated a major shift as the responsibilities for looking after children were no longer viewed as exclusively those of the mother but were seen as being able to be provided for through professional services.[60] While day nurseries and a casual nursing service were suited to the needs of mothers needing part-time relief from their responsibilities, child-care centres shifted that responsibility to government agencies. The provision of these services also recognised the possibility of women having identities as both mothers and workers. The possibility of these multiple identities for women was to be conceptualised by 1970s feminism in terms of women's 'dual roles'.

But the chief preoccupation of organised feminism in the 1940s and 1950s was with equal rights for women to enter the workplace and for women as wage earners. In this context, the drudgery of the housewife became an argument for why women should be full-time wage earners. Jessie Street, for whom the core principle of feminism was, as Marilyn Lake argues,[61] 'the necessity of women's independence', declared that 'Woman's unpaid work in the home undermines her independence, restricts her liberty and limits her development and opportunities in many fields.'[62]

Muriel Heagney, a powerful advocate for the needs of working-class women, had similarly shifted her focus by the 1940s to being primarily concerned with the need for women to have access to adequately paid full-time work. She no longer argued for the financial independence of women in the home but sought to establish this for women outside the home. And equal pay became central to the platform for feminism of the period, although it was also divisive of feminism during this time.

Heagney had been an early advocate of equal pay for women in her various capacities associated with the union movement and Labor Party politics in the 1920s. She continued her campaign during the depression and played a central role in the founding of the Council of Action for Equal Pay (CAEP) in 1937. But she fell out with Jessie Street during the war. Street argued for a more gradualist programme of reform whereas the CAEP, under Heagney's influence, maintained a strong commitment to demanding the full male rate for female workers. Changes to the kinds of work that women were doing after the war as well as divisions within the Council about the appropriateness of its political stance led to its demise in 1948. In this same year Heagney published her book, *Are Women Taking Men's Jobs?* which broke new ground as a serious study of women's labour and the poverty and discrimination suffered by Australia's working women.

While the focus of organised feminism remained on equal pay for paid work, the position of the housewife received attention from time to time over the next ten years. In the Australian context, Margaret Harland wrote in 1947 of the difficulties of housewives since the second world war and how their attempts to improve their lot had been 'met by stony silence by our legislators'.[63] She argued that raising a family should be recognised as the married woman's job and that the state should recompense her for this work, not just through child endowment but through an adequate system of pay so that she has money for her own use. In Britain, Alva Myrdal and Viola Klein published a book in 1956 on 'Women's Two Roles' that was to have a significant impact in the development of feminist discourse during the 1960s in Australia. They argued that 'the social isolation of the modern housewife is a powerful motive for women to seek employment outside their homes'.[64] They questioned why research was needed into why married women were seeking paid employment when the same question was not asked of married men, and concluded that both middle-class and working-class women were finding that 'only through a job, a culturally defined job, will they be liberated'.[65]

Myrdal and Klein's arguments were taken up by Jean Blackburn and Ted Jackson in Australia through a Fabian Society pamphlet published in 1963 in which they asked 'is the concept of the housewife who drudges her life away in an already spotless suburban home becoming rather absurd?'[66] They reviewed a range of studies that had sought to discern whether housewives were discontented, but found that the evidence was inconclusive. Nevertheless, they argued forcefully that by leading the life of a full-time housewife, women were wasting their talent and needed to enter the workforce for 'their own happiness and mental health':[67] 'The circumscribed domestic round, the absence of productive satisfactory work, and the social isolation engendered by the prevailing suburban cult of privacy all tend to make the housewife a frustrated, intellectually inbred person, who having little else upon which to lavish her attention, is in danger of fussing unmercifully over her children.'[68]

These arguments about the dissatisfactions of the housewife were to be powerfully echoed only a few years later by Betty Friedan, as we have seen in the previous chapter. They also relied on the understanding of paid work that was to become so important to second wave feminism. This movement adopted as unproblematic the view that paid work was essential to an individual's sense of fulfilment. Tom Lutz traces this 'hedonization of the work ethic' to the 1920s, when work for the professional and managerial classes became something to be done because it is fulfilling rather than because of a protestant ethic. In this period, he suggests, the work ethic was in the process of being resurrected and refurbished, 'not as a frame for moral living for the working class but as an answer to the boredom and alienation for the professional and managerial class, as an individual and class tonic, as a hedonized pathway to progress.'[69]

He notes that in this period too the housewife began to emerge as a nervous or bored figure whose mental health became of popular concern and for whom paid work became a possible solution. In the 1940s in Australia the major social changes of this period appeared to have prompted other concerns so that the drudgery of the housewife was more a national preoccupation than her boredom. But in the 1950s that drudgery was translated more into a boring rather than tiring experience and the solution proposed was precisely paid work.

The issue of the bored housewife will be revisited in Chapter 5. What is of more interest to us in this chapter is the way in which 1940s feminism sees the housewife as a figure who has particular responsibilities, powers and concerns that feminism seeks to represent – in the sense of giving voice to her concerns – assisting her to speak in her own name. In the 1950s we then see an important shift with the housewife now being represented in the sense of feminism seeking to speak on her behalf as a figure who needs to be rescued from her plight – rather than enabling her to speak for herself. She appears by this time as an identifiable if problematic figure within feminism. She is represented as victim, suffering from boredom and futility, in an argument about the equality of women and the social and political necessity of ensuring that women's talents are appropriately recognised and valued. It is this view that 1960s and 1970s feminism extended and elaborated. Yet at the same time, as we will see in the following chapter, alternatives to work as fulfilment were being offered increasingly to women through the popular magazines of the 1940s and 1950s.

Notes

1. Town Clerk's report, 10 February 1947, Ryde Municipal Council records.
2. Kate Darian-Smith, *On the Home Front: Melbourne in Wartime, 1939–1945*, Oxford, Oxford University Press, 1990, p. 97.
3. Kay Saunders and Raymond Evans, 'No Place Like Home: The evolution of the Australian housewife', in Kay Saunders and Ramon Evans (eds), *Gender Relations in Australia: Domination and Negotiation*, Sydney, Harcourt, Brace & Jovanovich, 1992, pp. 175–96.
4. Darian-Smith, *On the Home Front*, p. 96.
5. New South Wales Parliamentary Debates, House of Assembly, 22 November 1944, p. 1139.
6. Appendix 1, Interim Report of the National Health and Medical Research Council on the Decline in the Birth Rate (Interim Report of the NHMRC), 1944, p. 9.
7. Ibid.
8. Annexure G, Statements made by the women themselves in response to a public invitation to state their reasons for limiting families, Interim Report of the NHMRC, 1944, p. 70
9. Ibid., pp. 70–90.
10. New South Wales Parliamentary Debates, House of Assembly, 22 November 1944, p. 1138.
11. Transcript, 'A Woman's World?', *Women's Session*, Presented by Clare Mitchell, AA C3224/1, Box 4, 13 June 1947. See Chapter 5 for discussion of the *Women's Session*.
12. Denise Riley, *War in the Nursery: Theories of the Child and Mother*, London, Virago, 1983, p. 7.
13. Valerie Walkerdine and Helen Lucey, *Democracy in the Kitchen: Regulating Mothers and Socialising Daughters*, London, Virago, 1989.
14. Marilyn Lake, *Getting Equal: The History of Australian Feminism*, Sydney, Allen and Unwin, 1999.
15. Judith Smart, 'Private, Public and Political: The Efflorescence of the Housewives' Associations in Eastern Australia, 1915–1960', unpublished conference paper, presented at the Australian Historical Studies Association Conference, Melbourne, 1994, available from author.
16. Judith Smart, '"For the Good That We Can Do": Cecilia Downing and Feminist Christian Citizenship', *Australian Feminist Studies*, 19, Autumn 1994, pp. 39–60.

17. Ibid., p. 41.

18. Ibid.

19. Mrs (Cecilia) John Downing and Bill Newnham (interviewer), 'The Housewives' Association and a Bill of Rights for the Home', *Women's Session*, presented by Sheila Hunt, AA SP 300/1 Box 7, 28 September 1949.

20. Catriona Beaumont, 'Citizens Not Feminists: The Boundary Negotiated between Citizenship and Feminism by Mainstream Women's Organisations in England, 1928–39', *Women's History Review*, 9 (2), 2000, p. 425.

21. Bill of Rights for the Home, as presented to the Premier of Victoria (Mr Holloway) on 4 February 1948, Federated Housewives' Association, *Records* 1945–53, Mitchell Library, MLMSS 4155/H 3896, Sydney.

22. Ibid.

23. The Housewives' Association of NSW, '[Aims]', *The Housewife*, January 1954, p. 27.

24. New Housewives' Association, 'Report of Canberra Delegation, 5 April 1948', Chatswood Branch, Correspondence and Reports, Mitchell Library, MLMSS 6229, Sydney, 1947–1948; 'Housewives' June Conference to be Historic Occasion', *The New Housewife*, 6, June 1949, p. 1; Pat Ranald, 'Women's Organisations and the Issue of Communism', in Ann Curthoys and John Merritt (eds), *Better Dead Than Red: Australia's First Cold War, 1945–1959*, Sydney, Allen and Unwin, vol. 2, 1986, pp. 41–57, 191–4.

25. 'Ban the Bomb and Banish High Prices', leaflet, Janie Overton papers, File on Women's Day, Women's Movement and Union of Australian Women 1940–71, Mitchell Library, MLMSS 6968/1, Sydney.

26. Lynette Finch, 'Could "Winnie the War Winner" Organise Women?' *Hecate*, 10 (1), 1984, p. 20.

27. Progressive Housewives' Association, 'Objectives 1946', *Records*, Australian Archives, A6122/45 Item 1291, Canberra; 'New Housewives' Association Constitution 1948/1949', Janie Overton papers, File on Women's Day, Women's Movement and Union of Australian Women 1940–71, Mitchell Library, MLMSS 6968/1, Sydney.

28. Barbara Curthoys and Audrey McDonald, *More than a Hat and Glove Brigade: The Story of the Union of Australian Women*, Sydney, Union of Australian Women, 1996, p. 7.

29. *Sydney Morning Herald*, 26 May 1945, p. 9.

30. *Australian Women's Weekly*, 2 March 1946, p. 18.

31. Peter Spearritt, *Sydney Since the Twenties*, Sydney, Hale and Iremonger, 1978, p. 78.

32. Graham Allan and Graham Crow (eds), *Home and Family: Creating the Domestic Sphere*, London, Macmillan, 1989, p. 9.

33. Carolyn Allport, *Women and Public Housing in Sydney, 1930–1961*, unpub-

lished PhD thesis Sydney, Macquarie University, 1990, p. 237.

34. J.T. Purcell, 'Home Sweet? (a Study of the Housing Problem)', unpublished manuscript, 1 March 1954, semi-personal file of J.T. Purcell, 1953, 1969, File No. 7/7580, New South Wales State Archives.
35. *Australian Women's Weekly*, 12 September 1956, p. 2.
36. *Australian Women's Weekly*, 25 May 1946, p. 33.
37. *Australian Women's Weekly*, 14 April 1945, p. 32.
38. Dorothy Hewett, *Bobbin Up*, Melbourne, Australian Book Society, p. 50.
39. Ibid., p. 185.
40. Ibid., pp. 75.
41. *Australian House and Garden*, February 1949, pp. 24–7.
42. Carolyn Steedman, *Landscape for a Good Woman*, London, Virago, 1986, p. 108.
43. *Australian Women's Weekly*, 28 June 1947, p. 354.
44. Steedman, *Landscape for a Good Woman*, p. 81.
45. Judith Brett, *Robert Menzies' Forgotten People*, Sydney, Pan Macmillan, 1992, pp. 44–6.
46. Ibid., p. 52.
47. Ibid., pp. 56–8; see also *Australian Women's Weekly*, 6 August 1949, p. 32.
48. Brett, *Robert Menzies' Forgotten People*, p. 73.
49. Ibid.
50. See, for example, Edward Said, 'Reflections on Exile', *Granta, After the Revolution*, 13, 1984, pp. 159–72.
51. Jenny Bourne Taylor, 'Re-locations – from Bradford to Brighton', *New Formations*, 17, 1992, p. 92.
52. David Harvey, *The Condition of Postmodernity*, Oxford, Basil Blackwell, 1989, p. 292
53. Michel de Certeau, *The Practice of Everyday Life*, S.F. Rendall (trans.), Berkeley, University of California Press, 1984, p. 117.
54. Iris Marion Young, *Intersecting Voices: Dilemmas of Gender, Political Philosophy, and Policy*, Princeton, NJ, Princeton University Press, 1997, p. 148.
55. Ibid., p. 159. Young's reference to the home as a possible site for resistance here draws on the work of bell hooks in *Yearning: Race, Gender and Cultural Politics*, Boston, Southland Press, 1990.
56. Quoted in Young, *Intersecting Voices*, p. 149.
57. Lake, *Getting Equal*, p. 173.
58. Ibid., pp. 103–4.
59. Heather Radi (ed.), *Jessie Street: Documents and Essays*, Sydney, Women's Redress Press, 1990, p. 37.
60. Lake, *Getting Equal*, p. 196.

61. Marilyn Lake, 'Jessie Street and "Feminist Chauvinism"', in Radi (ed.), *Jessie Street*, p. 21.
62. Radi (ed.), *Jessie Street*, p. 43.
63. Margaret Harland, *Women's Place in Society*, Melbourne, F.W. Cheshire, 1947, p. 25.
64. Alva Myrdal and Viola Klein, *Women's Two Roles*, London, Routledge and Kegan Paul, 1956/1968, p. 83.
65. Ibid., p. 189.
66. Jean Blackburn and Ted Jackson, *Australian Wives Today*, NSW Fabian Society Pamphlet, 1963, p. 2.
67. Ibid., p. 35.
68. Ibid., p. 24.
69. Tom Lutz, '"Sweat or Die": The Hedonization of the Work Ethic in the 1920s', *American Literary History*, 8 (2), 1996, p. 262.

–3–

Dream Stuff

All she wanted to do was work until she and Alec had saved up enough to get the deposit on their house . . . that beautiful dream house on the little block of land out in Blacktown, that one with the pink and black bathroom, real tiles and the kitchen with the stainless steel sink, and the new baby in the frilled bassinet on the front porch.

Dorothy Hewett, *Bobbin Up*[1]

In September 1950, the *Australian Women's Weekly* ran a contest inviting 'home-makers' to submit designs for a new three-bedroom house because, as the magazine proposed, 'the people who know all about houses and the running of them are the women homemakers'.[2] The *Weekly* offered a total of £4,000 in prizes for the best designs, with a first prize of £2,000 – enough to build a modest suburban house in the early 1950s.[3] During the post-war period the modern family home assumed a special place in the national imaginary, reflected in this injunction to housewives to think about how their ideal home would look. The *Weekly's* competition suggested that readers could sweep away the shortcomings of traditional, or as they were described, 'pre-war', homes. Badly designed from the point of view of the home-maker, the traditional pre-war home represented 'errors of judgement . . . perpetuated in costly bricks and mortar in many big and small houses'. Because architects did not have to 'apply the problems of practical living' to their plans, their 'design mistakes' could cause a lifetime of inconvenience for housewives: 'Once built in they are there to stay. . . . Bad arrangements of rooms and long treks from kitchen to living quarters give hundreds of housewives fallen arches, and weight-lifting feats with clothes baskets up and down steps to the laundry shorten both tempers and lives.'[4]

This chapter outlines how magazines and newspaper feature articles which discussed the new look and design of the post-war period initiated far-reaching changes to the capacities of the housewife. This call to women to participate in planning and decorating their 'dream homes' certainly allowed the magazines to attract new readers and advertisers; yet it also reflects the ways in which the housewife was able to exercise a new kind of agency. As we have indicated in the previous chapters, during the post-war period, women were no longer excluded from the design and planning process, seen simply as 'users' of the home, but intimately involved in constituting it. Increasingly decribed as 'experts' on everyday life, invited to think about better ways of organising the space of the home, they became 'modernisers' of domesticity. Beatriz Colomina has suggested in her essay on modernist architect Adolf Loos, published in the collection *Sexuality and Space*, that gender relations are not just reflected in space, but produced by spatial organisation: 'Architecture is not simply a platform that accommodates the viewing subject. It is a viewing mechanism that produces the subject. It precedes and frames its occupant.'[5] Mark Wigley argues in the same volume that this point has often been overlooked by a feminist history of the home as a space to leave behind: 'The implied familial narrative of feminism growing up and leaving the secure private domain of the house for the public sphere exempts the house itself from analysis. . . . The specific mechanisms with which it constructs space need to be interrogated before its effects can be resisted.'[6] Cultural histories such as Colomina's and Wigley's suggest that domestic space needs to be recognised as an agent and ground of a gendered subjectivity, rather than simply the outcome of individual choice and taste which can be relegated to an invisible, private domain. Further, as Joel Sanders has suggested, the boundaries between architecture and domestic design, or more specifically between modernist myths of male architectural authorship versus feminised mass consumption, need to be understood as inscribing the particularly modernist portrayals of the 'gay decorator' and the 'emasculated architect'.[7] This division between 'masculine' architectural science and 'feminine' design practice, and the ascription of agency only to the former term, is problematic, Sanders and others have suggested, and needs to be rethought in terms of interdependence and mutuality: 'the surfaces of our buildings work like the clothing that covers our bodies; both are coded to enable us to articulate the various identities that we assume every day'.[8] As we argue here, the reorganisation of the post-war home questioned distinctions between public and private identities, and the intrusion of the public gaze onto home life gave the housewife a chance to construct a new, modern identity as an author of domestic space.

In addition to women being constituted as subjects of modernity through this call to play an active role in home design, women's and home magazines placed a great deal of emphasis on planning the home as planning the future. Domesticity was to be at the core of what a post-war world would be about. A number of authors have pointed to the way in which domesticity became central to ideas of the modern citizen in Australia in the 1950s. Domesticity, as John Murphy argues, was now not a means of retreat from public affairs but an expression of one's citizenship.[9] The decade or so after the second world war was by no means a homogeneous period. As we showed in the previous chapter, conservatism and anxieties about change vied with discourses of hope and optimism. But the language of progress dominated. Women's role was both to imagine a better future and to make these dreams reality. This chapter therefore looks closely at how women as housewives were made the key figures of this new domesticated modernity via mass

circulation publications during the 1940s and early 1950s. The arguments discussed in the previous chapter about women at home which concerned the
women's organisations of the 1940s – the improvement of their working conditions
as a public good – were weakened by the shift of responsibility for domesticity
from public authorities towards the family as a group of private individuals, a shift
which was organised around forms of consumption. Rather than a form of work on
behalf of the whole society, housework during the 1950s was increasingly constructed as a form of labour that benefited only one's immediate family. The housewife as consumer therefore was offered a new set of emotions in home-making
linked to the power to dream about the perfect home, and the perfect family. The
final section of this chapter raises questions about how this merging of the figure
of the housewife with the landscape of suburbia in this period shaped a possible
rejection of the very term 'housewife' during the mid- to late 1950s.

The Housing Problem

Several important shifts in the ways that Australians lived laid the foundations for
a post-war housing crisis immediately after the war, and also for the long boom
that followed. As was noted in the previous chapter, the housing situation during
and immediately after the end of the war was a great source of deprivation, and
provoked many reports and investigations that linked the national decline in fer-
tility to housing conditions. The scarcity of decent housing was a topic which
appeared regularly in magazines and newspapers during the 1940s, and despite
calls to heroically 'make do' under the restrictions of wartime rationing, it was a
constant source of protest. One woman, exasperated with her housing situation,
wrote to the *Australian Women's Weekly* in 1943, which reported that 'like scores
of other [readers, she had] included a plan of the home she hopes to own one day':

> We are living in an upstairs flat with no conveniences, a pocket-handkerchief backyard,
> and a dark and draughty staircase. There is always a smell of gas from leaky gas pipes
> and the bathroom is so dark we have to put on the light to see to wash. There is a narrow
> passage where the westerly winds whistle in the winter, and the house never sees the
> sun. I have no sink at all for a getaway for the water, and have to carry same down two
> flights of stairs several times per day. The people in the downstairs flat share the bath-
> room, lavatory and laundry. My contention is that life under these conditions is not
> worth living. I drew this rough plan . . . just to show the idea I had of a lawn courtyard,
> where small children could play in the sun but not get the wind, also where members
> of the family could sunbake without the prying eyes of neighbours and of passers-by.
> The mother can see her children from any of the rooms. In wet weather they can still
> have their exercise by the accommodation of the all-round verandah. . . . I think it is
> high time something was done to encourage the building of a better type of home for
> the people.[10]

The vision of the modern home described in the letter reflected both a retreat from the public gaze of the neighbourhood, and an intensification of the private space of the home, but more importantly it demonstrates that the housewife, from her vantage point of the pre-modern home, was able to speak on behalf of 'the people'. A woman 'almoner', or social worker, at Sydney's Crown Street Women's Hospital also spoke to the need to modernise home life when she wrote that 'The housing shortage is one of the greatest contributing factors to . . . maladjusted wartime marriages': 'It is difficult enough for young people to adjust themselves to a marriage which was interrupted by the war. It is a great deal more difficult when the adjustment has to be made to an already overcrowded household.'[11]

An Army Education Service discussion pamphlet published in 1945 titled *Our Population Problem*, and aimed at men about to make the transition to civilian lives, proposed that family life and the security and future of the nation were linked. It raised the spectre of 'a vast Asiatic expansion' swamping 'the desired [and ideal Australian population of] 20 millions . . . with 1,000 Asiatics to the north of Australia'. The pamphlet argued that population growth in countries like India and China following their future industrialisation would eventually engulf the Australian family: 'if we Australians wish to preserve our way of life we must be prepared not only to take immediate steps to increase our net reproduction rate . . . but also to conduct a vigorous migration policy'.[12] A lack of detached housing for families was posed by this Army Education Service pamphlet as one of the answers to the question of why women did not have more children: 'modern flats are too small and babies are unwanted in them. Parents should not be encouraged to try to rear a family within the restricted limits of flats, but proper housing should be found for them.'

For the few years after the war, housing problems continued to be central to this anxiety about population decreases. The winner of a contest for the best letter on 'the frustrations of life today' in 1947, Mrs Ivy Murray of Balmain, described how 'housing difficulties, the high cost of living and the shortages of essential food and clothing' adversely affected her family, and contributed to a sense of 'losing herself':

My main frustration is that I am slowly losing my personality and that the bright, happy person my husband married has disappeared. In two short years I have become a neurotic, nagging woman. The war cannot be blamed, because most of the war I was a single girl. . . . We are only a young couple, but by the time things get back to normal (if they ever do) we will have been so frustrated in our early married life that all our incentive will have disappeared. We were so full of hopes and plans when we married, but very little remains. The Government should make a law to have all houses built with every modern convenience and labor-saving device. It would give the younger people a new slant on life and induce them to populate the country, besides helping them to lessen the divorce rate. When a woman loses her personality she loses her husband.[13]

The figure of the downtrodden housewife and her lot of 'primitive' housing conditions was also used to mobilise anti-government sentiment during the late 1940s, when the Chifley Labor government was blamed for the housing crisis and ongoing shortages in commodities and basic services: 'Some time ago the Prime Minister [Mr Chifley] promised us that we were about to enter a new Golden Age, but to most women his promise is like the pot of gold at the foot of the rainbow – a pleasant fairy story for children.'[14]

The image of the underdeveloped home and the suffering housewife persisted after the change of leadership to the Menzies conservative government in 1949, but this was shifted to a private complaint, rather than a public problem. A report in the *Sunday Telegraph* in 1950 claimed that over 50,000 people in New South Wales sought medical and psychiatric help because of 'steadily intensifying nervous illness caused by their inability to get homes'.[15] The Victorian Assistant-Director of Mental Hygiene was quoted in this report as saying, 'Many people living in cramped quarters or with relatives have become mentally unbalanced. To be at ease mentally, people must live as they want to live.' The solution offered to this condition for now was to redesign the home, rather than change the role of the housewife. This solution, however, provided women with the ability to shape the conditions of their existence, and this played out in a variety of ways which we examine in the next section of this chapter.

The Housewife Speaks

A widespread re-location of the population from the inner cities to the suburbs took place following slum clearance schemes initiated during the 1930s. While a greater proportion of Australians started buying their own detached and planned homes after the war, and moved from rural areas to urban areas, this was accompanied by a long-term decline in employment in the personal and domestic service sector.[16] The homes that most Australians lived in – or aspired to live in – were reconfigured to match these changes in the modes of everyday life.[17] As Jennifer Craik has observed, during this period interior design replaced household management as the focus of domestic ideology. Practices of interior decoration, she contends, combine expressions of 'personality with goals or ambitions, as well as aesthetic conventions in the projection of a public image of homelife'.[18] Home magazines articulated interior design *as* a form of household management in the 1950s. Whether budgeting for a new house or renovations, deciding on the kind of home the family would live in, or how it would be furnished, women were given a new capacity to shape (their part of) the world during the 1940s and 1950s. As Peter Biskind notes of 1950s films such as *Giant* and *Pillow Talk*,[19] female characters shaped the space of the home and, in doing so, shaped and controlled man's environment. Biskind argues that 'Interior decoration becomes a metaphor for women's power to make over man's world, his values, in her image.'[20] Decoration of domestic space was not simply a cinematic trope, but was envisioned in the print culture of the same decade as creating a specifically gendered version of modernity. Women, as the agents of the modernisation of the home, and by extension everyday life, explored a different modernity from the kind of masculine vision that focused on transforming the sublime and grandiose spaces of industrial culture. Re-making the home and the suburb as a small-scale utopia, a more humble version of modernity, proliferated in popular cultural forms outside the national vision of economic development.

Both middle-class and working-class women were expected to play the housewife's role. For working-class women, the two main forms of home-based economy disappeared in the 1950s firstly with the shrinking of the domestic sector as a traditional area of women's employment and secondly with the diminishing contribution of boarders and lodgers as a source of domestic income. These former activities of outsourced domesticity were transposed into a new form of household economy: the task of producing oneself and one's own family as modern individuals. Work in the home became less physically arduous, yet it did not disappear completely. The modern housewife who re-made her home in the image of middle-class domesticity was not only making her household labour more efficient, comfortable and pleasurable, but also producing modern citizens.[21]

The housewife became an increasingly visible and vocal subject in the public sphere, mobilised around planning and housing issues, and appearing at the intersection of governmental and market discourses. In this way, she transcended traditional class divisions, but only at the expense of emphasising gender differences. For example, an advertisement for the Colonial Sugar Refining Company's 'Cane-ite' wall and ceiling boards published in the *Australian Women's Weekly* in 1947 echoed this extension of the housewife's perspective into commerical and public culture: 'Every housewife will agree that there should be more women architects to design homes from a woman's understanding viewpoint.' Thus women were regarded as classless, modern consumers *and* able to become architects, and were placed in dialogue with the discipline of architecture about what kind of domesticity would better suit them. While women architects were hardly in evidence in the pages of the *Weekly*, Walter Bunning, an architect and officer of the Department of Post-war Reconstruction, wrote an article for the magazine during 1944 inviting readers to send questions about post-war housing to himself and another architect, Hal Savage, which would be answered in a radio programme to be held in early January of the next year on the ABC. Bunning spoke to the readership of the *Weekly* both as subjects of modernity and as workers in the home:

Women will play a big part in the designing of post-war houses, will bring a new awareness, a scientific awareness to their post-war jobs, whether it is planning a meal or planning a home. . . .

Scientific planning will be applied to every part of the post-war house. Convenience in running the home in order to do away with difficult and laborious cleaning and ease in the preparation of meals, will be two of the main objectives. This will release the housewife from uninteresting routine duties to spend her leisure moments in more creative work.[22]

In a more comprehensive effort to 'discover what sort of homes Australian women want after the war', the Department of Post-war Reconstruction, in conjunction with *Woman* magazine, sponsored a series of articles about 'Planning the Post-war Home' during the early 1940s. The study – which was also published as a booklet titled *The Housewife Speaks*, aimed at Department-sponsored community discussion groups – asked women readers to indicate what they considered to be the ideal house size, layout and design for their family, as well as canvassing the need for community centres, nurseries, supervised playgrounds, shopping and transport facilities. The Department's survey of Australian women, via *Woman*'s readership, showed that 'there is widespread interest in home planning': 'in many instances readers not only answered the question by indicating "yes" or "no", but wrote letters when they felt the questions needed more comprehensive handling'.[23]

Mrs Mary M. Ryan, the only woman member of the Commonwealth Housing Commission established in 1943 as part of the Post-war Reconstruction project, gave an address titled 'Homes of the Future' to the National Council of Women in Adelaide in September 1944, in which she called for women's everyday experiences to be revolutionised: 'We must design housing for the future, not for the past or merely for the present. Any attempt to preserve the past must fail.'[24] During her tenure on the Commission, Ryan drew on her own experiences as a country housewife living in a house without running water or electricity to assess the proposals brought before it.[25] She was less than enthusiastic about many proposals brought before the Commission because they 'hark back to the old way of life':

The people for whom we should be building houses are young people who are now working hard in the Defence Services and the factories.

The mothers of the future will be the young women who are now in uniform or overalls. The background of their life will be quite different from that of their parents. They will be used to living together or working in groups, and to sharing many aspects of their lives. It is certain they will not lead the same lives as their parents.[26]

Ryan's embrace of modern architecture was an embrace of a modern social order: 'Housing in its fullest sense will help people to live the type of lives adapted to their economic conditions. At present it retards them. Badly designed houses prevent people from taking advantage of the scientific developments of the age.'[27] While the state investigated the future shape of the Australian home and family, according to the home-making magazines of the post-war period, planning and dreaming, then choosing and buying were now the key activities of home-making, and these activities were becoming increasingly gendered. Planning the home became a feminised activity, while building itself (and working to earn the money to invest in housing) remained masculine. A woman writing in *House and Garden* magazine endorsed the opinion of the pre-war home expressed by Ryan when she declared 'I'd like to blow up my kitchen':

> The saner alternative, of stripping the whole place and replanning with modern equipment, won't help in this case. For my kitchen, like seventy-five percent of those in homes to-day, isn't just badly arranged. It's badly built. Too small and crowded for family use, placed like an after-thought in the coldest and darkest corner of the house, and with essential things, like sink and stove, and doors all in the wrong places. ...
>
> It's a sad little kitchen – sadder because it's so common – but at least it has one merit. It has taught me to know exactly the kind of kitchen I'll build when I put a match to that bomb, and to find out what kind of kitchens appeal to other women of the same mind. And that's surely something![28]

Magazines showed young couples how they could participate in this new way of imagining the Australian home. It was now not enough to find an affordable home and furnish it with what was to hand. A kind of second-order consumption with the consumption of images, ideas, designs, diagrams, and so on, as much as actual goods, became the foundation of home-making.

At times the imagination of the ideal dream home replaced more material forms of home-making activity with the delays and shortages of materials so prevalent during and immediately after the war. As the manufacturer of 'Electric Servants', Australian General Electric advertised that planning for a Hotpoint kitchen would fortify morale 'with a dream of happiness for a day that will break ... this year ... next year'.[29] Early and informed preparation was advocated. The housewife became the co-ordinator of a team of home-building experts from the architect, to the builder, to the painter; she was to ensure that all parts of the home resolved into a harmonious whole. An advertisement for Masonite recommended that, while saving and purchasing were delayed, the imagining of the home could begin while shortages persisted; it instructed housewives, 'Start now to design your future home':

> Observation ... thought ... a pencil, paper and ruler are all you need to start planning a really 'liveable' home. True, you can't build it just yet, but an ideal home doesn't just 'happen'. It results from months of planning and thinking – planning and thinking that should start NOW.

Start a 'Home' notebook. Write down all those features in your present home that irk you; that make work and unnecessary steps – and your ideas to correct them. As you visit the homes of your friends from time to time observe points that appeal to you. Record those, too . . . .[30]

This dreaming about home, based on the limitations and shortfalls of existing realities, took precedence over the involvement of the architect. Experts were to assist them but the couple was placed at the centre of the home design:

When you have finished your planning, both of layout and materials, go to an architect. His training and experience will save you many times his moderate fee. He will quickly show you what is practicable and what is impracticable in your plans. He will be able to knit your ideas into an economical compact whole.[31]

A constantly shifting border between commonsense and fantasy was articulated in terms of feminine and masculine knowledges. A 1945 Army Education Service discussion pamphlet warned men that while they had been away at war their wives would have been thinking a great deal about the form of the post-war home:

The interior set-up of your post-war home may be safely left to the women. They are all a-tingle with electric ideas these days. They know all there is to be known about electric stoves, washing machines, bath heaters, irons, toasters, mangles, radios and radiators, refrigerators . . . and all the other electric gadgets. You will crackle when you get into your new home. You might even fuse if you don't watch your step. Perhaps that will happen when you come to pay the bill.

Women are all agog about insets, shower recesses, drop tables, flat doors, button door knobs, round corners for all rooms, and two-way larders for the tradesmen. . . . They are clamorous for concrete ramps from kitchen door to drying ground, chutes for rubbish, hot water by the turn of a tap.[32]

The man's part in this division of labour was 'to earn enough to keep this ideal home going and your wife happy inside it. She will run it. . . . You will do a spot of washing-up yourself and like it. Be grateful if you are not asked to take a hand with the weekly washing.'[33]

During late 1945 and early 1946, the *Australian Home Beautiful* (*AHB*) magazine featured a series of articles about home planning told from the point of view of Joanna, a young woman awaiting the return of her fiancé, Peter, from military service.[34] The cover of the magazine published as part of this series showed a smiling young woman looking at an architectural model of a modern one-storey home (figure 3.1). The extremity of scale between the house and the woman places her in control of the 'whole' of the home: she is made giant-like and all-seeing, able to imagine herself and her family in miniature living inside this perfect space.

Figure 3.1 Cover published in *Australian Home Beautiful,* March 1946, woman looking at model house. Cover illustration for Mary Jane Seymour, 'Joanna Plans a Home – Part 6'. By permission of *Australian Home Beautiful*.

In the first article of the series, titled 'The Dream', Joanna has already started planning her ideal home and wants to start a family as soon as Peter returns from military service. Joanna is an enthusiastic modernist, and the couple debate design philosophies as they formulate the plan of their new house. When Peter suggests 'a nice big entrance hall with a clear run right through [for children to play in]', Joanna counters with the (modern) opinion that:

> Passages were out of date and she hoped to have wall to wall carpets everywhere, and anyway the children could have a sandpit to play in out in the garden. That wasn't much good when it rained was Peter's comment, and the poor little things had to have a place somewhere or else it was no good building a house at all.[35]

Luckily, before Joanna and Peter can get into an argument about hallways and carpets, Spike, a fellow war veteran, calls and invites the couple to visit his house:

> So they went. It turned out that Peter's friend was an architect, though he wasn't practising then, but doing a war job. He had built a nice little house for himself two or three years before, and there were lots of things about it that Joanna liked very much. She liked the general arrangement of the rooms, the ample but unobtrusive provision of cupboards and the feeling that the house might be easy to run. Details, too, caught her eye and were mentally jotted down.[36]

Joanna's attention to detail reveals exactly how this new agency was constituted for women in the practice of home-making. As the author of this series argued, contemplation of domestic minutiae was not a frivolous or time-wasting activity. The modern challenge to make the home anew drew on women's authority on day-to-day living, moving domestic design firmly into their domain:

> It was amazing, Joanna thought, how much time one could spend on this business of planning a home. And the deeper one got into it the more fascinating it grew. For the last two months she had been going around the furniture shops and looking with new eyes at her friends' color schemes with the object of working out a furnishing scheme of her own. The time had not been wasted, for she felt that when the time came to make the actual decisions she would be infinitely more capable of advancing her own ideas and combating any fantastic notions with which her friend Spike might have imbued Peter.[37]

Home design magazines such as *AHB* circulated examples of latest design theory in application, and, most importantly, they provided a point of reception and negotiation for the sometimes brutal terms of rational modernist home design. The *AHB* reported on the results of a competition held by *The Melbourne Sun* (published by *AHB*'s parent company), in which 'Two leading architects, a prominent master-builder and the editor' chose one design from nearly 500 entries. The winning entry, from 'Mr Jeff Harding, ARAIA, of Balwyn, Victoria', displayed 'several modern trends in today's architecture': 'One is the linking of the interior with the out-of-doors. Another is the generous use of glass (which serves the same purpose). A third is the exchange of gabled roofs for very low pitched or perfectly flat ones, and finally the growing practice of definitely planning for future extensions.'[38]

The modern home, freed of 'traditional' fussiness, architectural muddle and unneeded walls and surfaces, reflected the new sense of boundlessness and possibility of the post-war society. When giving anonymous advice on how to improve readers' plans, Mr X., an architect responsible for a column called 'Considering the Plan', affirmed women's need for houses that would be less demanding of their time. Mr X. thought that a reader, Mrs S.F., wrote 'feelingly' of her design for the home from the perspective of the housewife. Her letter explained her thoughts for how her future house would bring about a more streamlined existence:

> I am sending to you my plan of a home I wish to build. I have lived for 14 years in a long, single-fronted villa, with kitchen right at rear, nearly 60ft from back to front door, so I must have walked untold miles answering door bells and nursing the family when ill. So I am determined my new home shall be central in every way, and step-saving. Also, my husband and I are keen gardeners, and our back garden is always a mass of blooms and tidy lawns, but no one ever sees them unless they peek out the bathroom window. So I have planned my house round the garden, so to speak. I think the lounge view and dining room windows ought to reflect the Glory of the Garden.[39]

While Margaret Lord, author of a popular text on contemporary Australian interior design, ridiculed 'Early Modernism' as the 'Operating Theatre Period', she acknowledged that it had been a necessary interlude in the 'clearing of clutter and ornamentation' from the home.[40] The advantages of, and opportunities for, modern home design were debated in newspapers and magazines by experts like Lord, who expressed both a modern desire for unity between all domestic activities and a new regard for the housewife's time. Many articles gave hints on time-saving and domestic efficiency, but it was increasingly recognised that no matter how efficient the housewife, her work was 'burdensome'. A cartoon in the *Daily Telegraph* showed what would happen if roles were reversed and 'Mum worked union hours' (figure 3.2).

The Importance of Looking

Through articles about how to dream and plan for one's home of the future, as well as drawings, images and advertisements for homes, magazines like the *AHB* and the *Weekly* helped their audiences visualise the modern home well before readers

Figure 3.2 George Sprod, 'If Mum Worked a 40-Hour Week', *Daily Telegraph*, 17 July 1947, p. 13. By permission of Newspix/News Ltd.

were able to experience it themselves. Three advertisements for Masonite, published between 1944 and 1950, show how new ways of seeing brought about by mass production and consumption constituted home as the site of modernity. The first advertisement, published in early 1944 – and displaying a very similar concept and layout to the *AHB* cover described above – showed a woman looking at miniature model of a modern nursery room, and gave the '"Inside" Story of a Post War Home', demonstrating the varied uses of Masonite as a building material and basis of modern built-in furniture (figure 3.3). The new surfaces and storage spaces of the home were not yet in material form, but a vision of desire:

> With her mind's eye every woman in Australia to-day can see her 'after-the-war' home. All through the war years she has planned it, mentally perfected it, longed for it.
>
> In a hundred dreams she has seen the day when restrictions and regulations all disappear; when builders build once more; when Masonite can be released from the grim requirements of a nation in arms, and play its happier role in the attractive architecture of peacetime homes.

The second showed a woman in 'new look' dress, characterised by its small waist and wide skirts, behind a miniature model of a modern family house (figure 3.4). The text above the model declared:

> There's a 'New Look' for homes too . . . but it is not just a vogue or a passing whim. As far as houses are concerned the 'New Look' will 'stay put' . . . The main problem in home-building today is to get maximum comfort, style and convenience in minimum floor space at the lowest possible cost. A 'New Look' home is one in which this problem is completely solved . . . one which always looks as though it cost far more than it did . . . and 'feels' larger than it is.

This pleasure in looking – both in terms of looking at the modern house, and in the new kinds of 'looks' (on to the garden, at other parts of the house, at spaces now made into features such as the kitchen and living areas) generated by the new house designs of the 1940s – exceeds the distanced and alienating Lacanian 'gaze' that has haunted feminist theory since the 1980s. As Karal Ann Marling has noted:

> The very construction of the [new consumer] artifact [of the late 1940s] makes it clear that looking and viewing were central acts of consciousness. In the most fundamental ways, the New Look is about looking, too – about distinctive forms, eye-catching patterns and textures, and attractive colors; about looking at people and their clothes and being looked at in turn; about thinking about looking. Looking: not the judgemental 'gaze' of contemporary feminist theory, but something more like a scrupulous, pleasurable regard for both shape and surface.[41]

The obsession with the outside of things articulated a palpable optimism. But the need to be able to see, to look out on, suggested a need too for control, for security, and for the management of one's everyday world. Yet the subject of this

Figure 3.3 Masonite, '"Inside" Story of a Post War Home', *Australian Women's Weekly*, 8 January 1944, p. 24. By permission of Australian Hardboards Ltd.

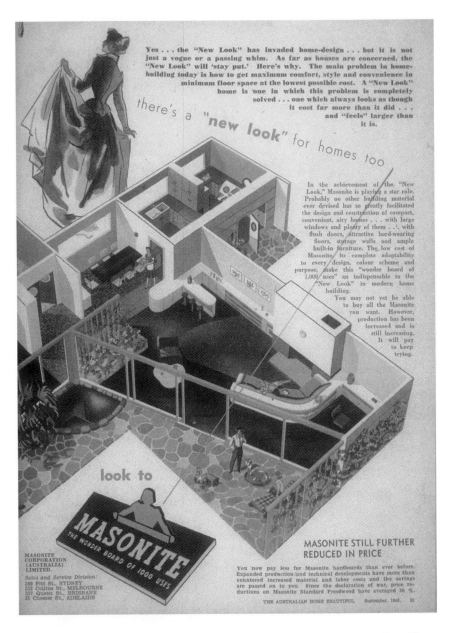

Figure 3.4 Masonite, 'There's a "New Look" for Homes Too', *Australian Home Beautiful*, September 1948, p. 21. By permission of Australian Hardboards Ltd.

looking was the housewife – it was she who was in control, doing the looking, and insisting that the look was right, that it was modern.

The third Masonite advertisement showed a drawing of a couple embracing as they look out through the windows of a modern lounge room to a newly planted suburban garden, suggesting that the choice of Masonite as a building material would 'speed up construction time and hasten that thrilling day when you are "on the inside looking out"' (figure 3.5). The dream of the perfect home was here a dream of being *inside* modernity, rather than excluded and separated from its benefits. This modernity was portrayed as particularly *photogenic* and *international* in the magazines. Accompanying an article in the 'Joanna Plans a Home' series in April 1946 were pictures of a 1940s house built for a Californian family. The photographs showed a large living room with floor-to-ceiling windows looking onto a garden. The article recounted the heroine's outing to

> a cocktail party given by a newly introduced American friend of hers who had settled in Melbourne early in 1940 and built a very modern house. Joanna was not keen, as a rule, on going to parties where she hardly knew anyone, but she had heard a lot about this house from Marilyn, who was continually raving about it, that she felt she might as well go along and see what it was really like. Although privately she did not expect it to be out of the ordinary or that it could tell her anything she did know already. For by this time Joanna was beginning to feel that she was something of an authority herself on houses and furnishing.[42]

The photograph's caption explained that the house had been designed by a 'Hollywood architect':

> Picture-goers may possibly have seen the name – they have almost certainly seen the work – of Richard J. Neutra, an American architect who has created some sensational effects for the screen and for those who act on the screen. He was one of the first exponents of the idea of bringing garden and house together.[43]

With her new-found enthusiasm for modernism, Joanna too 'loved the idea of linking the house and garden with great sliding windows – though naturally her own scheme would be on a much more modest scale'. Despite her previous musing on her ideal house, which involved decorating her house with 'period pieces' as well as her 'former' prejudices against modernism, 'She admired the handsome settee which divides the living room from the dining area, and was tickled by the quaint design of the chairs.' *AHB* indicated that Joanna had not discovered this modern scene all on her own, but had been 'shown the picture in a magazine called "Interiors"'.[44]

The setting of the 'cocktail party' reveals the new functions of the middle-class home, as it now provided in its open-plan design a way of being public in private

Figure 3.5 Masonite, 'When You're on the Inside Looking Out . . . Count the Savings Made by Masonite', *Australian Home Beautiful*, September 1950, p. 19. By Permission of Australian Hardboards Ltd.

space. This house enshrined a new level of comfort in its ability to entertain large groups of people without crowding or anonymity.

> Joanna had never before seen such a modern interior designed and carried out so completely to the last detail. Several things struck her. The room had a cosy air, there were no dark or remote-seeming corners, yet there was still plenty of room to move about.
>
> She noticed how the various party groups formed and re-formed easily, wandered out onto the terrace and back again, found somewhere to sit and put down a glass – often a problem at cocktail parties – without interruption or effort.[45]

This discourse of the dream home resolved lived contradictions between home as a place of work and a site of relaxation for women, at the same time as it expressed a new desire for harmony between women's and men's spheres in the discourse of family togetherness. The reorganisation of the flows between previously carefully policed boundaries – between clean and dirty areas and visible and invisible activities – actually reverses earlier forms of domestic organisation. Davidoff and Hall in their study of the middle-class home in *Family Fortunes* identified new uses of domestic time, and new regulations of domestic space in the early nineteenth century that have been foundational to the modern idea of home. They distinguish two stages in the modern segregation of living and housing: firstly, when productive work was banished from the domestic; and, secondly, when cooking, eating, washing, sleeping and other 'backstage' activities were separated from polite social intercourse and assigned special places for each function.[46] The post-war home, freed of 'traditional' fussiness and architectural compartmentalisation, reflected the new sense of boundlessness and possibility of the spectacular post-war society. The dream home, by combining activities imagined as separate in one overall space, overcame categorical oppositions between nature and culture, and public and private, by integrating activities that were previously separated. Internal contradictions were still present in the 'family togetherness' ideal, however, and these tensions manifested in the figure of the housewife as an indeterminately private and public figure. The housewife stood at the door of this new home, both worker and mistress. As *AHB* described her, she was 'gracious mistress, but housemaid too'.[47] Yet by bringing the whole family together, and installing the housewife's work at the social and physical centre of the house, this realisation of the dream home worked very hard to eliminate the tensions that women felt in simultaneously fulfilling incompatible roles.

On the Kitchen Front

Houses were described as 'servantless', and were invested with ideals of family togetherness both in internal layout and in provision of outside play areas where children could be watched by mothers through kitchen windows. A pamphlet advertising George Hudson 'Ready Cut' housing, which offered several designs 'based on the *very latest architectural and interior decoration trends*' of 1950, featured the 'Bellevue':

> Our new three-bedroom home will instantly appeal to the woman who prefers a larger *kitchen* than most [12 × 12]. Viewed from all aspects this is a most substantial looking home; and is an excellent example of the modern trend for large multiple windows. *It is every inch a home in the family sense.*[48]

Endless dreams of the elimination of labour were directed towards the kitchen. Indeed, *AHB* reported that US architects thought it the 'most important room in the house' and regarded 'its fittings and planning as a scientific problem of how to prevent household drudgery' (figure 3.6). In the ideal (North American) kitchen,

> Cupboards, stoves and sinks are just the right height; you don't have to spend half your life crouching on hands and knees. Long cupboards give yards and yards of bench space, and these, like the floors, are covered with brightly colored plastic, which is virtually indestructible. It also makes cleaning easy, for if you wished you could hose the place down. . . .
> The latest gas and electric stoves are streamlined in all colors from white to lipstick red. They have time clocks and push-button controls like a radio, so that you can go shopping or to a card party and depend on it that your gas or electric stove will start the roast on its way at three or four o'clock. About one stove in four in New York is automatic.[49]

Functionalism may have envisaged the kitchen as a laboratory for food preparation, but home magazines illustrated for their readers how the modern kitchen could also be invested with pleasure. Decoration and design came together to banish the unpleasant aspects of housework. An advertisement for new synthetic paints, which offered a greater range of colours, sought to assure readers that their home could be 'glamourised' by colour, and that a change in attitude towards housework occasioned by modern interior decoration would lessen the physical toil associated with domestic work. The advertisement showed a woman in tennis clothes talking on the telephone underneath the slogan 'Brighter house – lighter work': 'Moderns have found that beauty in the home and happiness and health for themselves go hand in hand, all thanks to 'Dulux'. There's no drudgery in cooking in a kitchen fit for a princess! There's no hardship in cleaning a bathroom that's a delight to your sense of beauty!'[50]

An article titled 'Getting Your Kitchen Out of Hobble-Skirts' in *House and Garden* magazine showed how the principles of efficiency and pleasing interior design were related. By showing 'What scientific planning did to 'Jenny's kitchen', the magazine demonstrated the 'glamour' possible in ordinary housework in the

Since the Lazy Susan holds the many materials used at the mixing centre, cupboards above the counter are left for equipment and supplies usually stored below the counter or in more out-of-the-way places. The wall cabinet above the mixing centre has shelves for mixing bowls, measuring spoons and cups, casseroles, and other accessories.

With a quick turn of the selector switch on her electric range, the home-maker can set either her oven, deep well unit or appliance outlet for automatic cooking while she is busy with other things. Indicators regulate the starting time, the duration of cooking, and the stopping time.

THE MOST
IMPORTANT ROOM

AMERICAN architects are treating the kitchen as the most important room in the house. They regard its fittings and planning as a scientific problem of how to prevent household drudgery.

In addition, any one of a dozen firms will plan individual kitchens, and show how their appliances would be best fitted together.

Cupboards, stoves and sinks are just the right height; you don't have to spend half your life crouching on hands and knees. Long cupboards give yards and yards of bench space, and these, like the floors, are covered with brightly colored plastic, which is virtually indestructible. It also makes cleaning easy, for if you wished you could hose the place down.

These modern kitchens also adopt the principle that carpenters learnt years ago: every piece of equipment has its allotted space, and as many pieces as possible are in plain view. This cuts out all the rummaging and emptying a whole cupboard just to find "that wretched little flat saucepan."

A knife expert discovered last week that a family cook uses a knife about 129 times daily, so the logical place for knives is in a rack on the wall like screwdrivers. The place for saucepans is in a large closet like a broom cupboard, with all the utensils hanging from nails by holes in the handles.

Toasters and electric mixers are in almost constant use, so it is quite pointless to shove them to the back of a cupboard. Every time you set up the equipment it takes about 10 minutes. Good Housekeeping Institute solved the problem by building a little garage in the corner of the main cooking counter. Then, when it is needed, all you have to do is slide it straight *Please turn to page 47*

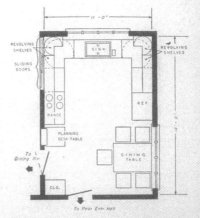

The U.S. Bureau of Human Nutrition and Home Economics evolved this small kitchen featured, without the plan, in the April, 1950, issue.

Figure 3.6 'The Most Important Room', *Australian Home Beautiful*, June 1951, p. 21. By permission of *Australian Home Beautiful*.

right setting (figures 3.7–3.8). The kitchen renovations depicted by the magazine foreshadowed changes to house design: 'For the past generation the trend has been towards smaller and smaller kitchens, but the reaction has now begun. More and more people want bigger kitchens, and will sacrifice dining rooms to get them.' This expansion of the kitchen zone reflected changes to middle-class living that meant:

> Kitchens have become the real living space in many homes. The glamorous gleaming cupboards and equipment are made a sparkling background in many homes to a convenient and dainty little alcove which starts off as a breakfast nook, but invariably finishes up as the family eating place for all informal meals.
>
> Color, too, has made the kitchen of today one of the most liveable rooms in the house. Daring and colorful kitchen set-ups are commonplace. The color does a lot for the housewife's morale, too!

While the same article suggested that 'There is real fun in planning a modern kitchen – Try it,' men were also invited to think about how they could reconstruct the space of the home to improve the lot of their wives. A 'Service correspondent' writing to *AHB* in 1945 wanted to use 'some spare time . . . plotting improvements to his home in the South and would like to know how he may some day make his wife's kitchen something like the advertising sketches he sees in magazines without spending the small fortune some of them would certainly cost'.[51] The magazine's carpentry expert advised that some small adjustments to the plan should be made, and 'the height of the fittings . . . should be suited to the one who will use them most. This provision, together with the equally important one of avoiding every unnecessary step, is the basis of success in arranging a kitchen which, whether simple or elaborate, will make the war bride's lot a truly happy one.'[52]

The discourse on the 'fun' and 'glamour' of housework was an attempt to render the physical and material aspects of housework invisible, as McHugh argues, to constitute it not as work, but as 'non-labour', reflecting a masculinist and bourgeois understanding of economy and society that has persisted since the early nineteenth century. This discourse, which posits the role of housewife as a form of being rather than a job, locates 'appropriately "feminine" women outside work, production, and the market, whatever the material realities of the home and the workplace'.[53] Planning was understood as pleasurable rather than a chore, and housework itself had to look effortless and housewives even happy in their role, no matter what kinds of work and worries they faced. A photo essay in the *Daily Telegraph* showed women how to 'look glamorous in the home' (figure 3.9): 'looking attractive isn't any more difficult in the house than when you're going out – you merely have to work to a schedule'. Signs of the dirty and taxing work of cleaning, such as aprons, headscarves or 'grubby gowns and slippers', should be

Figures 3.7-8 Photographs of Jenny's kitchen before and after, in 'Getting Your Kitchen Out of Hobble-Skirts', *Australian House and Garden*, December 1948, pp. 24-7. By permission of *Australian House and Garden*.

Figure 3.9 'Glamor at Home', *Daily Telegraph*, 16 January 1947, pp. 16-17. By permission of Newspix/News Ltd.

eliminated in case 'luncheon visitors' arrived early, or, more importantly, one's husband came home unexpectedly. The front and backstage of the home, given the new visuality of home-making, had to be scrupulously managed so that the house-wife did not look 'tired' or 'untidy' in comparison to pretty 'business girls' who would look 'fresh.'

The problems associated with maintaining this discourse of housework as 'leisure' – while the post-war industrial system increasingly drew attention to the conditions of workers – was partially solved through the introduction of 'labour-saving devices' that offered technological solutions to political problems during the 1950s. The objective of new technologies for cooking and cleaning was to eliminate labour and get the housewife's working week down to a manageable level. They did not necessarily eliminate the figure of the housewife herself, but they did highlight the demanding working conditions she faced. A photo-montage and accompanying article in the *Daily Telegraph* outlined the working day of 'an average housewife with a husband . . . and three children' ranging from five years to four months. The article showed that she was responsible for preparing and cooking '160 pounds of food', for a '1150–piece washup', and for making '35 beds', despite having a cleaning lady and a number of 'modern devices to help her with her chores' (figure 3.10). The claim for better working conditions for women in the home, in parallel with the working man's rights, was picked up by a Masonite advertisement which promised that 'We're getting nearer to a 40–hour week for housewives' and showed a woman and child, dressed for town, leaving their very modern kitchen in a hurry (figure 3.11).

> Amidst a chorus of demands for shorter working hours, the only voice hitherto inaudible is that of the housewife. But madame relies more upon practicality rather than politics. She knows that if she can streamline her kitchen, cut down her daily itin-erary, reduce the time now taken up by pacings to and fro, her working week will shrink without controversy or impassioned argument.

While the 'revolving shelves', 'pull-out table' and 'built-in cutting-board with catch-all for peelings' promised in the Masonite advertisement might have saved hours of domestic labour, they did not fully de-politicise the domestic sphere. But the process of dreaming about the perfect kitchen sometimes revealed a wish to transcend this occupation too. Many articles discuss designs and projects to get the kitchen to do the work by itself, particularly in plans that anticipate machinery to eliminate dirt and rubbish from the home. An exhibition home featured in the August 1946 issue of *AHB* was the result of 'more than 100 manufacturers, engi-neers and designers exhibiting their best and most advanced products and mate-rials. Germ-killing equipment, inter-phone system, built-in radios and television set, automatic dish-washing and waste-disposal units, infra-red bathroom fixtures – these are but a few of the many gadgets contained in the experimental house.'

Figure 3.10 'The Housewife's 100-Hour Week', *Daily Telegraph*, 16 October 1947, p. 11. By permission of Newspix/News Ltd.

Figure 3.11 Masonite, 'We're Getting Nearer to a 40-hour week for Housewives', *Australian Women's Weekly*, 8 February 1947, p. 44. By permission of Australian Hardboards Ltd.

The kitchen in this model house resembles the control centre of a space-ship, with its pedal-operated hot and cold water outlets for the sink, and the placement of a large wind-screen-like window above the work space (figure 3.12).

The kitchen contains numerous labor-saving and step-conserving devices. Stain-proof walls are lined with plastic roll-up doors. The model stands beside a jet-propelled dishwasher. Jets of hot water propel the dishes in sudsy water. Sink is equipped with electric waste disposal unit. The range, at left, has four rear gas burners, with work space in front. Frozen food container, air-vented vegetable container, table-height refrigerator, a sterilizing lamp, a 'sewing centre' are a few of the other features.

An article in the same year on the 'Kitchens of Yesterday and Tomorrow' reported that 'From overseas come books, magazines, booklets and catalogues, telling of the wonders that are being evolved for the better working of the entire house but particularly for improvements in the service quarters.' These designs were illustrations of the ways in which the kitchen in the middle-class home had been transformed since the era of servants:

From being regarded as the domain of the cook, the maid and the cat, the kitchen has become the workshop of the mistress. The old cry of the irate cook, 'You keep out of my kitchen,' has given way to the invitation, 'Do come in and see my kitchen.' Moreover it is too true that in former times scant consideration was given to the comfort and convenience of the maids who spent their days and most of their evenings in the kitchen – hot by day and badly lighted at night.

The article included sketches from the *Architectural Forum* of two different kitchens (figures 3.13–3.14). The first showed 'the ultra-modern, de-luxe "factory" – all glass and glitter', which was contrasted with the second, 'the efficient workshop in which the equipment is arranged on more conservative lines'. The caption accompanying the images revealed that a poll conducted by *McCall's* magazine had found that 'a majority of women voted for the quieter scene', demonstrating that some forms of modernity were seen as impractical and therefore undesirable.

From the literature of international architects, manufacturers and designers 'which ranges from clamant advertising to optimistic forecast', the author noted that

Kitchen planning will tend more and more to (a) include and improve the facilities for taking meals in the kitchen area; (b) link the diningroom and the garden with the kitchen; (c) place the kitchen so as to provide an outlook on to the near garden or (note our cover design) the distant view, if any. In California the out-of-doors aspect is, of course, more noticeable than in England.

Corner of living room showing the massive fireplace flanked by built-in radio and phonograph (left) and television set enclosed at right. Most of the furniture was especially made to harmonise with the architecture of the house.

Luxury characterizes the master bedroom. The over-sized bed measures 6 feet by 7 feet. The grey multi-cord bedspread is sculpture-quilted in the same design as the wallpaper. Arm-rests for reading, recede into the headboard of the bed when not in use. Beside the bed is an inter-communication receiver connecting with every room in the house and a master control board governing the lighting and radio systems for the entire house.

The kitchen contains numerous labor-saving and step-conserving devices. Stain-proof walls are lined with plastic roll-up doors. The model stands beside a jet-propelled dishwasher. Jets of hot water propel the dishes in sudsy water. Sink is equipped with electric waste disposal unit. The range, at left, has four rear gas burners, with work space in front. Frozen food container, air-vented vegetable container, table-height refrigerator, a sterilizing lamp, a "sewing centre" are a few of the other features.

The barbecue enclosure has its own fireplace, sink and food storage units. The table and benches are of bleached redwood to match the exterior siding of the house.

Australian Home Beautiful, August, 1946. Page Nineteen

Figure 3.12 Photos of young woman in kitchen with large window looking out onto the backyard. 'A Dashing Experiment in Building – Model Home That Cost 220,000 Dollars', *Australian Home Beautiful*, August 1946, p. 19. By permission of Australian Home Beautiful.

Figure 3.13-14 Drawings of new kitchen designs, W. A. Somerset, 'Kitchens of Yesterday and Tomorrow', *Australian Home Beautiful*, January 1946, Cover and p. 40. By permission of *Australian Home Beautiful.*

Kitchens of Yesterday and Tomorrow

by W. A. SOMERSET

WHEN a writer for this journal recently toured the stores and factories to see what might be new in kitchen equipment she found the market very bare. But on every hand she heard promises of new or improved appliances to make life easier and better for the housewife.

From overseas come books, magazines, booklets and catalogues, telling of the wonders that are being evolved for the better working of the entire house but particularly for improvements in the service quarters.

The fact is that in recent years the kitchen has undergone a complete transformation in character. From being regarded as the domain of the cook, the maid and the cat, the kitchen has become the workshop of the mistress. The old cry of the irate cook, "You keep out of my kitchen," has given way to the invitation, "Do come in and see my kitchen." Moreover it is too true that in former times scant consideration was given to the comfort or the convenience of the maids who spent their days and most of their evenings in the kitchen—hot by day and badly lighted by night.

From a browse over the literature already referred to—which ranges from clamant advertising to optimistic forecast—it would appear that:

Kitchen planning will tend more and more to (a) include and improve the facilities for taking meals in the kitchen area; (b) link the diningroom and the garden with the kitchen; (c) place the kitchen so as to provide an outlook on to the near garden or (note our cover design) the distant view, if any. In California the out-of-doors aspect is, of course, more noticable than in England.

In equipment, advances are promised in the design and efficiency of stoves. This is more apparent in English than American homes, again a matter of climate. Solid fuel stoves are increasing in popularity and new types are coming to light. Of one new insulated solid fuel cooker a writer says: "These cookers incorporate a water heater, supplying 250

Tomorrow's sink of unbreakable glass with close-down lid, concealed lighting and floor pedals for inflow and outlet of water.

gallons of hot water a week at 140 deg. F. They are all continuous - burning; this means that hot water is always on tap, an important point, for however many labor - saving devices there may be in the house, adequate supplies of hot water will always be the basis of easier housework. "Flue-cleaning is unnecessary when a solid-fuel continuous-burning cooker is in use, and in some oven-heat is controlled by adjustment of a simple thermostat. In the very small house, heating, cooking and hot water supply can now be combined cheaply and well from a single fire.

Ovens with glass doors are almost commonplace.

Sinks are mainly improved by the use of new materials, the combination of washing and rinsing bowls and the substitution of pedals for taps. Where taps are employed there is a tendency to place them on the wall above rather than on the faucets.

Lighting has advanced a long way from the old single electric globe in the middle of the room, suspended from the ceiling on a length of flex (that our one-time contributor the Night Watchman used to describe as "the fly walk"). Glareless lights are now placed at points where they will give best service and it will not be long before much of the kitchen lighting, as well as that of the whole house, will be done by fluorescent tubes, one advantage of which is that the rays they emit are cool.

In England at the moment wartime conditions, not yet overcome, have made some curious economies of space necessary. In one magazine is the photograph of a combined kitchen and bathroom but, at the other extreme, the current issue of "Ideal Homes" reproduces a photograph of a kitchen which is backed by the bathroom. The wall is hollow and takes all pipes and wires for gas, electricity and waste water. The novelty in this case is salvaged aluminium. The workbench, sink cupboards and drawers are of aluminium alloy faced with anodised aluminium sheets backed with cork for insulation against sound.

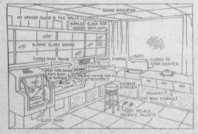

Sketches from the Architectural Forum of two kitchens. They represent first the ultra-modern, de-luxe "factory"—all glass and glitter—and second, the efficient workshop in which the equipment is arranged on more conservative lines. In a poll conducted by McCall's magazine a majority of women voted for the quieter scene.

Australian Home Beautiful. January, 1946. Page Thirteen.

While the spaces within the kitchen themselves became more transparent – 'Ovens with glass doors are almost commonplace' – a total merging of the kitchen with the rest of the house was not yet (and perhaps never would be) possible:

> In England at the moment wartime conditions, not yet overcome, have made some curious economies of space necessary. In one magazine is the photograph of a combined kitchen and bathroom but, at the other extreme, the current issue of 'Ideal Homes' reproduces a photograph of a kitchen which is backed by the bathroom.

While she did not embrace the idea of a combined kitchen/bathroom, Joanna, the modernist heroine of the *AHB*, was indeed planning her ideal house around the kitchen. Starting out by 'reading everything she could get hold of and looking at her friends' houses with more attention than usual', Joanna then began 'to visualise some of the things she would like to have in her house':

> A nice big living room with doors direct into the garden so that one did not have to go out of the front or back doors every time was the central theme. She wouldn't cramp her style with a mere dinette but would insist on a dining room big enough to have friends to dinner occasionally. A modern kitchen, of course, and somewhere out of doors, a spot both sunny and sheltered which could be reached from all three, so that one could take lunch or afternoon tea outside without any fuss and without having to tear through the entire house to get more hot water or the cheese or the jam. Bedrooms she was rather hazy about. It did not seem to matter much about them so long as they were near the bathroom – a modern bathroom of course – but she would like the bathroom to be out of sight of the front door. She remembered a friend's house, quite a smart one too, where it could be quite embarrassing if the bathroom was accidentally left open.[54]

The kitchen was placed at the centre of 'all three': living, dining and outdoor spaces. And, as Joanna's 'haziness' on bedrooms shows, the centrality given to the boudoir and parlour in the Victorian-era house had been devolved to the new zones of living-room, courtyard and patio in the post-war middle-class home. Countless advertisements and articles explained that one's choice of home furnishings reflected one's taste and personality. A new intimacy was accorded to the work of buying and choosing household furnishings, as a 1951 ad for Vantona Bedcovers in *AHB* indicated:

> FURNISHING of your bedroom reveals your self – that is why a lovely Vantona Bedcover tells all the world that you appreciate fine things . . . See the whole range of Vantona Bedcovers – you'll find there's one to give the right look to your bedroom – and expression of yourself.[55]

The bedroom in the middle-class home was marginal at this time in comparison to the emphasis placed on the living areas, including the kitchen, but it was invested with a new importance according to advertising culture of the period. The bedroom was hardly somewhere that one needed to demonstrate to other people one's taste for 'fine things'. Even in the 'backstage' areas of the modern house, one's personality was on display.

As these articles show, the passing of the housewife, despite all this labour-saving and calls for better working conditions for women at home, was for now still unimaginable, as she represented a powerful way of organising her family's consumption. The *AHB* believed that as futuristic as the 1950s kitchen might look to readers, 'it will be as outmoded as the hand-pump within a couple of decades'. Yet the housewife was still at its helm:

> Ranges are on the drawing boards now which will defrost frozen meals and heat them all in a minute. This will mean an end to hot kitchens and unpleasant odors. Housewives will buy these meals in partly cooked form, and this will wipe out tiresome cooking and endless preparation. . . .
>
> Then kitchens will become of less importance. In fact, meal preparation may be so simplified in another 20 years that the kitchen may be brought into the living room. There it will occupy a corner behind cupboard doors. The hostess will come home with the guests, and with martini in hand she will gaily chat away and whip up that meal in two minutes.[56]

The article concluded that 'All this may sound like dream stuff to you, but it is only dream stuff because it is a few years ahead.' The process of dreaming about the modern home was portrayed as a gendered activity, appearing in this dream as the point of intersection between mass production and individual agency. The dream of the future housewife was to become the absolute consumer. Consumption without labour is figured here as the *telos* of modernisation. This is exemplified by the narrative of the kitchen developed in the magazines: a space transformed from slave's dungeon, to laboratory, to neatly stowed cupboard. The housewife is still visible at the narrative's end, despite her role as a cook simplified to a mere pusher of a few buttons on the microwave. For all that, domesticity – now a practice of display and appearance – even though a proper task for a modern subject, was still women's activity and the home a gendered space. These kinds of home improvements, without a narrative of progress, sit uneasily against the con-troversies over policy and political arguments that were advocated by women's organisations and discussed in the previous chapter. This discourse of self-expres-sion through discerning consumption and generating the 'right look' reflects an increasing exteriorisation of the self through consumption and display. Nicholas Brown has suggested that 'the transparency of the modern home was crucially mediated by women, and by feminised preoccupations with social standing, refined further and further away from the (masculine) world of occupation and closer to the (feminine) search for personality'.[57] This modern search for personality through consumption, and its increasing visibility, however, raised the possibility that housewifery was an occupation, with working hours, equipment and training. As the final section of this chapter explores, during the 1950s this tension between the housewife as a certain 'personality' or identity and housework as form of labour that should be recognised as such contributed to an uneasiness about speaking as a 'housewife'.

The View from the Kitchen Window

In this survey of narratives surrounding the transformation of the post-war home, it is evident that the gendering of home design produced a new agency for women, and raised questions about domestic working conditions. The 'view from the kitchen' illustrated in the advertisements and magazines provided the means to begin to argue about the conditions of housework, but it did not provide a coherent political agency. This agency was informed by a new social intelligence or set of knowledges accorded to the female subject in the home. The woman in the home was encouraged to become a small-scale utopianist and a technician of space, whose work, just as much as other more traditional kinds of housework, was to dream about and plan the perfect home. The woman-at-home became a position from which to speak, principally as a consumer, but also as a subject hailed by governments. The housewife was drawn into the public sphere through a narrative of progress, which was materialised through the modernisation of the home. Thus the architect was becoming the judge of good home design, but not the source of its imagining. The modern home was construed as giving visual pleasure to its occupants, as well as allowing them to inhabit both inside and outside, amalgamating certain versions of the public and private. The housewife's task was to understand these latest ideas and adapt them to her family's needs; to make home life more productive. Women became increasingly responsible for tasteful home decoration, mediating the wild profusion of goods in the market to construe proper consumerism as an expression of 'self', a reflection of the well-cultivated inner person. Women's participation in the modern world was figured as the modernisation of domesticity, which paralleled a fascination with the previously 'backstage' activities of cooking and cleaning. The interior design discourse translated wider social changes into an everyday version of modernity particular to women's culture in the post-war period.

This discourse continued in to the 1950s, and by the end of the decade, a narrative of completion of the self in suburbia was offered to women in magazines such as the market-dominant *Women's Weekly*. They insisted, for example, on behalf of famous women who had turned down careers to become full-time housewives, that even after a career as a celebrity or sportswoman, one could become a 'satisfied housewife' and find fulfilment in designing new homes and looking after husbands and children.[58]

Yet articles in other, less widely circulated magazines rejected the housewife role outright, and considered it a touchstone of oppression. Margot Parker, a columnist for *Woman's Day*, declared that when she even tried to write about domesticity, 'so massive is my detestation of domestic duties and so intense my passion for throwing myself into what I call My Real Work (which is typing) that the first day I came over all peculiar, shrieked at the prospect and Went Out'.[59] Parker's column parodied 'time-and-motion experts' who dogged 'the footsteps of women around their homes, with stop-watches at the ready. Timing them and writing nasty things about them in their reports.' Parker argued that the 'time-wasting' that such studies found in the women's domestic activities paid 'little heed to a housewife's need to be creative and Express Herself' by making lamingtons, needless shopping trips or talking on the telephone to friends. Her account of the non-productive labour of housework disputed the very terms of a discourse that sought to make women regulate their housework and become more efficient. 'What [the experts] don't realise is that housewives like to do their marketing every day so that they can get out of their solitary confinement for a spell and maybe meet and talk to other women temporarily released into the exercise yard.'[60] Douglas Wilkie, who had published an article titled 'Housewives – Wake Up!' in *Woman's Day* on 21 April 1952, replied to a series of readers' letters asking for a 'campaign plan' for housewives to organise with a follow-up piece, 'Be Politically Active or Remain Animals', on 7 July. Wilkie's conclusion was that 'Unless women surmount their political inertia they'll remain nothing but animals – charming, pretty, delightful and wholly necessary animals, but relegated, most of them, to the muddier and drearier end of the human farmyard.'[61] A letter from an Adelaide reader published on the same page called to the magazine's readers to recognise that 'women, and especially the mothers of young children, shoulder the heaviest of the community's burdens'.[62] Her letter echoed the demands of workers to limit working hours and establish time for the pursuit of self-improvement and relaxation:

> It's a common thing in our society for mothers of pre-school children to work a seven-day week of 90 hours or more 52 weeks of the year. Under these circumstances they cannot possibly bring up their children according to the teachings of child-care authorities. The whole situation is bad for mothers and deplorable for the children.[63]

These changes expanded the role of the women at home to such an extent that the possibility of speaking of such a person as 'the housewife' began to sound inadequate. Nan Hutton, a 'housewife' correspondent for *Woman's Day*, wrote in her regular column 'One Woman's Day' in 1955 that the demands of modern home management had made the title 'housewife' redundant, and the persistence of the term prevented women from recognising their own self-worth and resulted in them 'underestimating [their] value'. The collective description 'housewives' was old-fashioned, belonging to 'Mrs Beeton's day, where women were required to be housekeepers and very little else'.[64] Hutton declared her irritation at having 'to describe myself as "housewife"' on the census form and income tax declarations:

> 'Housewife' implies that a woman who is running a home is engaged only on the rather dreary tasks of keeping the place clean and cooking hearty imaginative dinners, a creature subjugated to domestic routine, whose badge of office is the apron, and whose vision of life is limited to the view from the kitchen window.
>
> I wish I could invent a better word for the job that I try to do, and that women like [my friend] Helen accomplish so superbly. Sometimes I am asked to give the 'housewife's view' on some problem, and whenever that happens, I want to protest: 'But there's no such viewpoint, or, if there is, I can't give it to you.'[65]

An emerging middle-class view of the housewife role as insufficiently modern, and therefore limiting and 'backward', is articulated in Hutton's characterisation of a 'view from the kitchen window'. More importantly, though, the way she questions her own ability to speak on behalf of all women at home demonstrates how vulnerable the housewife as a collective figure, embraced equally by all women, had become. Both working- and middle-class women were increasingly able to express a desire for more than this limited view towards the end of the 1950s. Such a rejection of the housewife role cannot be seen exclusively as a stepping-stone to the public sphere. The way that Hutton retreats from a single label can also be seen as a call for a recognition of the private sphere as the ground for a new subjectivity that is more subtly positioned between public and private; hence her petition to be seen as more than just a 'housekeeper' subjugated to routine. Her description of her role as a job, and her claim to raise the status of housewives, demonstrates just how extensively the role and significance of the housewife had changed in the post-war period. This expansion of housewifery had advanced to such an extent that the housewife's tasks become excessive and even impossible to truly achieve. As our analysis of the inscription of gender in domestic space during this period has shown, women were increasingly the object of a modern regime of visuality that took hold more fully during the 1950s at the same time as they became the subject of looks and gazes within the home. In this new world of looking and having, a set of parallels between *working in the home* and *being a woman*, or gendered labour and gendered identity, were hardened and fixed. Women such as Hutton were both rejecting their role as 'just' workers in the home and creating a subjectivity that was no longer part of its furniture.

In the narrative of progress and futurity outlined in the magazines, the modern, technologised home, full of the latest 'conveniences', was split away from the world of everyday life, which is by nature repetitious, non-productive and non-progressive. The recurring, mundane practices of home-making paled in comparison with the glowing images of consumerism. The seeds of dissatisfaction would take root in this gap between representation and reality, as foreshadowed by Hutton. This dissatisfaction would flower more fully in the 1950s in the notion that the housewife role was totally and irredeemably boring, and women's responsibility for the home a form of imprisonment. The problem of the housewife constituted in these terms became a questioning of the relationship established during the nineteenth century between the space of the home, (non-)labour and women's political and class identity, which we will explore further in Chapter 5. The next chapter, meanwhile, investigates how the representation of women's labour in the home changed during this time in film narratives. As we will see, the split between glamour, fun and pleasures of these new regimes of consumption, on the one hand, and the dreariness, physical labour and sheer overwork of the domestic sphere, on the other, were to play out in important ways in depictions of troubled housewives in Hollywood films of the 1940s and 1950s.

Notes

1. Melbourne, Australasian Book Society, 1959, p. 175.
2. 'Hints for Plan-a-Home Contest', *Australian Women's Weekly*, 30 September 1950, p. 17.
3. Victorian Fabian Society, *The Housing Crisis in Australia*, Melbourne, Spotlight Press, 1958.
4. 'Hints for Plan-a-Home Contest'.
5. Beatriz Colomina, 'The Split Wall: Domestic Voyeurism', in Beatriz Colomina (ed.), *Sexuality and Space*, New York, Princeton Architectural Press, p. 83.
6. Mark Wigley, 'The Housing of Gender', in Beatriz Colomina (ed.), *Sexuality and Space*, p. 331.
7. Joel Sanders, 'Curtain Wars: Architects, Decorators, and the 20th-Century Domestic Interior', *Harvard Review of Design Magazine*, 16, Winter/Spring 2002, pp. 1–9.
8. Ibid., p. 9.
9. John Murphy, *Imagining the Fifties: Private Sentiment and Political Culture in Menzies' Australia*, Sydney, University of New South Wales Press & Pluto Press, 2000, p. 10.
10. Lilian Bond, Drummoyne, NSW, quoted in 'Ideal Homes . . . of Tomorrow', *Australian Women's Weekly*, 22 May 1943, p. 31.
11. Mrs Elsie Fordham, 'Home Shortage a Cause of Marriage Troubles', *Australian Women's Weekly*, 22 April 1944, p. 13.

12. Army Education Service, *Our Population Problem*, Discussion Pamphlet 7, Melbourne, Ramsay Ware Publishing, 1945, p. 17.

13. 'Housewife Wins Letter Contest', *Daily Telegraph*, 6 February 1947, p. 14.

14. Zelie McLeod, 'Life Today is One Big Frustration for the Housewife', *Daily Telegraph*, 30 January 1947, p. 15.

15. Eric Bell-Smith, 'Lack of Homes is Driving Them Insane', *Sunday Telegraph*, 8 January 1950, p. 13.

16. Peter Cuffley, *Australian Houses of the Forties and Fifties*, Knoxfield, Five Mile Press, 1993; Alastair Whyte Greig, *The Stuff Dreams Are Made Of: Housing Provision in Australia 1945–1960*, Carlton, Vic., Melbourne University Press, 1995.

17. J.S. Gawler, a practising architect after the first world war and deputy chair of the Commonwealth Housing Commission in the 1940s, traces these changes to the 1920s: 'Other housing ideas came along. We bought American magazines and many of them had house plans and photos published every month, particularly the *Ladies' Home Journal*; thus was introduced the Californian bungalow, or "bungle-oh", as some called it. It had some good points; it freed the small house from the drawing room, introducing the idea of a living room connected to the kitchen by a door, introduced the breakfast angle, and built-in furniture. The domestic servant had quite disappeared for most people and the house plan was adjusted. The kitchen had good cupboards, the pantry disappeared and so did the scullery; instead there was a small wash-house or laundry often as a separate outbuilding. The kitchen became a room the housewife could ask her friends to enter.' J.S. Gawler, *A Roof Over My Head*, Melbourne, Lothian, 1963, p. 53.

18. Jennifer Craik, 'The Cultural Politics of the Queensland House', *Continuum*, 3 (1), 1990, p. 208.

19. *Giant*, Director, George Stevens, Script by Fred Guiol and Ivan Moffat, Warner Bros, 1956; *Pillow Talk*, Director, Michael Gordon, Script by Stanley Shapiro and Maurice Richlin, Universal, 1959.

20. Peter Biskind, *Seeing Is Believing: How Hollywood Taught Us to Stop Worrying and Love the Fifties*, New York, Pantheon Books, 1983, p. 290.

21. Ruth Schwartz Cowan, *More Work for Mother: The Ironies of Household Technology from the Open Hearth to the Microwave*, New York, Basic Books, 1983, p. 100.

22. Walter Bunning, 'Your Home . . . After the War', *Australian Women's Weekly*, 1 January 1944, p. 21.

23. Department of Post-war Reconstruction, *The Housewife Speaks*, Sydney, Associated Newspapers, c.1945, p. 2.

24. Mary Ryan, *Homes of the Future*, 1944, Typescript, JAFp SOC 1855, Canberra, National Library of Australia, p. 1.

25. Carolyn Allport, 'The Princess in the Castle: Women and the New Order Housing', in Women and Labour Publications Collective (eds), *All Her Labours: Embroidering the Framework*, Sydney, Hale and Iremonger, 1984, p. 166. Ryan, a member of the Country Women's Association and former hospital matron in the town of Portland near Lithgow, New South Wales, used her experience as a pre-war housewife to argue for her position on the Commission when she was challenged by members of more radical women's organisations: 'Although I am only a humble housewife, my position on the commission is of equal status with the men, and each of us was particularly mindful of the women's point of view and were watching the interests of the housewife and the woman in the home' (Mary Ryan, Unpublished Diary, Book III, p. 95, quoted in ibid., p. 166). Allport also notes that Ryan 'became more and more impatient with the drudgery of her own housework as the work of the Commission focused on ways of reducing household chores for the woman in the home', writing in her personal diary during this period, 'I don't take very kindly to the housework when I get home, especially the scrubbing, sweeping, polishing, washing, etc. that has to be done day after day in these wretched little cottages with no conveniences of any kind to make the daily grind a little easier' (Mary Ryan, Book II, p. 10, quoted in ibid., p. 134)
26. Ryan, *Homes of the Future*, p. 1.
27. Ibid., p. 3.
28. Rachel Dent, 'I'd Like to Blow Up My Kitchen!' *Australian House and Garden*, 4 (3), March 1950, p. 44.
29. Hotpoint, 'Today is the Time to Plan To-morrow's Kitchen', *Australian Women's Weekly*, 14 February 1942, p. 32
30. Masonite, 'Start Now to Design Your Future Home', *Australian Home Beautiful*, June 1945, p. 2.
31. Ibid.
32. Army Education Service, *Home Life*, Discussion Pamphlet 9, Melbourne, Ramsay Ware Publishing, 1945, pp. 11–12.
33. Ibid., p. 13.
34. During 1946 the Australian government relaxed wartime restrictions on printing, allowing *AHB* a print run of 40,000 per month. According to an in-house history of the magazine, 'Post-war editors Roy Simmonds (1946–1951) and Keith Newman (1952–59) saw the circulation spiral upwards to beyond 100,000 in the building and do-it-yourself boom of the late 1950s.' Julie Oliver, *Australian Home Beautiful: From Hills Hoist to High Rise*, Sydney, Pacific Publications, 1999.
35. Mary Jane Seymour, 'Joanna Plans a Home: 1 – The Dream', *Australian Home Beautiful*, March 1945, p. 8.
36. Ibid., p. 9.

37. Mary Jane Seymour, 'Joanna Plans a Home: 4 – She Visualises an Ideal Kitchen', *Australian Home Beautiful*, October 1945, p. 14.

38. 'Best of 400 Small House Designs', *Australian Home Beautiful*, October 1945, p. 15.

39. Mr X., 'Considering the Plan', *Australian Home Beautiful*, August 1945, p. 38.

40. Margaret Florence Lord, *Interior Decoration: A Guide to Furnishing the Australian Home*, Sydney, Ure Smith, 1942, p. 42.

41. Karal Ann Marling, *As Seen on TV: The Visual Culture of Everyday Life in the 1950s*, Cambridge, Mass., Harvard University Press, 1994, pp. 14–15.

42. Mary Jane Seymour, 'Joanna Plans a Home: She Finds Out There Are Still Some Things to Learn About Furniture', *Australian Home Beautiful*, April 1946, p. 9.

43. Ibid.

44. Ibid.

45. Ibid., p. 10.

46. Leonore Davidoff and Catherine Hall, *Family Fortunes: Men and Women of the English Middle Class 1780–1850*, London, Hutchinson, 1987, p. 359.

47. *AHB* quoted in Nicholas Brown, *'A Cliff of White Cleanliness': Decorating the Home, Defining the Self*, Urban Research Program Working Paper No. 48 (ed. R. Coles), Urban Research Program, Australian National University, Canberra, 1995, p. 13.

48. George Hudson Pty Ltd, *How to Build Well and Save Money with a George Hudson Pty Ltd 'Ready Cut' Home*, Sydney, George Hudson Pty Ltd, c. 1950, n.p. Pamphlet held at Mitchell Library, Syndey, ref. no. 643.209944/1. Emphasis ours.

49. 'The Most Important Room', (see figure 3.6). The second paragraph is taken from p. 22 of the same article.

50. Dulux Paints, 'Smart Girl . . . She's Got the Right Angle on Housework', *Australian Women's Weekly*, February 1950, p. 14.

51. Alex Smith, 'Carpentry in the Kitchen – Suggested Improvements', *Australian Home Beautiful*, January 1945, p. 26.

52. Ibid., p. 38.

53. Kathleen Anne McHugh, *American Domesticity: From How-to Manual to Hollywood Melodrama*, New York, Oxford University Press, 1999, p. 76.

54. Seymour, 'Joanna Plans a Home: 1 – The Dream', p. 8.

55. Vantona Court Bedcovers, 'An Expression of Yourself?' *Australian Home Beautiful*, December 1951, p. 40.

56. 'The Most Important Room' (see figure 3.6), p. 22.

57. Brown, *'A Cliff of White Cleanliness'*, p. 17.

58. Pat Sobey, 'Family First for Margo Lee – She Turned Down a Hollywood

Career', *Australian Women's Weekly*, 25 April 1956, p. 15; Paula Walling, 'Film Star Happy in Housewife Role', *Australian Women's Weekly*, 11 July 1956, p. 23; Winifred Bissett, 'Shirley – Hurdler to Housewife: Olympic Champion is Happy as She Knits October Layette', *Australian Women's Weekly*, 1 May 1957, p. 5.

59. Margot Parker, 'We All Hate Housework!', *Woman's Day with Woman*, 28 July 1958, p. 23.

60. Ibid.

61. Douglas Wilkie, 'Be Politically Active or Remain Animals', *Woman's Day and Home*, 7 July 1952, pp. 4–5.

62. Margaret Forte, 'What We Need is a Pressure Group', *Woman's Day and Home*, 7 July 1952, p. 5.

63. Ibid.

64. Nan Hutton, '"Housewife" is Not an Apt Description', *Woman's Day and Home*, 12 December 1955, p. 25.

65. Ibid.

The Three Faces of Eve

In this chapter we further trouble the understanding of women's lives in the 1940s and 1950s as shaped by dominant ideologies of the home as women's proper place. By analysing a set of post-war films that feature housewives as main characters, we show that the 'woman's film', rather than being concerned with promoting domesticity as women's proper social role, actively explored a tension between discourses of modernity and femininity. We suggest that the housewife in such popular cultural forms of the period had to work through the problem of the modern individual's relationship to home: that is, the discourse of self-determination that requires the modern self to be completed in the public world of work. Gender complicates the housewife's story: she must become a modern citizen, yet still complete her feminine subjectivity 'at home'. We suggest that popular films of the 1940s and 1950s therefore reveal subtle yet profound changes in a historically formed emotional ambivalence about the figure of the domestic woman.

In this respect, our argument builds on the analysis of the woman's picture developed by Mary Ann Doane in her 1987 book, *The Desire to Desire*. In a set of 1940s films aimed at a female audience, Doane identifies narrative conventions that operate to exclude women from occupying identities of maternal reproduction and economic production simultaneously.[1] We argue, in a parallel but different vein, that these conventions figure the domestic as a contested space of subjectivity for both women and men. Films produced for a female audience in the 1940s and 1950s worried over the questions that also concerned women's magazines and marriage guidance manuals: how much should a woman care about her home? How should she deal with the tension between her desire for own identity as a modern individual and the inevitable sublimation of her self into her social roles as mother and wife? What did the good (and bad) housewife do, and what did she look like?

Family and home in these films offer a space of realisation for female identity outside the world of work. In the films that we study, the domestic embodies the place at which modern life could be 'brought home', representing the fragile locus of a new world that had been promised before the war. In the following discussion of the films *Mildred Pierce*, *Come Back Little Sheba* and *The Three Faces of Eve* (made in 1945, 1952 and 1957, respectively), we examine different stages in the constructions of the figure of the housewife in Hollywood cinema from the 1940s and 1950s.

The films analysed in this chapter are predominantly Hollywood productions, despite the Australian focus of this study. There are several reasons for this, the most obvious being the limited Australian feature film production during the war and post-war period. From 1940 to 1960 only one urban-based Australian melodrama was produced – *A Son is Born* in 1946 – following the modest success of 1939's *Mr Chedworth Steps Out*.[2] The overwhelming flow of Hollywood-produced films into Australia, and world-wide, after 1940 was in part due to the growing dominance of American product in feature film production throughout the 1920s and 1930s, and a set of major American distribution companies that enforced distribution of their product over others, a situation that had been criticised in Australian trade papers throughout the 1930s. Pressure on the Australian film industry of a limited domestic market and stiff competition from the better-funded and organised American product, combined with wartime restrictions on film investment, resulted in the closure of the major Australian studio, Cinesound, in 1940. By 1939, the USA was the source of over 1,000 movies screened in Australia, representing 80 per cent of feature film imports into the country, with only 15 per cent from the UK and 5 per cent from other countries.[3]

All the films examined here were screened in Australia during this period, and all rework the position of home set up in the masculine narrative of modernity – as a place to leave behind – and articulate a different relationship to domestic space. We suggest that significant transformations in the figure of the 'housewife' occurred during this period. These films demonstrate an important shift in representations of housework that resonates with the transformation of the home outlined in the previous chapter. During this time the cinematic narrative of housewifery moved from a form of gendered *labour* to an inflexibly gendered *identity*. These films pick up on, and offer solutions to, the tensions we have described in the preceding chapters which surrounded women's role in a modernised domestic sphere. The positioning of the housewife as a form of gendered identification, rather than a practice, further contributed to the need for women to distance themselves from it. What was offered as an alternative to such an identity was not clear in the post-war era, as the feminist subject was yet to arrive on the scene.

Homework and Housework

Representations of women at home in the films of the 1940s and 1950s suggest that the identity of the housewife was under pressure during the post-war period from competing discourses that each defined femininity in quite different ways. Characters in these films often debate the cultural and economic value of women's work both inside and outside the home, and the plots of 'women's films' often deal with conflicts between different roles and expectations of women: mother, wife, worker, consumer, and so on. Studied over time, films aimed at female audiences particularly demonstrate contemporary changes in views about the agency of the housewife. In the 1940s, feminine identity was economically defined as 'invisible', as women's work was unpaid, voluntary or temporary (although, of course, many working- and middle-class women did work). Yet culturally, femininity was becoming highly visible as it became the site of the shaping of new consumer identities contributing to these tensions. Further adding to the complexity of this figure, a proper femine subject was constituted and interrupted by other forms of identification additional to gender (particularly sexuality, class, race, nation).

These intersecting social categories were repressed within Hollywood texts that sought to homogenise a diversity of female subject positions under the sign of the domestic. The cinematic housewife was overwhelmingly a white, middle-class construction, and often contrasted with her 'other', represented as a black or working-class, or both, women, working as her domestic servant.[4]

In this chapter we wish to focus on how these tensions within the housewife figure were barely containable, and point to how these films problematise a certain vision of modernity through a splitting of the figure of woman into two, opposed classed and gendered identities: the working woman and housewife.

An alternative experience of modernity is explored for women, which questions how home fits into modern social structures. This alternative modernity is constructed through the ideology of separate spheres that Nancy Armstrong has identified in her study of women's writings of the eighteenth and nineteenth century. This gendered modernity was imagined through a separation of home and work that is seen by Armstrong as cohesive and transformative, rather than oppressive and isolating for women. The household in these writings, she argues, is represented as a centrifugal force tempering the effects of the marketplace as a centripetal force.[5] Armstrong observes that the 'writing of female subjectivity opened a magical space in the culture where ordinary work would find its proper gratification and where the very objects that set men against each other in the competitive marketplace served to bind them together in a community of common domestic values'.[6]

Despite this desire for an alternative modernity shaped by such domestic values, the home modernised and brought up-to-date in the twentieth century by the latest domestic and communications technology and the popularisation of techniques of child-rearing, relationship management, dietary and health advice has remained unassimilable to the site of the real action of modernity: the public sphere figured in the world of work and the streets of the modern city. The desire to be modern, to participate in self-determining goals and achievements outside the home, while maintaining links to family and tradition, are shown to be the terms of women's modernity in the films we examine. Like the nineteenth-century novel, such films open up a similarly 'magical' space in which feminine faults and virtues are magnified into entire characters. These films explore the gendered divisions between the public and the private, the marketplace and the domestic; the home becomes a hinge between masculine and feminine views of the world that play out in emotive ways.

Cinematic melodrama was increasingly connected with the 'woman's film' – only described as a coherent body of films much later in the 1970s and 1980s – as both forming and addressing a particularly female audience in the 1930s.[7] Hollywood melodrama was consolidated in the 1940s with lavish budgets and high-profile stars of studios such as Universal and MGM. Warner Brothers, a studio that had signed a series of female stars to long contracts (including Bette Davis and Joan Crawford), actively sought female writers for a series of quality pictures for these leading women after 1941 to take the place of male directors who had joined America's war effort. Because women were assumed to be the main audience of these films, melodrama fell into the divisions between high and low culture and has been long associated with a presumed submission to manipulative cultural practices: escapism into over-sentimental and unrealistic scenarios. Thus the 'unfulfilled housewife' often appears as the archetypal viewing subject of melodrama, a characterisation Molly Haskell railed against (and in part constructed) in her book *From Reverence to Rape*, first published in 1974:

> Among the Anglo-American critical brotherhood (and a few of their sisters as well), the term 'woman's film' is used disparagingly to conjure up the image of the pinched-virgin or the little-old-lady writer, spilling out her secret longings in wish fulfilment or glorious martyrdom, and transmitting these fantasies to the frustrated housewife. . . . At the lowest level, as soap opera, the 'woman's film' fills a masturbatory need, it is soft-core emotional porn for the frustrated housewife. The weepies are founded on a mock-Aristotelian and politically conservative aesthetic whereby women spectators are moved, not by pity and fear but by self-pity and tears, to accept, rather than reject, their lot. That there should be a need and an audience for such an opiate suggests an unholy amount of real misery. And that a term like 'woman's film' can be summarily used to dismiss certain films, with no further need on the part of the critic to make distinctions and explore the genre, suggests some of the reasons for this misery.[8]

Declarations such as this inaugurated an important critical project to re-examine these films as feminist critics sought to jettison the assumption that they were purely 'emotive', without redeeming intellectual content. Subsequent to Haskell's book, these films were critically re-evaluated by film historians in the 1970s and 1980s as containing the seeds of an ideological critique of the bourgeois family and capitalism in the cold war era, thus transcending emotion with rational analysis. In 1981 Geoffrey Nowell-Smith, in the journal *Screen*, argued that

> Melodrama can thus be seen as a contradictory nexus, in which certain determinations (social, physical, artistic) are brought together but in which the problem of the articu-

lation of these determinations is not successfully resolved. The importance of melo-drama . . . lies precisely in its ideological failure. Because it cannot accommodate this problem, either in a real present or in an ideal future, but lays them open in their shame-less contradictoriness, it opens a space which most Hollywood forms have studiously closed off.[9]

The critical project of the 1980s reinscribed distinctions between public and private that were carried over from the nineteenth-century ideal of domestic wom-anhood. But, rather than looking for 'ideological loopholes' in the films, and reading the subversive feminist messages 'behind' the texts, it is possible to look for the ways in which these films produced gendered subjectivity: that is, how they showed women how to be women. Through its address to women at particular his-torical moments – specifically in the ways in which these films establish a dis-course of frustrated affect, or emotional blocks, rather than a form of false consciousness – the woman's film represents a rich site of analysis of ideas about women and the structuring of feminine subjectivity.

These tensions are developed through a melodramatic structure of feeling that manifests in characters' lives as an emotional economy of excess and lack: the housewife is either tragically indifferent to or over-invested in her home and family; she is either insufficiently open to modern ideas of the home or marriage or she is a victim of modernisation by embracing it too intensely. This problema-tisation of the housewife – as a mode of femininity caught between tradition and modernity – certainly contributed to the devaluation of women's work and the pro-jection onto the figure of the domestic woman of negative traits of over-mothering, immersion in the private sphere and excessive consumption. Yet this problem of modern womanhood also revealed the dimensions of social change and the new role of women in the market economy of the post-war period. The narratives of the films we examine construct the married woman as facing a series of limited options. At the one extreme, she can become like a man and express an autonomous self, which means she must be opposed to her family and focused on the world of work. At the other end of the spectrum, she can throw herself into femininity and her own identity in her family to the point of living her life through others and circumscribing their own expression of autonomy. The equivalence of the role of housewife with a feminine identity is the exact problem of these films, and one that their main characters must resolve or resign to by the end of the last reel. The 'desire to desire', named as the subject of these films by Mary Ann Doane, is the problem of the fictional housewife; however, her task in these films is more precisely the desire to desire 'properly'.

This problematisation of female subjectivity that we explore through an analysis of such films is not equivalent to the pathologisation of the housewife that emerged in a number of key texts before and after the 1950s. From Freud's essay on the hysterical teenager Dora and her house-obsessed mother, to Friedan's *Feminine Mystique*, the effects of boredom and frustration associated with the housewife rest on a wide-spread projection of lack of power and failure of individual development onto the persona of the woman at home.[10] In the 1950s and 1960s a dissatisfaction with the capacities and responsibilities of housework among early second wave feminists cast the emotional state of the housewife as a case of arrested or incomplete development within the terms of modernity: her daily life was characterised as being about repetition rather than progress; her association with cleaning, child rearing and dreary routines of shopping made her a worker who produced no product; and her spatial confinement to the home placed her crucially outside the urban and public world of mass culture and the dynamics of spectacular changes and developments in modernity. As this chapter on the films of the period will show, however, any vision of the domestic as temporally and spatially other to modernity was not easily accepted in the popular cultural forms that were shaping female subjectivities of the time.

Definitions of Melodrama

Melodrama has been claimed to be a 'genre whose conventions make ideologies "visible and watchable"'.[11] It has also been defined as 'the genre of domesticity' and, as such, is particularly important to feminist cultural studies.[12] Critics in the 1970s and 1980s, influenced by Peter Brooks' 1976 study of melodrama, identified it as an intrinsically modern cultural form for the ways that it 'makes the [modern] world morally legible'.[13] They re-evaluated the 'low' cultural form of melodrama in order to seek out its 'ideological failures'. Melodrama was thus 'discovered' in the 1970s and 1980s as the scene of a narrative resistance to a total ideological closure of the meanings of femininity. While this focus on transgressive content has been the motivation for many feminist studies of melodrama, such feminist critical work in the 1980s was also significant for the ways in which it drew attention to the historical nature of categories of feeling and sentiment.[14] Because melodrama works through an opposition between romance and the ordinary, its structure of feeling begins with the material of everyday life and expands and hyperbolises emotions contained within it. This opposition produces the emotional economy of melodrama, and foregrounds its modes of storytelling in everyday life. Feminist investigation of melodrama as a genre has uncovered the ways in which the domestic as the private sphere has been figured as the space of emotions. By drawing on Raymond Williams' notion of 'structures of feeling' as a recognition of the ways in which political change, social categories and subjectivity are related, we can understand how the films of the 1950s spoke to feminist critics of the 1970s and 1980s.

Through the concept of a 'structure of feeling', Williams connected emotions to historical phenomena and social categories:

For what we are defining is a particular quality of social experience and relationship, historically distinct from other particular qualities, which gives the sense of a generation or of a period. The relations between this quality and the other specifying historical marks of changing institutions, formations, and beliefs, and beyond these the changing social and economic relations between and within classes, are again an open question: that is to say, a set of specific historical questions. . . . We are talking about characteristic elements of impulse, restraint, and tone; specifically affective elements of consciousness and relationships: not feeling against thought, but thought as felt and feeling as thought: practical consciousness of a present kind, in a living and interrelating continuity.[15]

Williams distinguishes feeling ('meanings and values as they are actively lived and felt') from ideology ('formally held and systematic beliefs'), noting that they are of course interrelated in practice: 'Methodologically, then, a "structure of feeling" is a cultural hypothesis, actually derived from attempts to understand such elements [affective elements of consciousness and relationships] and their connection in a generation or period, and needing always to be returned, interactively, to such evidence.'[16] Feminist analyses of the themes of women's repression and suffering, mistaken guilt and cathartic innocence in melodramatic texts have represented melodrama as 'a (social) safety valve', yet this critical 'structure of feeling' about the form itself demonstrates changing relationships of women (as intellectuals) to domesticity. While Laura Mulvey has argued that the function of 1950s Hollywood melodrama was to 'provide an outlet for [ideological] inconsistencies . . . by touching on sensitive areas of sexual repression and frustration; its excitement comes from conflict not between enemies, but between people tied by blood or love', it is possible to understand melodrama as a form of training of the emotional subject.[17] Through watching melodrama, we participate in the realisation of the inequities of these family ties. Melodrama produces these ties as both emotional and social bonds through such conflict, rather than simply providing an outlet for the audience to vent collectively inexpressible or unspeakable emotions.

The kinds of emotions associated with domesticity in melodrama reflect historical shifts in subjectivity, and the organisation of emotion along gender lines. The emotional mode of melodramatic heroines has been called 'hysterical' by Lacanian-influenced feminist theorist Joan Copjec, in an interesting discussion of melodrama as a feminised sublime. However, the ways in which melodrama uses an hysterical mode to amplify 'the gestures of suffering', according to Copjec, is not a sign of women's irrationality or the text's unreality, but 'like wrestling', 'in a world which is unsure what justice should look like', the genre 'manages justice . . . so that virtue always wins out'.[18] Sentimentality in Western culture has been a feminised affect, emerging at an historically specific moment of the construction of gender and domesticity.[19] Copjec explains,

My initial premise is this: crying was an invention of the late eighteenth century. I offer as proof of this thesis the fact that at this precise historical moment there emerged a brand new literary form – melodrama – which was specifically designed to give people something to cry about. . . . I suggest . . . that we pay closer attention to this modern social imperative in order to distinguish crying in the modern sense . . . and for the wholly new emphasis in art and art criticism on the sentimental, emphatic relation between spectator and character – to distinguish this modern crying from all the lachrymation of earlier times.[20]

Despite ongoing critiques of the opposition between emotionality and rationality (such as those developed by Jaggar and Kaplan[21]), critics of classical Hollywood cinema, with some notable exceptions, have tended to repeat the 'ideological' rather than the 'affective' reading, either discussing them as damning critiques of the status quo, or as morality tales that punish deviant or rebellious characters. Peter Biskind in his extensive and detailed analysis of films of the 1950s judges their message as either conservative or pluralist.[22] In a more complex analysis, Kathleen McHugh, in her discussion of housework in Hollywood films in *American Domesticity*, has shown the kinds of sublimation of other differences, specifically class and race, that gender performs in these films. McHugh argues that the prominence of the figure of the middle-class woman in melodramatic genres elides both the representation of and the real labour of black or working-class women in the home. She observes that the housewife, as a construction of a white, middle-class, heterosexual femininity, has often been taken as the feminine per se.[23] The housewife, as a highly visible figure of the modernisation of gender during the twentieth century, came in the 1940s and 1950s to stand for the completion and assumption of a proper feminine identity, of the natural completion of womanhood. McHugh quotes Angela Davis on this point: 'Although the "housewife" was rooted in the social conditions of the bourgeoisie and the middle classes, nineteenth-century ideology established the housewife and mother as universal models of womanhood.'[24] The challenge remains to understand these films as simultaneously social and textual, as working towards a set of meanings at the same time as these meanings were shaped by forces outside the text. As Barbara Klinger has noted in her study of Douglas Sirk, the context of reception, or the ways in which we view film at any given time, are always guided by 'systems of intelligibility and value' that, rather than offering one true reading over another, 'help us understand the role history plays in negotiating and renegotiating meaning'.[25]

As our study is concerned to show, the gendering of women's work in the home created some unstable and untenable divisions between public and private, home and work. While acknowledging the invisibility of issues of class or race in the image of the happy, clean, post-war home, this chapter departs from some of these assumptions about the housewife as a stable, unchanging figure of gendered culture, and asks instead what shifts and changes in representations of women in the home occurred during this period. Popular film genres such as the melodrama articulated an address to a female consumer that was crucial in constructing a sphere of difference and distinction for women's agency in the 1940s and 1950s. No one film can be judged as ultimately conservative or progressive, as the films are complex, open texts. The characters are often contradictory and non-heroic, and their motivations are often multiple and obscured by their circumstances. Most of all, they show the domestic as an ambiguous and liminal space, in need of constant work to maintain its value as a home, or a psychical and emotional space, and not just a house, which is just a physical location. The previous section of this chapter argued that women's modernity was imagined in popular film through a rhetoric of domesticity, drawing on traditional ideas of separate spheres. This section has suggested that melodrama as a cultural form reflects and constructs a 'structure of feeling' for women's modernity. We will now examine these arguments in more detail through *Mildred Pierce*, a film from the 1940s that has long puzzled feminist film critics with its rather confused and intricate representation of the 1930s and 1940s housewife.[26]

Putting on the Apron

Mildred Pierce has been categorised as both film noir and melodrama. The distinction between the two genres has been drawn in the 'loss of home [that] becomes a structuring absence in film noir'.[27] Film noir also represents a domestication of crime and transgression. Instead of an inherent criminal tendency or evil in the heart of men, the novels and films of film noir that deal with women characters emphasise the ordinariness of crime, rather than diagnose its cause as moral decay. All of James M. Cain's three novels that were made into classic film noir – *The Postman Always Rings Twice*, *Double Indemnity* and *Mildred Pierce*[28] – establish relationships between strong female characters and men who work only intermittently or in very routine occupations. The couples commit murder or embezzlement because of a mixture of lust and a desire for the freedom that money brings, rather than a pathological need to murder or destroy. Based on Cain's experience as a journalist, the novels emphasise the ordinariness and prevalence of violence, and locate it in the suburbs and small towns rather than the big city, an alienated public sphere. Cain's novels, and the films made of them, show that the housewife-next-door is capable of murder if she is pushed by circumstance and the lack of a good male provider.

The film of *Mildred Pierce*, directed by Michael Curtiz in 1945, exemplifies this merging of melodrama with film noir. Cain's 1941 novel, from which it was adapted, recounts a classic melodrama in realist style, but the film frames this melodrama with two noir segments depicting a murder and the hunt for a killer. Mildred, (played by Joan Crawford) has to survive after her marriage ends suddenly and she is left with two children to support, Kay and Veda. Mildred left school at seventeen to get married to Bert, who loses his fortune as property speculator in a new suburb in Los Angeles in the early 1930s. Bert, unlike Mildred, who is a semi-skilled labourer in the home, still sees the home as a site of leisure, lazing around reading the newspaper and resenting Mildred for nagging him about his household duties.

Mildred Pierce merges melodrama with film noir by depicting a married woman as a protagonist – rather than using private detectives or policemen as central characters – and displaces public violence from the heart of the film noir plot onto the domestic – onto ordinary women and men, rather than the *femme fatale*. The focus on failed men (rather than good and bad girls) makes femininity distinctly more ordinary and less threatening to the social order than the failed masculinity embodied in shiftless, over-consuming and unproductive men. These gendered types appear in a set of films that depict the massive social changes associated with the economic depression of the 1930s, the transitional period of work and thrift during the 1939–45 war, and then the relative affluence of the 1950s.

Like many melodramas, films like *Mildred Pierce* show the housewife dealing with life at home despite an absent or inadequate husband; most usually they are widows and divorcees. They explore the question of how women who find themselves alone might deal with the modern world on their own terms, while still maintaining the image of domestic womanhood. These women use their experiences in the private sphere to their advantage in the public sphere, becoming waitresses and restaurant and service industry entrepreneurs. They negotiate the damning diagnosis of being 'just a housewife', as an employment agent describes Mildred Pierce, explaining why she is only offered demeaning jobs as a domestic worker when she looks for work after her husband leaves, rather than as a receptionist, which is her preference.[29] During Mildred's search for work during the depression of the 1930s, the skills of home-making can only translate into the most menial paid work, as another character eventually explains to her:

> All right, you wanted to know why that lady offered you a job as a waitress, and why I recommended you for this. It's because you've let half your life slip by without learning anything but sleeping, cooking, and setting the table, and that's all your good for. So get over there. It's what you've got to do, so you may as well start doing it.[30]

Mildred is determined that her children will have greater opportunities in life than she and Bert have had. In the first flashback sequence, which allows her to tell her life story, she explains:

> I was always in the kitchen. I felt like I'd been there all my life except for the two hours it took to get married. I married Bert when I was seventeen. I never knew any other kind of life. . . . Just cooking and washing and having children.[31]

Following Bert's departure to live with the 'other woman', Mildred finds work as a waitress and saves enough money to build up her own chain of highly successful restaurants. Because of her experience as a wife and mother, she extends her domestic duties efficiently and professionally into the public sphere. She quickly figures out that despite a lack of ready cash during the depression, and perhaps because of wide-spread economic hardship, many people want home-cooked food in an atmosphere of domestic comfort. She senses, however, that there is a kind of shame associated with serving food to other people, and hides her waitress uniform from her children, only working when they are at school.

The film's main scriptwriter, Catharine Turney, believed that the noir framing story was introduced for several reasons: firstly, as an attempt to attract a wider audience; secondly, because the plot did not seem particularly suited to a feature film; and thirdly, because of the censorship code, which meant that Mildred's daughter had to be punished for the crime of sleeping with her mother's second husband. Turney explained in an interview in the 1980s that the studio would not film the script if it was directly adapted from Cain's realist style:

> I had to compress it quite a bit, but I wanted to stay with the novel the way it was as much as possible. I liked the novel very much. But the property went on the shelves for a time because nobody wanted to do a movie about a housewife who made pies. It wasn't very glamorous or interesting to people at the studio. No actress wanted to play it, no director wanted to do it period. It was finally [producer] Jerry Wald who revived the project and talked Joan Crawford into doing it. . . . She was in her mid-thirties at the time and didn't want to play the mother of a sixteen-year-old daughter who stole the man from her.[32]

Turney also credits Wald with turning 'the thing into a murder mystery':

> The novel is very different from the movie. In the book, Veda, the bitchy daughter, really does have a good voice, and she comes through in the end, so you have the feeling that she's really going to go on and accomplish something. Which makes Mildred's sacrifices for her and belief in her worthwhile. But Jerry didn't want that. He wanted the murder. And then, the flashback structure was his idea as well. . . . I think his approach had something to do with the censorship that was in force. If a girl transgressed, she had to be punished, according to the framework of the Johnson-Hays office.[33]

What does remain in the film after the producer's intervention, as in the Cain novel, is the occupation and location of the main character in the home. Although she becomes more than 'just a housewife' by the film's ending, as Turner suggests above, this posed the problem of ensuring that the film's star remained attractive and glamorous while she was playing a home-maker. The housewife-turned-business woman played by an established star must constantly maintain her distance from the frump, and clothing such as Mildred's fur coat and the use of heavy make-up help her to solve this tension. Veda, during a fight about her marriage to the son of a rich family, alludes to this when she tells Mildred that despite her 'new hairdo and some expensive clothes', she is nothing but 'a common frump, whose father lived over a grocery store and whose mother took in washing' . Particularly telling is the appearance of the apron that Mildred wears when working in the kitchen, both at home and in her business, which allows the kind of manual and dirty work that she does to be distanced from the love scenes. The apron in the film moves around characters (being worn by Bert's ex-business partner, Wally, and Mildred's black maid), as both the material symbol of maternal labour and an eroticisation of the domestic scene, anticipating the 'new look', as discussed in the previous chapter, which emerged as a mode of a sexy yet domesticated femininity in the late 1940s. *Mildred Pierce* suggests that domestic labour, when transposed to the public sphere, reverses notions of gender and class. This is literalised in a scene in which Wally, Bert's former business partner and investor in Mildred's business venture, is put to work in the restaurant kitchen and Mildred ties his apron strings. By putting on the apron, Wally figures ongoing shifts in the organisation of gender in the 1930s and 1940s (figure 4.1).

Figure 4.1 Butterfly McQueen, Joan Crawford and Jack Carson in *Mildred Pierce,* 1945. Film image by permission of Warner Bros. By courtesy of George Eastman House.

This redistribution of the affect of domestic labour is most explicit in the novel, when Veda reveals to Mildred that it is exactly her *lack* of class sophistication and role as a domestic worker that her shiftless playboy lover, Monty Beragon fetishises:

> Really, he speaks very nicely about your legs. He has a theory about them. He says a gingham apron is the greatest provocation ever invented by women for the torture of man, and that the very best legs are found in kitchens, not in drawing rooms. 'Never take the mistress if you can take the maid', is the way he puts it. And another thing, he says a pretty varlet is always agreeably grateful, and not too exacting, with foolish notions about matrimony and other tiresome things. I must say I find his social theories quite fascinating.[34]

Monty deals with the problem of his own ambiguous social position and lack of traditional masculinity by sexualising Mildred's lower-class identity. Yet this speech obscures the real dilemma of the downwardly mobile, post-war gentleman: Monty is unable to provide, so Mildred must work. Her management of the 'Pie Wagon' causes her constant preoccupation with smelling of grease from fried chicken, so her lavish spending on clothes and cars and her ambition for her daughter to achieve fame as a singer or movie star are signs of her need to escape the domestic and abject nature of her work. Mildred's double life at work and home in order to maintain her new middle-class status makes her responsible for the way that Veda has turned out. When arrested for Monty Beragon's murder, Veda blames Mildred: 'It's your fault I'm the way I am – Help me.'

The class transformation of Mildred's family through consumerism is posed as antithetical to the puritanical achievement of spirituality through hard work. Published in 1942, the same year as the release of Cain's book, Phillip Wylie's diatribe on modern motherhood, *Generation of Vipers*, demonstrated an emerging anxiety about the influence and role of mothers in the modern family.[35] Wylie claimed that American women's tendency to emotionally over-invest in their children's success was a widespread social problem. Controversially, he accused contemporary mothers of living through their children to a degree that was detrimental to their development of an independent and healthy identity. This paradox of the modern mother is embodied in Mildred's story of self-actualisation through her daughter, Veda, especially apparent after Kay, her younger tomboy daughter, dies of pneumonia. While her story reveals a stark lack of choice and limited options in the face of husbandly desertion, Mildred's refusal of the domestic-angel model of womanhood allows her to make many instructive mistakes in her rearing of her children. She transgresses several social conventions in her divorce through her successful working life, economic support and then remarriage to an unemployed man of higher social standing than herself, and finally in pretending to be Monty's murderer to save her surviving daughter from jail. The emotion evoked by

Mildred's story is an 'outlaw emotion', in Alison Jaggar's terms. Such emotions, she says are 'distinguished by their incompatibility with the dominant perceptions and values'.[36] Jaggar identifies 'outlaw emotions' as 'potentially or actually feminist emotions'.[37] *Mildred Pierce*, because of the ways in which it merges the codes of film noir with the narrative of maternal melodrama, complicates any simple story of maternal sacrifice. This new post-war development indicates that rather than a clear separation of good and bad mothers, these discourses could be embodied in one character at different times. This complex 'structure of feeling' around women, work, consumerism and domesticity emerges in the depiction of Mildred as a housewife in a fur coat with a gun. By assembling a series of incompatible spheres of experience (housework, crime, the city, suburbia), the film demonstrates the ways that these phenomena have never been unrelated.

Posing some bother for feminist film critics, the film's final shot reunites the glamorous fur coat-wearing Mildred with the scene of the domestic abject: when Bert and Mildred exit the Justice building to the left of screen into a new post-noir dawn, two women wearing headscarves and pinafores scrub the hallway on their hands and knees. As Linda Williams has argued, this shot 'literalises' the relationship between middle-class and working-class women.[38] It also foreshadows the re-inscription of housework onto a low 'other' and the complex relationship of the middle-class woman to the household economy of the migrant worker in the global economy. Further, this final shot of the film foregrounds the labour of housework, and demonstrates the 'splitting' of housewife as gendered subject: the middle-class woman defined through the labour of consumption and able to exit the domestic scene into the public sphere not as 'just a housewife' but in the discourse of equality, alongside her husband. The working-class woman is still defined by her labour, and the work of cleaning and tidying up persists. What the shot also anticipates is the splitting of the housewife into a subject and object in feminist debates around housework in the 1970s and 1980s. While most people do have to do some housework, the 'housewife' as an identifiable persona associated with a particular historical period represents a key transformation in feminist constructions of self, in the passage from home-making as an activity undertaken by women to an identity belonging to some (insufficiently modern) women.

The Childless Housewife

A 'social problem' film of the early 1950s, *Come Back Little Sheba* constitutes the relationship between economic conditions and women's agency in a very different manner.[39] The film, adapted from a successful stage play by William Inge, a disciple of Tennessee Williams, also traces the consequences of a pre-war marriage, but showed that just staying at home was not enough for women to make their husbands happy. Once high-school sweethearts, 'Doc' and Lola Delaney were forced into marriage during the 1930s because Lola was pregnant. Doc dropped out of medical school and became a chiropractor to support his new wife and child, but their baby daughter died. Now a reformed alcoholic, Doc avoids his frumpy wife and dreary and neglected house by attending AA meetings and doing late-night '12–step work' with other ex-alcoholics (figure 4.2).

Figure 4.2 Shirley Booth and Burt Lancaster in *Come Back Little Sheba*, 1952. Film image by permission of Paramount. By courtesy of George Eastman House.

The film opens with Lola Delaney answering the door in her chenille dressing gown in the late morning. Without her husband's knowledge, she has advertised a spare bedroom for rent, and Marie, an art student at a local university, wishes to take it. Doc is at first offended that his wife would consider taking in a boarder – 'Not the Delaney's, they don't rent rooms' – but seems charmed by Marie and her innocence, and allows her to move in without telling his wife because, as he says to Marie, 'It's my house.' It becomes apparent that Lola, who cannot have any more children, has displaced her grief over her miscarriage by directing her affection to 'Little Sheba', a missing dog that she constantly looks for throughout the film. Lola seems to have no other activities to fill her time, apart from waiting for the postman, who never brings her letters. Lola takes on a mothering role, as if Marie were her daughter, and this relationship triggers her to reflect on the loss of her child and the decay of her beauty. She asks Doc if he is sorry that he had to marry her; 'you didn't know I'd get old and fat and sloppy'. Because she has no children and invests very little time in doing housework or cooking, her life is lonely, uneventful and isolated. She is portrayed as nostalgic for her high school days and her own past popularity – 'the "it" girl who danced the Charleston'. Lola's slovenly behaviour is contrasted both with the youth and beauty of the teenage girl and with the hard work and thrift of the devoted mother of four, Mrs Kaufman, who lives next door. Doc comments that Marie must spend a fortune on bath powders and salts as their bathroom 'smells like a lilac factory', while Lola confesses that she is 'too tired to wash her face'. Mrs Kaufman advises 'you should get busy, Mrs Delaney' to forget the loss of Little Sheba. When visiting Lola while she prepares a formal dinner for Marie and her home-town fiancé, Bruce, Mrs Kaufman declares, 'Why, you've done all your spring-cleaning in one day. I certainly have to hand to hand it to you, all the years I have been saying Mrs Delaney is a good-for-nothing, sits around the house and never even shakes a dust mop.'

Doc seems to blame Lola for his having to drop out of medical school and not becoming a 'real' doctor. He tells Lola that most alcoholics are 'disappointed' men, although exactly what he is disappointed in he does not say. The depiction of Lola as a failed housewife seems to confirm that he should be disappointed with his life because, despite overcoming alcoholism with the help of AA, he still struggles with drink. He is shown to be in constant danger of relapse, especially when Marie's sexuality is on display, and she is shown too vulnerable to the advances of the racy Turk Fisher, her college boyfriend. When she flirts with Turk, Doc is torn between attraction to her and disgust at her sexual freedom.

In a touching and amusing scene, Lola listens to a radio programme during the middle of the day, during which rhythmic 'primitive' drumming starts to fill her lounge room. Lying on the couch, Lola starts to move her hands as if in a trance. The radio announcer's deep and hypnotic voice fills the room:

> Taboo . . . it's taboo radio listeners – your fifteen minutes of temptation. Leave behind your routine, the dull cares that mark your daily existence, your little worries, the daily confusion of the workaday world, follow me to where lithe natives dance on a moonlight isle where pagan spirits hold sway . . . the restless surging white shore . . . won't you come along? But remember it's taboo!

Lola's escape into the fantasy worlds of radio is paralleled in the film by Doc's compulsion to drink, but the couple have different reasons for their escape from the everyday. Doc is trapped in marriage to a woman who does not fulfil her role as a beautiful, happy, hard-working wife. He is shown getting his own breakfast and Lola makes no effort to look her best for him. When Doc finally goes on a drinking binge triggered by his mistaken perception that Marie has 'lost her virginity to Turk' the night before a special dinner with Bruce, he returns home drunk and violent to a distraught Lola, who has waited up all night. When he starts to destroy their crockery set, because it's too good for 'sluts', his long-suppressed hatred of Lola is revealed. He tells his wife to 'Scream all you want, you fat slut. Make the neighbours think I'm beating up on you.'

He reveals his highly contradictory expectation that Lola should be both a good domestic worker and display a proper kind of femininity. He is jealous of the guests, commenting that the prospect of company in the form of Marie's fiancé, Bruce, has made Lola freshen up and perform as a housewife should: 'You even combed your hair, even washed the back of your neck and put on a girdle.'

The film ends when Doc returns home from the City hospital after drying out. Lola has finally heeded the advice of Mrs Kaufman and spent her time wisely, making new curtains and painting the icebox. Both characters accept their failings as they accept their roles as husband and wife: Lola, coiffed and made-up, cooks bacon and eggs as she tells Doc of a dream that she found the dead body of Sheba, finally accepting the death of both her baby and its substitute. The final word is Doc's as he drinks his breakfast orange juice and declares 'It's good to be home.'

Themes of grief, over the loss of both child and child-substitute, are developed in the film narrative, and in particular scenes such as those that show Lola as waiting for something to happen, while lacking in purpose. Her husband seems bored with her and home; however, when faced with his own failings, he admits that he could have returned to medical school and restarted his career as a doctor when his parents died and he was given his inheritance. The film builds up a sense that the housewife, especially if childless, is out-dated, old-fashioned and obsolete. Only the final scenes of the film show her important role as Doc's loving wife when he breaks down emotionally and allows his need of her to become apparent.

The very ordinary setting and circumstances of Lola Delaney's story in *Come Back Little Sheba* stand against the bizarre and improbable plots of the film noir/melodrama cycle. The themes of boredom and empty time, sub-plots in the films of the 1940s, become dominant in realist films like this one. In these narratives of the domestic everyday, an affect of tedium tempers melodramatic excess, yet the relations between women's lives, their consumption of cultural texts and the institutions that shape them remain the same. As the housewife passes from heroine, to possible deviant, to a figure of 'disappointment', to 'a study in frustration', she comes to signify a problematic figure of modern femininity during this period. The final section of this chapter examines a film that deals with the housewife as a 'personality fragment' that must be dispensed with in order for the truly modern woman to emerge.

A Doubled Plot of Femininity

By the 1950s, individual imperatives to monitor one's own life and ensure that all aspects of the housewife's existence were kept in check intensified in magazines and domestic management guides. The last film we examine, *The Three Faces of Eve*, reflects such an intensification of the gendering of home in the 1950s.[40] The film tells the story of Eve White, played by Joanne Woodward, who is a 'rather sweet, rather baffled young housewife' living in a small southern American town with her husband and a young daughter.[41] After unsettling her husband by behaving completely out of character, and suffering migraines and blackouts, Mrs White visits a psychiatrist. During these sessions another personality reveals herself within the body of Eve White: Eve Black, a sexy, uninhibited, outspoken and glamorous woman who supposedly expresses those parts of Eve White's personality that she has repressed. Eve White is demure, married and modest in her desires; Eve Black is outrageous, single, consumes irrationally and behaves irresponsibly. Eventually, guided by the therapist and by the end of the film, a third self called Jane emerges as a new persona, 'born' during the sessions: an intelligent, sensible, educated woman, who helps resolve and integrate the different facets of Eve's personality into a 'whole and healthy human being'.

The film is based on a case history of multiple personality written by two psychiatrists, Doctors Thigpen and Cleckley, who bestowed the names of Eve, 'White' and 'Black', on their patient, Chris Sizemore. Their popular book documenting the analysis was published in the same year as the film was released.[42] Both book and film represent the story of Sizemore, a woman with multiple personalities. Ian Hacking has discussed the ways in which Eve White's story and Chris Sizemore's diagnosis diverge in his magisterial study of multiple (or, as it is now classified, dissociative) identity disorder, *Rewriting the Soul*.[43] Here, we do not want to take issue with the truth or falsity of the psychiatrist's story, nor of the psychiatric condition of such a disorder, but to look at how these personality fragments are used to narrate a story of a gendered identity in the film.[44]

The case history of Chris Sizemore as Eve is located in the dynamics of an encounter between madness and housewifery in the popular imagination of the 1950s. The biographies of female multiple personality outlined in the case history *and* the feature film reflect significant assumptions about women's position between the worlds of work and home. These changes indicate that a sense-making structure, emerging from social and cultural conventions of femininity, overlaid the un-narratable or unacceptable parts of Sizemore's/Eve's story. This generic and melodramatic structure created a resonance for her life story with wider concerns and anxieties over women, mass culture and the domestic. The film version of *Three Faces of Eve*, as well as the book upon which it was based, can be located not just as pop psychology, but also under the rubric of the woman's film and, more specifically, within the genre of the maternal melodrama that emerged during the high point of classical Hollywood production in the 1930s and 1940s.[45]

The story of *Eve*, as a sub-genre of melodrama, emerges from the fascination of the woman's film with a doubled female identity in the many 'twin sister' plots of the gothic melodramas in the 1940s. Identified by film historian Lucy Fischer as a 'canon of texts on the female *doppelgänger*', the emergence of the genre of 'double films' in the late 1930s was marked by a divergence from the male double narratives in that they 'reflected established patriarchal assumptions about women'.[46] With titles such as *A Stolen Life*, *Cobra Woman* and *The Dark Mirror*,[47] Fisher argues that rather than reflecting an eternal conflict in the feminine psyche, the production of these films should be historicised to show that their generic features 'do not represent real poles of the female psyche but rather two opposing *male* views of woman'.[48] In these films, these two views were embodied by the same actress playing two separate characters. These stories represent a materialisation of a discourse on femininity as split into either the good twin – who is able to form properly managed heterosexual desires and a domestic identity by the end of the film – or a deviant twin – who loves excessively or obsessionally, and is disposed of either by murder, accident or suicide. Fisher's argument about the misogyny of this concept is persuasive. Despite being understood and discussed as the 'woman's film', this description of the genre was certainly misleading, because of its notable absence of women screenwriters or directors. The popularity of these stories with female rather than male audiences, however, challenges Fisher's reading of the films as misogynist.

A more nuanced understanding of these films is hinted at by Fisher herself, that this 'male' view of women in the 1940s 'would seem to have cultural determinants – since woman's *persona* was seen as divided, and its aspects as mutually exclusive'.[49] By the 1950s, this division fell across a different line, as 'normal' femininity was increasingly represented not just by a heterosexual woman who loved and was loved, but also by the middle-class housewife. Rather than the good and bad twins of the war period, of whom the evil one had to die to resolve the narrative, the post-war period established the housewife as the central figure of women's modernity inside these divisions.

Despite their decline in the 1950s beside the new cultural forms of television soap opera and drama, such melodramatic narratives organised and literally plotted out women's lives in the post-war period. The cinematic adaptation of Sizemore's story reworks an untidy and undirected sequence of events of suffering and trauma into a narrative of a woman's search for a modern self. Eve's 'split' identity reproduces the divided female subject explored in the 'twin' plots of these films, and this parallel with such cinematic convention may explain the attraction of producers and audience to the story of Sizemore a decade later. In the 1950s, a story as bizarre as Sizemore's could be efficiently transposed to a cinematic narrative as an *internal* conflict in women's identity: taking place in the same body, and the 'split' personality resolved by psychic integration into a 'whole' person rather than an exorcism of the evil element. Both the film and the book combine scenes of dissociation into a plot with fixed entry and exit points into Eve's inner life. Indeed, Thigpen actually advised Sizemore against revealing the persistence of her illness in her own book because it would create confusion for the reader if she neglected to include a neat and tidy ending.[50] In *his* story, like the dirt that the housewife expels from the domestic, the therapist performs a cleaning process on Eve's psyche to unearth and re-organise her traumatic memories, thereby maintaining the boundaries between self and other, inside and outside, health and sickness. In *her* story, the combined stresses of financial problems, her husband's unemployment, miscarriage, a forced abortion, strict social restrictions on what constituted a proper feminine identity, and her own fragile sense of home overwhelm her daily life and prevent any realisation of her desired capacity to love and build a safe place for her family to grow. According to Sizemore, these factors, rather than any inherent conflict in femininity or the female psyche, forced the different 'personalities' to take on the un-safe areas of sexuality, anger, work and child bearing, thereby creating the unstable and uncanny boundaries between self and other that Thigpen's version maintains. This sense of an uncanny and transgressive selfhood is reflected in the title that Sizemore had wanted to call her 1950s book, *Strangers in My Body*.[51]

The film uses flashbacks and special effects to portray the forces that 'fractured' Eve's self into 'two personalities battling for dominance'. The film also gives the viewer access to a panoptic yet intimate outsider's perspective on Eve, a perspective unavailable to Eve herself. Hacking establishes that representations of multiple personality used a panoptic vision from its earliest diagnoses in the 1880s, when multiple personality was visually recorded in Charcot's photographic studies of hysteria.[52] These splits and separations create suspense and fascination for the audience in the film because, as many critics have noted, melodrama works through a tragic structure of feeling that 'grants its audience greater knowledge than its characters possess, and this disparity produce pathos'.[53]

For the housewife self, Eve White, later observed by the integrated self, Jane White, the practice of reading sentimental poetry and classical literature offered a way of transcending her unhappiness and personal problems. Eve Black, however, finds her alter ego's reading habits 'the quintessence of dullness. They leave her cold in the literal sense as well as the spiritual.'[54] Eve Black prefers to spend her evenings in nightclubs and afternoons in movie theatres, and actually participates as a performer in clubs by singing and dancing, to the amusement of her suitors and the displeasure of her husband (and Eve White). In a therapy session she takes pride in her role as amateur nightclub singer and pop chanteuse:

'Her face will be a sight to see if you tell her about the time I was out at the Lido Club. Had some champagne cocktails with a fellow there. I like to sing you see . . . I put some charge into it when I got to "Rockin' and Rollin'" – *Rockin' and rollin'/All night long . . .'*

With a little toss of her head she carried a snatch of the tune for a moment.

'But what really sent 'em,' she said, 'was when I stood there in the middle of that dance floor with the spotlight on me and let 'em have "Sixty Minute Man".'[55]

The split between different areas of everyday life is figured here in the separation of black popular culture from white culture, regional tradition from urban modernity. The story of the two Eves embodies uneven development of the northern and southern United States, associating the 'lowly' and primitive Eve Black with the South as the excluded subtext to the American narrative 'of capitalism and modernization, of individualism, materialism, education, reason and democracy'.[56] In the film, as the two Eves become less dominant, the character's southern accent, most noticeable in Eve Black, fades until it is almost gone in the speech of the educated Jane. However, because the film figures this national and economic difference as a split between housewife and her 'others', it subsumes these national and racial tensions within a feminine struggle for identity. This gendered narrative constructs the conflict between incompatible elements of the female persona as primary and prevailing over other social and cultural divisions.

Both the film and Thigpen and Cleckley's book strongly textualise the particular historical circumstances of Chris Sizemore's life as romance narrative and journey of discovery. Both stories coerce the details of a still living woman with a psychiatric disorder into a kind of über-narrative of feminine identity and ego psychology that stands for all women – most strikingly in Thigpen and Cleckley's re-naming of Sizemore as the essential, eternal and biblical 'Eve'. The notion of Eve's deeply split and contradictory 'immature' feminine identities as either saintly housewife or good-time bad girl works in Thigpen and Cleckley's version because it operates from widely held understandings of these subject positions as conflicting social imperatives of womanhood: one could be either one or the other in the same body, but never both in the same self.[57] For the female viewer, the story of the fictional Eve offers a resolution of all these tensions in the figure of a 'modern woman' (Jane) who manages these multiple and conflicting pressures and finally integrates all aspects of her sexual, maternal and economic identities as a wife, mother *and* worker. Her character only achieves this difficult task of self-completion and self-understanding with the help of analytic techniques mediated by her psychiatrist. These changes are visually expressed in her assimilation of both good and bad Eves into a sexy yet sophisticated style of dress and a modest beauty. Jane's labour of self-production involves her keeping up with the latest fashion and beauty (at this point in the film her hair-do rises abruptly upwards into a back-teased and lacquered beehive anticipating the styles of the early 1960s), through proper expression of her femininity in remarriage and reunion with her child, and most crucially through the articulation of her personal and most interiorised life story with familial and public history through memory work and analysis.

Yet in one very striking way, this film – highly popular although criticised at the time and later as unbelievable and ridiculous – represents a very important shift away from aspects of the woman's picture discussed in Mary Ann Doane's book *The Desire to Desire*. In 1940s melodramas and film noir aimed at a female audience, Doane identifies narrative conventions that exclude women from occupying identities of maternal reproduction and economic production simultaneously. By the mid-1950s, this exclusion did not seem to be so obvious or easily held in representations of women in films and other texts. Jane White is a working woman, and she is able to remarry and drive away with her reunited family (and second husband) at the end of the film.

The film's extrapolation of an exceptional, individual case to a foundational dilemma for all modern women points to some key tensions around the figure of the housewife in popular culture in the 1940s and 1950s. These tensions revolve around a series of shifting balances between social, family and individual desires and constraints for women. The film plays out these desires in the tensions between the housewife as figure of lack and boredom against the working woman as feminine fulfilment and self-actualisation; between women's struggle for economic independence and self-determination against their primary roles as carers and home-makers; and within the zone of popular culture itself as a problematic source of pleasure and consumption in opposition to the moral and upright institution of the family. In the final section of this chapter we map responses to these films, which were framed as a problem of modern femininity.

Harpies like Mildred

Several writers during the 1950s used the films to argue that modern women were leaving behind traditional values of domesticity. Damon Mills, a writer in the Australian publication *Monthly Film Guide*, accused Hollywood of never being 'sufficiently impressed by the womanly virtues of honour, nobility, courage, faith and moral fortitude'.[58] Films which featured strong female characters holding the family together in times of trouble were made in the 1940s, in narratives such as *I Remember Mama*, *Mrs Miniver* and *Meet Me in St Louis*, yet these films were at the time, and have been since, far less noted and discussed as constituting a separate genre.[59] Mills read the 'shrewish' Mildred Pierce as 'typical' of the type of female 'protagonist' (not worthy of being called a 'heroine') of 'nearly all film dramas we see – women who are concerned only with winning rich husbands, scoring over feminine rivals, gaining a luxurious existence, fighting to keep worthless children in that same luxury'.[60] Mildred herself was an example of a tendency to present as 'normal behaviour' a main character as a

> woman whose mind could not rise above gutter-level to place a value on anything. Her whole conception of life was that it should provide bodily well-being of the most luxurious order obtainable for both herself and her ill-bred trollop of a daughter, and that any means that would secure this end were legitimate – however twisted and unjust they may seem from a well-balanced viewpoint.[61]

Even worse were the films that showed the lives 'of numberless Hollywood husbands whose wives do not understand them'. Such movies 'owed their success to their pandering to a lachrymose, artificial and vulgar sentimental feeling in this matter possessed by many women'. These films

> almost sanctified the illicit relationship around which their stories were built, ringing the heads of their leading feminine characters with haloes of righteousness, whereas in cold actuality the best that could be said of these women would be that they were weak and misguided.[62]

Overall, Hollywood was guilty of inflicting 'agony by pictures recording the dubious moral activities of women' like Mildred Pierce. The author did not explain whether the agony was his own or more widely social. This sort of vision of popular cinema as a directly degrading force does not demonstrates that such films were either morally wrong or, from the 1970s critical position, entirely ideologically correct, but reflects an ongoing debate over the representation and reception of woman's film which forges an association between cultural consumption, economic conditions and women's agency. We advocate a different perspective, that is, that by looking at how these films figure changes to the figure of the housewife as 'woman as wife-companion' and the home as a space of self-completion, they ask us to see what has been left out of history.[63] The material presences of home in the suburban house as setting and locus of action in these films uncovers the relationship of representation and the everyday: 'a significant insignificance' in that these things are so taken for granted that they do not warrant filming or narration. Our account of these films shows that what is the unrepresentable material of the maternal melodrama is what is lacking from Eve White and Lola Delaney's lives as a drab housewife. What 'Eve Black' (and Mildred Pierce to some extent) enjoys and excels at is everything that everyday life is not: glamorous clothes, dancing, flirting, singing, travel, fame, attention. Located outside the everyday yet taking it as a departing point, these films examine the possibility of a gendered version of modernity.

Melodrama – as it was manifest as a cultural form in the post-war period – by representing narratives of women's 'choice' between public and private, paid and unpaid work, demonstrates that female subjectivity was under negotiation. Precisely because family and love, work and money were shown in these films as mutually exclusive, and something women had to choose between, they generate an affect of forbidden passions and impossible circumstances. Yet they also question these very oppositions: because melodrama is grounded in realism and the everyday, these films show women in the home and the practice of everyday life. Herein lies a paradox that resonates throughout the history of the housewife. Because domestic labour is invisible to the economy and to culture, because it is part of the backstage operation of the production of the self and life, such labour is vary rarely documented on film, unless it is aberrant, unusual or strange. The figure of the housewife gathered up all the contradictions of modern life like those other contraband of modernity: dirt, never-ending repetition and ritual that exist outside linear time and resist transformation into progress and totality. So housewives on film, like Mildred Pierce, Lola Delaney and Eve White, are troubled, lazy, bored or mad because they are insufficiently modern women. The films usually end with a return to domestic reality, but with a change or transformation taking place in the characters, who have realised an essential error that they have made or who have given up their conflicting needs so that happiness is possible. When Veda is charged with murder, and Mildred is let off the hook in *Mildred Pierce*, Mildred's over-investment in her daughter's life is surmounted. Lola heeds her neighbour's advice in *Come Back Little Sheba* and demonstrates her love for her husband by taking better care of her house and herself, thus 'curing' his alcoholism. In *Three Faces*, Eve must give up both the dependency and passivity of her housewife persona and the irresponsibility and autonomy of her single girl persona so that she can take up the correct, modern femininity of the mature Jane and be a good mother. Although the films set up contradictions between women and work outside the home, they do not necessarily accept them. They show that they exist and direct the audience's attention to inequities in women's contemporary situation.

As Mary Russo has argued, feminism has been marked by a wilful ignorance of the ordinary and mundane.[64] The splitting of the identity of the housewife from the figure of the modern woman is one aspect of this absence. The emotional structure produced by these films offers a way of knowing how these social and political conditions impacted on women's lives. Because these films, and other popular cultural forms that engage melodrama, 'speak beyond the capacities of representation', they offer and provide a method to track what work representations of the housewife actually did in this period to produce a modern self.[65] The films show various stages in the transition from housewifery as a form of work, to housewifery as identity. The task of developing a gendered identity that matches up to the demands of modern life produces an unstable subject, and one that is open to feminist narratives of self-actualisation in work, but basic questions of the role of the home in modern life remain unresolved. While one can stop doing housework, the identity of the housewife is harder to cast off: an 'inadequate human being'. As we have argued in previous chapters, feminist critiques of representation must acknowledge this shift from a material economy of housework to an economy of the subject in order to begin to recognise the absences of second wave feminism's. In the next chapter we examine, through a case study of women's radio programming of the 1940s, the emergence of a feminist speaking position around the politics of everyday life, which anticipated and in some ways went beyond second wave feminist concerns.

Notes

1. Mary Ann Doane, *The Desire to Desire: The Woman's Film of the 1940s*, Bloomington, Indiana University Press, 1987.
2. *A Son is Born*, Director, Eric Porter, Script by Gloria Bourner, Eric Porter Studios, 1946, and *Mr Chedworth Steps Out*, Director, Ken G. Hall, Script by Frank Harvey, Cinesound Australia, 1939.
3. See 'Official Report by the Chief Censor of the Commonwealth Film Censorship for the Year 1939', in *Film Weekly Motion Picture Directory 1940/41*, Sydney, *Film Weekly*, 1941, pp. 8–9.
4. This is discussed at length by Kathleen Anne McHugh in *American Domesticity: From How-to Manual to Hollywood Melodrama*, New York, Oxford University Press, 1999. Anne McClintock provides an excellent account of the pre-history of domesticity and whiteness in the Imperial project in *Imperial Leather: Race and Gender in the Colonial Conquest*, New York, Routledge, 1995.
5. Nancy Armstrong, *Desire and Domestic Fiction: A Political History of the Novel*, New York, Oxford University Press, 1987, p. 95
6. Ibid.
7. Rick Altman, 'Rebirth of a Phantom Genre', in *Film/Genre*, London, BFI, 1999, pp. 72–7. Film historian Andrée Wright contrasts the scarcity of Australian productions during the war years with the burgeoning genre of 'woman's film' in the USA (Only ten Australian features were made as filmmakers were redeployed to make newsreels and propaganda films, and of the stories they portrayed most were war or military films such as *Wings of Destiny*, *Forty Thousand Horsemen*, *The Power and the Glory*, *A Yank in Australia* and *The Rats of Tobruk*. See Andrée Wright, *Brilliant Careers: Women in Australian Cinema*, Sydney, Pan Books, 1988, p. 88.) The bias of Australian productions to bush epic and 'transposed western'-style films even after the war (*The Glenrowan Affair*, *Captain Thunderbolt*, *King of the Coral Sea*, *Robbery Under Arms* and so on) has meant that domestic melodrama has been an absent genre in Australian cinema.

8. Molly Haskell, *From Reverence to Rape: The Treatment of Women in the Movies*, New York, Penguin, 1979, pp. 154–5.

9. Geoffrey Nowell-Smith, 'Minelli & Melodrama', reprinted in Christine Gledhill (ed.), *Home is Where the Heart is: Studies in Melodrama and the Woman's Film*, London, BFI, 1987, p. 74.

10. Sigmund Freud, *Case Histories, I. 'Dora' and 'Little Hans'*, James Strachey (trans.), Harmondsworth, Penguin, 1977; Betty Friedan, *The Feminine Mystique*, Harmondsworth, Penguin, 1983.

11. Mary Beth Haralovich, 'All That Heaven Allows: Color, Narrative Space, and Melodrama', in Peter Lehman (ed.), *Close Viewings: An Anthology of New Film Criticism*, Gainesville, University Presses of Florida, 1990, pp. 57–72.

12. Laura Mulvey, '"It Will Be a Magnificent Obsession": The Melodrama's Role in the Development of Contemporary Film Theory', in Jacky Bratton, Jim Cook and Christine Gledhill (eds), *Melodrama: Stage, Picture, Screen*, London, BFI, 1994, p. 122.

13. Peter Brooks, *The Melodramatic Imagination: Balzac, Henry James, Melodrama, and the Mode of Excess*, New Haven, Yale University Press, 1976.

14. Gledhill (ed.), *Home is Where the Heart is* (see note 9).

15. Raymond Williams, *Marxism and Literature*, Oxford, Oxford University Press, 1977, pp. 131–2.

16. Ibid., p. 133.

17. Mulvey, '"It Will Be a Magnificent Obsession"'.

18. Joan Copjec, 'More! From Melodrama to Magnitude', in Janet Bergstrom (ed.), *Endless Night: Cinema and Psychoanalysis, Parallel Histories*, Berkeley, University of California Press, 1998, p. 260.

19. The next chapter examines in detail the way that boredom, modernity and femininity have been interrelated. For now, it is important to remember, as Patricia Meyer Spacks has noted in her book, *Boredom*, the emergence of the description of person or text as 'interesting' came at the same time as someone or something could be called 'boring'. (Patricia Meyer Spacks, *Boredom: The Literary History of a State of Mind*, Chicago, University of Chicago Press, 1995.)

20. Copjec, 'More!', p. 249.

21. Alison M. Jaggar, 'Love and Knowledge: Emotion in Feminist Epistemology', in Alison M. Jaggar (ed.), *Gender/Body/Knowledge*, New Brunswick, Rutgers University Press, 1989, pp. 145–71; E. Ann Kaplan, 'Mothering, Feminism and Representation: The Maternal Melodrama and the Woman's Film 1910–1940', in Gledhill (ed.), *Home is Where the Heart is*, pp. 113–37.

22. Peter Biskind, *Seeing is Believing: How Hollywood Taught Us to Stop*

Worrying and Love the Fifties, New York, Pantheon Books, 1983.

23. McHugh, *American Domesticity*, p. 19.
24. Angela Y. Davis, *Women, Race and Class*, New York, Vintage Books, 1983, p. 229.
25. Barbara Klinger, *Melodrama and Meaning: History, Culture, and the Films of Douglas Sirk*, Bloomington, Indiana University Press, 1994, p. xvii.
26. Pam Cook, 'Duplicity in *Mildred Pierce*', in E. Ann Kaplan (ed.), *Women in Film Noir*, London, BFI, 1980, pp. 69–80; Julie Weiss, 'Feminist Film Theory and Women's History: *Mildred Pierce* and the Twentieth Century', *Film & History*, 22 (3), 1992, 75–87; and Linda Williams, 'Feminist Film Theory: *Mildred Pierce* and the Second World War', in Deidre Pribram (ed.), *Female Spectators: Looking at Film and Television*, London, Verso, 1989, pp. 12–30.
27. Vivian Sobchack, 'Lounge Time: Postwar Crises and the Chronotope of Film Noir', in Nick Browne (ed.), *Refiguring American Film Genres: Theory and History*, Berkeley, University of California Press, 1998, p. 144.
28. *The Postman Always Rings Twice*, Director, Tay Garnett, Script by Harry Ruskin, Niven Busch and James M. Cain, MGM USA, 1946; *Double Indemnity*, Director, Billy Wilder, Script by Billy Wilder and Raymond Chandler, Paramount, 1944; *Mildred Pierce*, Director, Michael Curtiz, Script by Ranald MacDougall, Catharine Turney (uncredited) and James M. Cain, Warner Bros, 1945.
29. James M. Cain, *The Five Great Novels of James M. Cain*, London, Pan, 1985, p. 401.
30. Ibid., p. 361.
31. Albert J. LaValley (ed.), *Mildred Pierce*, Madison, University of Wisconsin Press, 1980, p. 97.
32. Catharine Turney, 'Interview with Catharine Turney', in Lee Server (ed.), *Screenwriter: Words Become Pictures*, Pittstown, Main Street Press, 1987, p. 234
33. Ibid., p. 235.
34. Cain, *Five Great Novels*, p. 463.
35. Phillip Wylie, *Generation of Vipers*, New York and Chicago, Holt, Rinehart & Winston, 1955.
36. Jaggar, 'Love and Knowledge', p. 146.
37. Ibid.
38. Williams, 'Feminist Film Theory', p. 28.
39. *Come Back Little Sheba*, Director, Daniel Mann, Script by William Inge and Kettie Frings, Paramoun, 1952.
40. *The Three Faces of Eve*, Director, Nunally Johnson, Script by Nunally Johnson, Twentieth Century Fox, 1957.
41. This description of Eve is from Alistair Cooke's documentary-style introduc-

tion, which frames the rather unbelievable story of Eve by addressing the audience in front of the screen in an empty cinema. Cooke refers to her as a housewife several times in his narration of the film.

42. Corbett H. Thigpen and Hervey M. Cleckley, *The Three Faces of Eve*, New York, McGraw-Hill, 1957.

43. Ian Hacking, *Rewriting the Soul: Multiple Personality and the Sciences of Memory*, Princeton, Princeton University Press, 1995.

44. In her own accounts of her treatment, she indicates that Thigpen neglected the persistence of several other selves (up to twenty-two) associated with her identity disorder during this period, leaving her far from 'resolved' into a single identity at the end of his treatment. Unhappy with Thigpen and Cleckley's version of the events of her life and highly critical of the psychiatric treatment she received in the 1950s and after, she twice attempted to correct this misunderstanding of her condition and its 'cure'. She first tried to publish her own account of the analysis in the late 1950s, in *The Final Face of Eve*, but her co-author and publisher changed her version of events to more closely resemble the film. On Thigpen's advice, she did not reveal her identity to her closest friends and family as the subject of the film and did not see the film herself until the 1970s. Finally, her cousin published a book based on her diaries and interviews in the 1970s in which she provided an alternative ending to the 1950s books and film. (See Chris Costner Sizemore and Elen Sain Pitillo, *Eve*, London, Victor Gollancz, 1978; also published as *I'm Eve* by Doubleday in the USA in 1977.)

45. E. Ann Kaplan, 'Individual Response: The Spectatrix', *Camera Obscura*, 20–1, 1989, 194–9; Christian Viviani, 'Who is Without Sin: The Maternal Melodrama in American Film, 1930–1939', in Gledhill (ed.), *Home is Where the Heart is*, pp. 83–99.

46. Lucy Fisher, 'Two-Faced Women: The "Double" in Women's Melodrama of the 1940s', *Cinema Journal*, 23 (1), 1983, p. 26.

47. *Cobra Woman*, Director, Robert Siodmak, Script by Scott Darling, Gene Lewis and Richard Brooks, MCA/Universal, 1944; *A Stolen Life*, Director, Paul Czinner, Script by George Barraud, Karel J. Benes and Margaret Kennedy, Orion/Paramount, 1939; *A Stolen Life*, Director, Curtis Bernhardt, Script by Karel J. Benes, Catharine Turney and Margaret Buell Wilder, Warner Bros, 1946; *The Dark Mirror*, Director, Robert Siodmak, Script by Nunally Johnson and Vladimir Pozner, Universal International, 1946.

48. Ibid., p. 34, emphasis ours.

49. Ibid., p. 38.

50. Sizemore and Pitillo, *Eve*, p. 371.

51. Ibid., p. 368

52. Hacking, *Rewriting the Soul*, p. 5. By keeping a diary and writing notes and

letters, Chris Sizemore allowed her personalities to communicate with and demonstrate awareness of each other, and actually watched the documentary films that the psychiatrists made of her separate personalities in order to 'introduce' her two 'sides' to each other for therapeutic purposes.

53. McHugh, *American Domesticity*, p. 94.

54. Thigpen and Cleckley, *The Three Faces of* Eve, p. 158.

55. Ibid., p. 69.

56. Kathleen Stewart, *A Space on the Side of the Road: Cultural Poetics in an 'Other' America*, Princeton, Princeton University Press, 1996, p. 3.

57. Actually Chris Sizemore had several personalities around this time and after (see also note 44), many of them unnamed as they were not truly separate 'personalities' but could only be identified by their significant objects and hysterical obsessions: Freckle girl, Turtle lady, Bell lady, Banana Split girl, Strawberry girl, Blind lady, the Virgin, and so on.

58. Damon Mills, 'Of Harpies Like Mildred', *Monthly Film Guide*, August–September, 1950, pp. 9–10.

59. *I Remember Mama*, Director, George Stevens, Script by DeWitt Bodeen, Kathyrn Forbes and John Van Druten, RKO Radio Pictures, 1948; *Mrs Miniver*, Director, William Wyler Script by George Froeschel, James Hilton, Jan Struther, Claudine West and Arthur Wimperis, MGM, 1942.

60. Mills, 'Of Harples like Mildred', p. 9.

61. Ibid.

62. Ibid., p. 10.

63. Jackie Byars, *All That Hollywood Allows: Re-reading Gender in 1950s Melodrama*, London, Routledge, 1991, p. 156.

64. Mary Russo, *The Female Grotesque: Risk, Excess and Modernity*, New York and London, Routledge, 1994, p. vii.

65. Ibid., p. 167.

–5–

Boredom: The Emotional Slum

In 1947, the authors of *Modern Woman: The Lost Sex* declared that 'the social development which created the physical slum also created throughout society what may be termed the emotional slum',[1] and women were trapped within it. This bestselling book of the late 1940s and early 1950s claimed to describe the 'disordered' state of woman's psyche following 'the destruction of the home' during the Industrial Revolution.[2] The book's co-authors, sociologist Ferdinand Lundberg and psychoanalyst Marynia Farnham (also husband and wife), argued that women's personal lives had been affected by 'recent historical changes . . . [which made them] materially for the better but psychologically for the worse'.[3] They identified the Industrial Revolution as the catalyst for what they believed had been a decline in and decay of a fulfilling home life, and the beginning of a process of modernisation that involved no sense of progress. They blamed the Enlightenment 'Man of Reason' for this change in the home, with women and children his innocent victims. He had, they argued, introduced forces beyond his or anyone's control into everyday life:

> Educated European man of the seventeenth and eighteenth centuries was much like a home inventor who goes to the basement to conduct experiments that will give him a feeling of his own power. In the course of his gadgeteering he finally hits upon the one experiment that causes a great explosion. The explosion blows up the old house completely, and blows himself, his wife, the children and little baby out the windows. . . .[4]

Lundberg and Farnham borrowed the notion of the urban slum, as a central trope of the discourse of modernisation during the nineteenth century, to characterise this 'psychosocial' situation. It provided a powerful sense of the disjuncture that they believed existed between the private world of home and family and the public world of work and politics in the post-war era. This vision of the 'emotional slum' projected an atmosphere of incomplete psychological development onto women's private lives. This interior state was, according to Lundberg and Farnham, 'less easily recognized' than the more familiar underdevelopment of the urban ghetto marked by race and class. But women's emotional decline was not simply related to poverty, and 'knew no geographical barriers', appearing on 'Park Avenue, Wall Street and Fifth Avenue as well as Main Street, State Street and Constitution Avenue'.[5] Neither was it confined to North America, where Lundberg and

Farnham lived and worked: 'We may find it in England, where, geographically, it was first fully defined, although it did not originate there. . . .'[6]

By linking both the urban and 'emotional' slum to modernisation – a 'by-product of the factory system of production' developed during the Industrial Revolution – Lundberg and Farnham connected the modern economic system with a stagnant and degenerate femininity. They argued that modernisation – in particular, the separation of work and home – had undermined woman's social and economic roles, and devalued the everyday time and place of the home against an abstract and unified public sphere:

> She consequently no longer has security of position as a woman, a female being. Her femaleness is now treated as a coincidence, an unfortunate complication. Everything she undertakes is apt to be on a part-time basis, much of it having nothing to with being a woman – all of which makes for a great deal of confused surface variety in her life but adds up to little in the way of solid satisfaction, peace of mind, easing of deep inner tensions.[7]

These changes had gradually precluded women's 'natural' sphere of authority, the home, from any involvement in the narrative of modernity, which was based around ideals of progress formed through the separation of private and public spheres. The only way that 'modern woman' could participate in this new social world was outside the family sphere as a 'consumer-courtesan, living her own separate life, [with] her own money to spend'.[8] The wide availability and adoption of mass entertainment in a modern society was not a solution to, but the symptom of, the 'shock' felt by modern men and women following this 'destruction of the home':

> This emotional slum may be defined as existing wherever there is unhappiness and diversion on an unprecedented scale – movies, radio, phonograph, automobiles, yachts large and small, vacation resorts, television, sports amphitheatres and equipment, colorful magazines and newspapers, comic strips, elaborate toys for children, and an additional variety of appliances and devices for furthering feelings of momentary pleasure – is a rough yardstick of the extent to which people increasingly feel the lack of a capacity for enjoyment within themselves.[9]

The Lost Sex encapsulated women's emotional state in metaphors that evoked the mass destruction and organised violence of war, with chapters titled 'The Tidal Wave of Modern Unhappiness; or the Fantasy of the Firing Squad', 'Mother and Child: The Slaughter of the Innocents' and – the central problematic of the book – 'The Destruction of the Home'. The latter described modern women as suffering 'blast shock' from the explosions of the Industrial Revolution, and becoming 'displaced persons' after the 'home's destruction'. The authors argued that any '[u]nderstanding of modern women can never be complete without a preliminary understanding of what has happened to the home, over which women ruled as veritable queens for centuries . . .'. As a result of these changes, they concluded, '[w]omen were not freed of the home and its drudgery, as many have asserted. With the loss of the home, they lost other things, deeper things . . .'.[10]

Betty Friedan, writing nine years later in *The Feminine Mystique*, considered *The Lost Sex* to be a 'crude application of Freudianism', and a primary source and evidence of the powerful hold of the 'feminine mystique' in contemporary culture.[11] As Ruth Feldstein has recently argued, Lundberg and Farnham's book, together with Phillip Wylie's *Generation of Vipers*, first published in 1942, cannot be seen simply as a conservative reaction to 'the anxieties that shifting gender mores generated', because this 'mother-blaming' was not 'restricted to middle-class white women who needed to be "contained" within the suburban domestic sphere' and had been important to liberal analyses of families since the 1930s.[12] Friedan, perceived as working against this backlash, also reproduced aspects of the argument contained in *The Lost Sex*. She too borrowed metaphors of destruction and horror, familiar from wartime, calling one of her chapters 'Progressive Dehumanisation: The Comfortable Concentration Camp' and describing the post-war proponents of the feminine mystique as 'brainwashing' women. Like Lundberg and Farnham, she totalised changes wrought by processes of modernisation such as the way in which consumerism signified a new female vocation, encapsulating these changes in the term 'feminine mystique', and she characterised them as overwhelmingly negative for women. She diagnosed modern women as living in a state of boredom and dissatisfaction, thus becoming 'passive non-identities' and bad mothers, pathologically over-invested in their children. She argued that these dysfunctions were in the process of being transferred to the next generation via a form of compensatory 'destructive love', reflected in the 'ego-failure' of young American men.[13] As an account of the changes felt by the family in the post-war period, *The Lost Sex*, with its 'psychosocial' methodology and claims of women's exclusion from modern life, made a very similar diagnosis of the condition of 1940s womanhood to Friedan's of women in the 1950s in *The Feminine Mystique*. The solution that each book offered, however, was of course radically different. Lundberg and Farnham believed that women should return to their roles at home and give up their aspirations to a public identity, while Friedan called for a revolution in women's social position through their self-actualisation: 'a new life plan for women'.[14]

But by far the clearest theme that both texts have in common is the way that they deployed the modern housewife as a subject rather than an object of boredom. Starkly contrasted with the domestic happiness promoted in advertising, as discussed in Chapter 3, these books evoked a sense of emotional dis-ease and even stasis in the modern home. While they argued for different responses to this phenomenon, they both inquired into *gender* as a *locus of melancholy*.[15] In the inter-vening period between the publication of these books, the bored housewife took on a distinct shape and presence in the modern cultural imaginary. This figure, in both texts, is called on to represent both an *affect*, or emotional state, and an *agent*, or a means of change. By taking these texts together, and reading them against each other, it is possible to see what work this gendered figure – the housewife – and her associated affect – boredom – was called on to do in the post-war period, for both feminist and anti-feminist positions. Lundberg and Farnham located women's independence or 'masculinisation' as a cause of dysfunction. Friedan identified their dependency and passive acceptance of the 'feminine mystique' as the problem. But both texts used the 'modern feminine' to describe a person who experienced the ultimate indicator of a truly modern subjectivity: boredom as a response to social conditions, rather than an indulgence in moral weakness. Boredom for both texts implied a dwelling on the self and pointed to the ways in which the external conditions prevented the self from becoming fully actualised. During the 1950s, this newly collectivised awareness of women's social posi-tioning represented the grounds for moving concerns about domestic roles into public discourse. Not only did narratives such as these, which were determined to construct women as subjects of boredom, provide women with a means of self-consciousness, they also united women through a public expression of an intensely private experience.

This chapter seeks to map the background to such an emotional response to modern life, and particularly to unpack its gendered dimensions. We begin with a brief description of how women were described as the subjects of boredom in women's magazines of the 1940s and 1950s. Articles and letters to the editor in the *Australian Women's Weekly* demonstrate the point made earlier in this book that popular culture in this period was by no means providing a single monolithic message to women about their role in life. Far from painting an unambiguous rosy picture of the housewife as heroine, magazine articles discussed whether or not housework was a fulfilling occupation and how some women managed to juggle the demands of career and home. They further demonstrate that popular culture gave voice to a set of tensions about domesticity and achievement for women in this period. Just as the films discussed in the previous chapter worried over how women should manage the desire to define their own identities as modern selves with the seemingly inevitable sublimation of self required of them in their roles as wife and mother, so these magazines asked what women should do, how they should care about home.

We then go on to look at a rather different medium of communication – radio – and how a discourse on boredom and the home emerged in a very particular set of programmes directed to a female audience, similarly indicating the pervasiveness of these tensions in the structure of feeling of the time. These programmes particularly explored the dangers of the housewife becoming too immersed in the home, endangering not only her own identity but that of her family too. Women were being instructed on the importance of creating a life for themselves – and hence a home – still connected or open to the world. As the subject of boredom, modern woman needed to change her life. The question was: how far should she go?

'Time to Burn'

In 1958 an article in the *Australian Women's Weekly* by Margaret Burlace stirred up a storm of correspondence. She claimed that 'Women have time to burn'. She urged women to organise their time more effectively and to ensure that they had time to socialise with their friends and to undertake some recreational activities such as going to Workers' Educational Association courses. Her article included a weekly plan starting at 6.30 am, six days a week, and concluding each day with the evening meal. Without such a plan, she argued, women 'reduce their wasted time and energy to the ashes of self-pity. Frustration, boredom, and loneliness are the result.'[16] The first replies to Burlace's article tended to admonish her for the lack of humanness in her approach and of its insufficient flexibility to deal with the inevitable little traumas of children's lives. Subsequent letters tended to be more approving. All agreed that the housewife's life was a busy one but that it could be managed with the right attitude, with or without a plan. Other articles and letters during the 1950s expressed a similar view about the need for housewives to have recreation and some mental stimulation. An editorial in 1953, for example, praised a '36 year old Melbourne housewife' who undertook a Bachelor of Arts degree in her spare time while looking after her three children. 'No housewife and mother', it said, 'need feel that taking on this role automatically means being buried alive in a smother of domesticity.'[17]

In this same magazine, however, concerns emerged from time to time about the extent of demands on the housewife's time. Whereas political discourses particularly during and just after the war focused on the drudgery of the housewife in the sense of the difficulty and unpleasantness of home conditions, the *Australian Women's Weekly* by the 1950s seemed more interested in the hours she had to work. A male journalist in 1958 announced that he agreed with a prominent churchman, Dr Irving Benson, who had declared that housewives were 'shockingly overworked'. To determine his stance on the matter, the journalist had for a day taken over the work of a housewife with four children. After fifteen hours work his back was aching and he decided it was the hardest day he had ever had.[18] Other articles discussed the range of skills a housewife needed to draw on and a study that had measured the number of miles a woman walked in a day completing her tasks around the house.[19] None of these articles suggested that different arrangements should be made for the management of the labour of the home, although some suggested that women were not making effective enough use of 'labour-saving' devices while others raised the spectre of whether women should be paid for their household work.

Where as these articles discussed the difficulties of the full-time housewife, whether in terms of her boredom or drudgery, others explored the opportunities for women to be both housewives and career women. A Special Feature in the *Australian Women's Weekly* in 1957 discussed the emergence of the working wife who keeps her job at least for some time after marriage, runs an ordered home and leads a happy life. Her marriage was described as a companionate one in which there is more sharing of household responsibilities at the same time as she learns new ways of doing things that put fewer demands on her and save work.[20] Other articles declared that 'working wives are here to stay', some saying women were continuing to work until they had children in order to contribute to the family income, but others exploring the possibility of women continuing to work even after they had had children.[21] But an anonymous male author wrote an article in 1959 declaring that 'My wife works and I hate it!' He complained that their home and children were no longer properly looked after. While he could understand women going out to work for reasons of financial necessity, his wife worked because the children were all at school and she was bored.[22] The magazine calculated that 40 per cent of the letters that came in 'sackfuls' in response to this article were on the husband's side, 36 per cent on the wife's, while 24 per cent had sympathy for both sides.

What these articles and letters reveal is that popular magazines were far less monolithic in their approach to talking about women's lives in the 1950s than Betty Friedan and others have claimed. Similarly, advertisements, even though working to persuade women to buy the latest labour-saving devices, would often acknowledge the tensions about whether women's lives should combine domesticity and achievement precisely in order to sell their goods. While acknowledging women's boredom or ambivalence, advertisements sought to channel their emotions and the desires they signalled into a desire for commodities. An advertisement for Pyrex dishes in 1947 demonstrated that washing up could be so much 'fun' that even husbands would want to do it (figure 5.1), and by 1957, an increasingly sophisticated campaign to sell washing machines on Mother's Day promised to make 'Washday . . . a time of welcome relaxation' (figure 5.2). By giving voice to the seemingly private experience of boredom in these various ways, women's magazines articulated a sense in which women in the home lacked a proper set of tasks for life, at the same time as they explored, albeit in limited form, the way the organisation of everyday life in the modern world created this problem. This talk was *sotto voce* alongside the more comfortable images of domestic happiness. But it was opening up a space in which the problems of the housewife identity could be discussed.

Figure 5.1 'When Husbands Insist on Washing up . . .', Pyrex advertisement, *Australian Women's Weekly*, 5 July 1947, p. 44. By permission of World Kitchen (Australia).

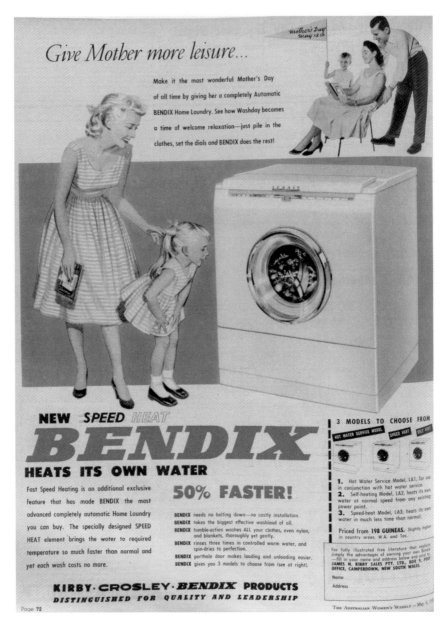

Figure 5.2 'Give Mother More Leisure . . .', Bendix advertisement, *Australian Women's Weekly*, 8 May 1957, p. 72. By permission of BT Appliances.

Housewives' Corner

The tensions highlighted above between consumerism, home and modernity are evident not just in popular culture such as film and magazines, but also in the broader history of women's media. As a key social institution, and an important cultural form of modern domestic life, women's programming on Australian radio from the 1920s demonstrates how these issues were handled in a 'public service' manner. Australia's national broadcaster, the Australian Broadcasting Commission (ABC), was established by an act of parliament in 1932. Taking over the various stations owned by the Australian Broadcasting Company, the nationalised Commission continued to use announcers and programmes during a transition period in mid-1930s. Building on the female audience established by the Company, during the next ten years the ABC established regular programmes for women. *The National Women's Session, Women's Magazine* and *Morning Magazine* were intended specifically to cater for the female component of the ABC's audience, which was imagined as massive potential audience, awaiting the arrival of radio's benefits.[23] The commercial – or what were originally referred to as 'B' – stations provided an alternative to the worthy and earnest talks from representatives of women's organisations that were a staple of programming on the ABC stations. The commercial stations offered instead a *Women's Radio Service* 'consisting mainly of reproduced music and fashion talks'.[24] The standard introduction/conclusion for the *Women's Session* stated that it was 'designed particularly for the service of the housewife'. The show ran from 10.30 am every weekday, first on radio station 2BL, and from 1946 on station 2FC. These daily *Women's Sessions* continued until the 1960s, when they were taken off air.

In 1933, May Couchman, the only female ABC Commissioner appointed in 1932 and an official of the Australian Women's National League, recommended that 'in order to attract the average woman of intelligence, something better would have to be offered' than the broadcasts for women the Commission had taken over from the old Australian Broadcasting Company. The ABC introduced more 'middle-brow' cultural fare such as book reviews, classical music and discussions of art in the hope of 'rais[ing] women from the atmosphere of the gas stove and the ironing board'.[25] An article published in the ABC's *Broadcaster* magazine in 1936 argued that radio was a central medium for the task of bringing the modern world into the domestic sphere:

> Nothing is more enervating physically to women or so stagnates the feminine intellect as the lack of fuel for fresh ideas providing material for thought and talk. Yet radio may break the monotony of normal home life for women who must necessarily spend the greater part of their life in the house.[26]

The new cultural form of radio was understood not only as being able to break the 'monotony' of the housewife's life, but also more concretely as a technology that could unite women isolated in their homes and literally bring them into dialogue with the public world.

The *Women's Sessions* were consolidated along these lines in war broadcasts such as 'The Kitchen Front' in the early 1940s. The question of what to include in programming was initially decided by time available in the daily schedule and technical restrictions, with the earliest broadcasts being fifteen-minute speeches live-to-air twice a day.[27] Under the direction of hosts based in Sydney, the *Women's Session* was extended into a magazine-style programme after 1944. Book reviews formed the core of many broadcasts, as well as 'staged' discussions of food shortages, food production, the Red Cross, discharged servicewomen, fashion, cooking, child care and travel. The most popular programme, in terms of audience share, was the West Australian programme, from 1944 directed by Catherine King, wife of an academic, Alec King, and daughter of Walter Murdoch, a Professor of English at the University of Western Australia. According to her biographer, Julie Lewis, King's aim was to 'provide the housewife with some mental stimulation' in addition to the 'service' items that were a staple of ABC programming.[28] Her programmes were presented in an authoritative yet intimate format, containing cosy and friendly 'talks' rather than the more one-way 'lectures', all underpinned by the host's warm 'personality'.

Both state-based programmes, such as King's, and the national broadcasts employed a notion of a democratic public sphere, giving voice to issues of public policy that affected the home and inviting politicians and representatives of women's organisations to give armchair talks.[29] The daily rhythms and intimacy of radio was believed to be well suited to women's culture, and talks were timed to fit with the rituals of morning and afternoon tea.[30] This ability of radio to operate in the 'background', to be aimed at, and taken up by, women whose minds needed to be occupied as an antidote to the mundane and repetitive chores that made up housework was one of the rationales for the *Women's Session* and determined its enduring format. The discussion surrounding the ability of women to listen for extended periods highlights the role of radio in the 1930s and 1940s as an activity that was considered to demand full attention. It was imagined that radio listening would take place in the living room, rather than the working areas of the house such as the laundry and kitchen. Women were expected to sit down, 'put their feet up' and listen to the sessions at morning or afternoon teatime.[31]

In May 1943, the ABC's Talks department held an informal meeting regarding the *Women's Session* and three female members of staff were invited to express their opinions. Three points are recorded in the minutes of this meeting: first, a view of the 'tremendous importance from a community and national point of view of fostering the activities and interest of home life'; second, the recommendation that the sessions should be at once 'practical, informative, educational and cultural'; and, third, the suggestion that a 'woman of personality and background who is outstandingly "microgenic" be sought as a compere'.[32] The session achieved these aims during the last years of the war by articulating how the domestic sphere related to the war effort, and its chosen speakers affirmed women's role in nation-building by speaking to the woman listener at home both as a 'citizen' and as the guardian of family life. In a talk originating from 4QR in Queensland, for example, a Miss Goulton described family life as the 'basis of national strength, health, greatness, and morale' and the maintenance of the 'home front' as the 'sacred duty and privilege of wives, mothers and sisters'.[33]

A 1941 session proposed, however, that after the war there might be 'no more private worlds for women.' This session particularly demonstrates how the form of radio offered a new medium for debate, in which listeners were invited to imagine themselves participating in and hence to be very much part of that imagined community of the nation.[34] It also shows how the ABC conceptualised radio as cultural form that could establish a new relationship between public and private spheres. This session dramatised a conversation between three women, Thirza and Elizabeth, 'two lucky housewives', and Edna, 'a poor business woman'.[35] Thirza responds to being called 'lucky' by Edna by dismissing a radio talk she recently had heard in which a woman had said 'that if only married women, in their homes, would realise that they're the luckiest people on earth, most of our Pre War and Post War problems would be settled'. Elizabeth agrees, and says 'it seems ridiculous to me, too, when it's becoming more apparent every day that women can no longer seclude themselves within their own four walls'.[36]

Elizabeth hopes that 'pressure won't be brought to bear on [women who have been working] after the War is over to force them back again into private life', but Thirza reflects on her experience after the end of the first world war:

> Well, Elizabeth, if the last Post war period is any criterion, pressure won't be needed. I remember well that, then, most of the women who'd worked like Trojans for the war effort said, in effect, 'Thank Heaven, that's over' – and of their own accord, they went back to their housekeeping and their petty social diversions.[37]

In response to this characterisation of 'most women' entirely interested in the petty matters of housekeeping and social diversion, Edna quotes an 'interesting article' by Pearl Buck, who had recently divided American women into three groups:

> First. The women who have a real vocation and so break down all obstacles in order to achieve their purpose – she thinks that's a small group. The second, also small made up of women like those you speak of, who're quite satisfied with domestic routine and not wanting to take any part in life. Then a very large third group – she calls them 'Gunpowder women' – who aren't satisfied, but don't know what they want. This group,

she thinks, are the women with time and potentiality for public service. She gives them that name because she thinks they only need a spark to make them a dynamic force in National life.[38]

The *Women's Session* imagined itself as a transformative cultural form, as the spark that would ignite women's dynamism. With the potential to harness this dissatisfaction, the only obstacle was women's self-recognition as bored and unfulfilled by domesticity. This characterisation of the majority of women as needing to be 'told what they wanted' was the teleology of the programme, and the subject matter of unfulfilling domesticity was its means. At times the session addressed itself explicitly to these 'Gunpowder Women', and sought to create them and give them a 'voice' through the medium of radio. It included their voices alongside the more didactic forms of lectures and talks, but it employed the notion of the listener as attentive and intelligent in order to generate an ongoing conversation about women and domesticity. Radio was the medium that would make women full 'citizens' in a democratic nation by taking them out of their own world and relating their personal domestic problems to those of others. A talk by Janet Mitchell on women in 'This Changing Australia' in 1942 argued that a woman would only become 'a citizen in the fullest sense when she feels passionately that the children of Mrs Smith next door should have as good an environment as her own children'.[39] She linked radio to women's embryonic citizenship, which, while it still began at home, would move beyond the domestic sphere:

> Is there any ground for the belief, widely held amongst women as well as men, that the average and typical woman, she whose interest centres in the home and children . . . she is still the typical woman, no matter what equality of opportunity has done for her sisters in business and the professions towards ensuring their economic survival . . . is either incapable of grasping or unwilling to grasp her place as a citizen with a responsibility towards the wider problems of the community. Thanks largely to the radio, the home keeping woman of to-day, whose circumstances and means limit her personal contact with men and women outside her immediate circle, has the chance of being well informed on world events.[40]

Radio, as it was conceptualised by the ABC, was imagined as having a privileged access to the domestic sphere, and the Commission particularly saw its role as addressing a unified audience of women who were awaiting enlightenment and were about to 'become citizens'. Despite this self-assurance about the coherence of women's interests, discussions of what the housewife should *feel* as well as *do* within the *Women's Session*, however, demonstrates how this ideal began to fragment as a result of an address to a mythical 'woman at home'.

Finding Time

An enduring topic of the *Women's Session* lay in solutions to domestic drudgery in the home. Over time, this search for ways to change the home for the better, and lighten the 'housewife's burden', gave rise to an increasing expression of feelings of boredom and isolation on the part of the woman at home. Women on the 'land' were particularly singled out for mention in relation to 'the most primitive and labour-making conditions' of rural domesticity.[41] Yet the problem of modern home life was constituted in terms of the 'survival of the race' and was a universal concern. Even guests to the programme who argued that women were 'lucky' to be housewives acknowledged the prevalence of feminine boredom because of the inherent isolation and monotony of home life. The solution offered by a dominant strand of discourse, then, lay in a transformation of domestic time, a revisioning of the home as neither 'shut off' nor isolated from the flow of public time. Advocating that women manage domestic time more effectively, as did the 1950s women's magazines articles discussed earlier in this chapter, these 1940s radio programmes envisaged women as having greater opportunity to become part of this public world.

This focus on time was not a new theme of home management, as studies such as Ruth Schwartz Cowan's have shown.[42] Home economics had long produced the household in the mould of the workplace, and in the twentieth century it sought to apply Taylorist theories to housework in the desire to achieve the efficient time management that domestic experts such as Catherine Beecher had advocated in the nineteenth century.[43] The discussions of boredom in the *Women's Session* reveal, however, that a new emphasis on futurity had entered the home that was radically different from these nineteenth-century ideas. The 'spare time' that would be freed up by modernisation of domesticity could potentially give rise to new and greater experiences of boredom, if it were not put to good use. The new time of the home constituted domestic space as part of the rest of the social world, infused with purpose and relevance to the life of the nation. Underpinned by the ideal of democratisation of culture that was the cornerstone of the ABC's public service philosophy as the national broadcaster, the *Women's Session* showed the way to this new temporal regime for the housewife: through participation in culture and community, she would become a fully modern person. In reality this discursive shift of 'home time' into a structure of progression towards a perfect domestic order further emphasised the contradictions of modernity and domesticity. This focus on the time of the home, and charging women with increased responsibility for it, repressed the affect of women who still found housework and motherhood, when balanced with some 'free time' and cultural interests, not to be a completely satisfying existence. The *Women's Session*, both because it attempted to speak to women at home, and because its hosts spoke as housewives themselves, did not seek to contain these contradictions, and this conflict between time, gender and selfhood in the domestic animated its daily schedule throughout the 1940s and 1950s.

Vera Wellings, in a talk in October 1941 on 'The Value of Time' to 'Women in the Post-war World', describes this new emphasis on time as a domestic commodity. She defined 'our main post-war problem' as 'the domestic one' and women as having 'a grave responsibility in our own sphere'. She told her audience that only women who were economically 'desperate' or career-focused would ever enter the job market after the war. For the rest, they were so fortunate to be able to choose their time and place of work that they should not be even in the slightest bit dissatisfied by it:

> If only the thousands of married women who have their homes and children could make up their minds that they are, actually, the luckiest people on earth I think we would have gone far towards solving not only the majority of our post-war problems, but a great many that face us today.[44]

Wellings described the wastage of domestic time as a 'murder'. The unstructured time of the home, if not brought under control, would result in ever-increasing anxiety, if women did not recognise that the home should be a model of production and progression towards higher goals:

> We lose time; we save time – and we kill time.
>
> And no murder could be more unforgivable. The most brilliant scientist can't resuscitate that particular corpse.
>
> To the young an hour or two lost here or there is of little consequence. But to the woman in the prime of her life lost hours bring a curious sense of apprehension. How is she ever to make up for that lost time – time goes so fast, and there is so much to do.[45]

Unlike the unmarried working woman, who had to 'rigidly' adhere to a domestic routine 'to keep her affairs and her person in good order and condition', the woman at home could fall into a 'fatal weakness' of putting things off. Unproductive 'chatting' would not make the deeper boredom go away, but simply postpone it and 'lose' more time. Women should feel proud if they could 'conquer' domestic boredom:

> But to the vast majority of women the successful organisation of a domestic day is a feat to be proud of. There are all those boring little details that must be attended to every day of the week – and on Sundays! It is fatally easy to put off a few of them to have a chat over the telephone – or over the fence . . . .[46]

War work had given women lessons in domestic management, providing a means of discipline for 'those of us who are inclined to lose time in this delightful but disorganising fashion'.

> Between finding time and saving it there is, perhaps, not so very much difference . . . . And having lost time, having found it and having recognised the fact that it can and must be saved, surely we need not simply kill it again.[47]

Time saved should be spent in useful activities, not in more idleness. The leisure of the future, which 'will inevitably come with the cessation of our war-work', should not be wasted: women should use 'spare time' to become involved in useful activities such as 'study circles', training in 'the art of leadership and public speaking', and fundraising for 'social services'.[48] Women should nurture their own inner life, and develop a mental attitude that would protect against boredom. Wellings ended her talk with a call to join the war of 'ideas and ideals', which had transcended a conflict over economics or trade:

> Whatever ideas you have [for planning the future] are of value. The important thing is to have them! Not to let minds wander vaguely on about the laundry, tomorrow's dinner and that awful tear in the school-boy son's pants!
>
> It is only by the collecting and coordinating of the ideas of the average woman, however dull and unoriginal she may think herself, that we can hope for any substantial improvement in our social status and mental development.[49]

A set of solutions to boredom was offered during the 1950s by speakers such as Maude Farr, introduced to her audience as 'a former NSW Inspector of Domestic Science Schools and at one time the only woman Inspector'. She gave an account of her philosophy about 'the important job of being a housewife', gathered during her many years of educational experience, denying that housework was boring in the first place:[50]

> Individual women, women's organisations and women's writings continually and stridently ask, 'Why should women be condemned to the drudgery of the home, to its dullness, to the performance of tasks that do not provide an intellectual outlet? Why should men have all the interesting work to do?'[51]

Farr argued that housework was neither drudgery, nor lacking in intellectual endeavour, if it was performed to 'modern standards'. Women were told not to belittle the 'dignity of their real work as wives and mothers', and not to feel humiliated, as one woman visiting New South Wales had done, when 'she had to record herself on official documents as "housewife"'.[52] When the host, Ida Jenkins, returned to the air after Farr's talk, she added her own opinion of what made housework so hard:

I think the thing most women complain about in housework is the repetition – doing the same things each day does become monotonous – but can you tell me of one job in the world that doesn't get monotonous when it's repeated? One of the big problems is, I think the aloneness of housework. In almost every job you see other people at work – you work with them, but the housewife is inclined to think she is the forgotten number.[53]

Nance Donkin, in a series of talks called 'Come Out of the Kitchen', argued instead for a time for the housewife apart from domestic chores. The first, 'What About Some Spare Time?', argued that the domestic sphere was limiting to women's spiritual growth and advocated pursuing some personal time as a cure for routine:

> I've never agreed with people – they usually seem to be either men or else women who never have been tied down to a domestic routine – who assert that the Home should be enough. As I see it, the Home is very limiting, both to your imagination and to your spirit. Don't keep the front door closed. It's keeping out a lot that's worthwhile. Come out of the kitchen, take a deep breath and lock the vacuum cleaner away for a while.[54]

This talk proposed that even the busiest housewife should have some 'spare time' in which she could read a good book or play tennis. Subsequent talks recommended spare time activities such as kindergarten work, millinery or dressmaking, woodwork or interior decoration, evening lectures and classes on architecture, child guidance, speech training, the 'History of Theatre', and listening to the Schools Broadcasts on the ABC to 'take us out of the kitchen'. These activities were canvassed as a way for women to 'let off the steam of boredom' before it built up in to an 'unmanageable' emotion such as anger:

> What do you do when you're so bored with the house and all it entails that you feel you could scream quite as long and effectively as a mill whistle. The steam needed to allow that whistle to scream is, of course, a mere drop in the boiler. It doesn't whistle just once. It does it over and over again, every morning at 8.15, or every afternoon at 5 .... Unfortunately, it's usually the family which gets the hot end of the steam. The family, which has done nothing to deserve it, except come home from school or from work wanting a bit of attention and a bit of food, suffers. And the housewife, feeling rather ashamed of herself, gets no proper relief at all.[55]

In her third talk, 'Taking the Irk Out of Housework', Donkin offered a portrait of the woman who had constructed her self entirely as a housewife and should now be loosened from the bonds of perfection:

> We all know the woman whose horizon is bounded by her back fence and the front door. She's usually tired, often nervy and rarely cheerful. Her conversation is an endless

repetition of domestic details, shopping and cooking and how it was such a good washing day she washed the curtains again. . . . This woman lives in a spotless house, which is not a home. It's such an uncomfortable place you're always in a hurry to get out of it. . . . She's tied herself down to this deadly routine because of an old belief that 'it's a woman's duty'.[56]

Such women were suffering 'Domestic Martyrdom', suggested to be an 'occupational disease' associated with the home, in keeping with other professional stresses which gave the businessman 'his ulcer', the pilot 'nerve-strain' and the clerk 'tired eyes'. Women's work, however, was 'more deadly than any of these because of the mark it leaves upon the spirit'. This disease 'attacks so gradually that a housewife can become a chronic before she's aware of it. Then inertia sets in and it's too late to do anything.'[57] Donkin's portrayal of the obsessive housewife demonstrates how the use of time had become a determinant of domestic happiness. Her ideas on how to cure boredom stopped short of asking that the whole household contribute to the labour required to manage the home for their benefit, or suggesting that women had the option of paid work instead, but it did recognise that the housewife was also a worker, and that she should be able to step out of her work role. This discourse on boredom, which linked time as a precious commodity that could not be 'wasted' to women's role as citizens of the future, constructed only women who concerned themselves with trivia, and thus repetitive time, as susceptible to boredom. While their consciousness was hardly imagined as able to be 'raised' along feminist lines, their mental labour was also valuable and could be 'collected' and 'coordinated' in order to improve women's collective destiny. This discourse attempted to prove that the existing gender system could be maintained, and improved, if women's time was properly managed.

But during the late 1940s, an alternative framework had emerged alongside this one. The *Women's Session* began increasingly to adopt the material generated by its listeners, and hosts started to read out letters sent in by the audience. Many of these letters contested the separation of spheres along gendered lines, and hence articulated a different perspective on the gender system sustained by the other sessions we have discussed. In 1947 the *Women's Session* initiated a series of discussions on whether marriage was a 'full-time career' and invited listeners to contribute by sending their opinions to the programme. This debate, conducted during October and November 1947, included guest speakers Mrs Bruce Mayne, Phyllis Burton (a woman doctor), Jill Meillon, Mrs Foristal and two 'schoolgirls', Phyllis and Lois. The final sessions in the series took up a wide-ranging discussion of housework, boredom and drudgery in the form of listeners' letters that were read out on air.

Mrs Bruce Mayne was the first speaker and she echoed the first perspective with her admission that 'Of course I believe in having interests outside the home, but I think they should be kept as interests and hobbies and not as an end in themselves.'[58] Lois, a thirteen-year-old pupil at Queenswood Ladies' College, also thought that marriage was a full-time career, with women 'the spiritual centre of the home', and portrayed the housewife as a creative being: '"It is not *what* we do, but *how* we do the things we do that puts us in the brotherhood of artists" and being a wife and mother is being an artist with a full time job.' She insisted that women should mask this world of work from the gaze of their husbands:

> Besides tending to the house, the wife must keep herself attractive to her husband. On returning home from work at night, the husband, physically tired and mentally weary, does not want to find his wife in the same condition as she would be if she were out at work all day.[59]

The first of the listeners' letters quoted painted a somewhat ironic picture of this social definition of the housewife's role which is worth quoting at length:

> What is expected of a wife? She must be a loving companion to her husband and always take a great interest in his career and in his hobbies. She must have charm of manner, not necessarily looks, to be able to welcome his friends to the home at any time of the night and day and she must always have an emergency larder and be able to toss up an appetising meal at short notice. She should behave like a mothercraft nurse and be able to bring up her babies well and efficiently. She must be a good cook. She must be able to talk intelligently about most things. She should be able to do a little carpentering and a little plumbing and not have to call in an expensive workman every time a little thing goes wrong.
>
> She should be able to put in a new fuse when the electric iron blows out. She should be able to service the car and keep it clean. She should have a slight knowledge of tailoring so that she can do little repairs to her husband's suit when needed. She should be good at the same sport as her husband – tennis or golf usually. If she is overweight she must diet and do shincutting exercises. She must be well educated and be able to help her children with their lessons. She must be good with her needle. She must be good tempered *at all* times. She must never be depressed. She must have a sense of humour. She must let her husband have some independence but not enough to get into mischief and bring disgrace on the family.
>
> If she lives in the country she must be able to make butter and keep poultry and so on. Perhaps help her husband muster sheep. She must be able to talk politics and discuss international affairs (banking, for instance). She must be able to take advantage of all that modern science offers her to make the work in the home less like drudgery. She mustn't be too tired in the evening to go out with her husband.[60]

This letter concluded that marriage could not be a 'full-time career' because women could not be limited only to the home if they were to be able to converse with their husbands as equal, intellectual partners, and they still had to train in some kind of work in case their husband died and left them 'penniless'. As part of the same debate, another listener's letter described a woman 'as a home-maker ... [participating] in a career where she can be a literally priceless asset to her country. She is building a democracy in a way that no other woman can do and it is an exacting, thought satisfying task.'[61] The inclusion of these letters – as well as the points of view advanced by women invited to speak on the *Women's Session* who repudiated or agreed with the proposal that marriage was a full-time career – constituted a space in which the ideal of 'the woman at home' was able to be discussed and even rejected. As indicated by a letter from a former teacher, and mother of four children under ten, the programme had transcended the very ideal in facilitating a discussion of it. For her it had sparked a sense of the disintegration of the idea of women's common interests and life ambitions:

I would like to ask why, whenever a discussion of this type comes up, people so readily assume:
a) That all women have the same capacity
b) That a woman whose entire interest is centred in her home and children is necessarily making a first-class job of it. Now, my own experience and observation have taught me otherwise, and I am becoming very tired of the habit of thought that classes all women together, like sheep. Just as there are women of limited capacity, so there are women who can successfully combine outside work with the adequate care of husband and children. It depends upon the person.[62]

In providing women's sessions, radio promoted the idea that women could be classed together as a unified group with common interests and desires largely to be found in the home. At the same time it facilitated debate that undermined such a notion, either explicitly, such as in this listener's statement, or implicitly, by enabling the different points of view of women to be heard and hence legitimating the fact that there were such different points of view.

But the programmes also enabled the expression of a point of view that would emerge further strengthened and elaborated in the late 1960s and 1970s by making a claim to be able to speak for all women as a unified group, but without foreclosing women's subjectivity. In February 1948, 'Mrs Lindsay Nicholas' compiled a scripted discussion between Mrs 'Contented' and Mrs 'Discontented' home-maker. Nicholas was also introduced by her maiden name, Hepzibah Menuhin, by which she was known as a concert pianist and as violinist Yehudi Menuhin's sister. Menuhin described herself as a 'gunpowder woman', and read out a blessing to the discussion in the form of a telegram from Pearl Buck 'from her home in Pennsylvania':

Greetings to the National Women's Session. I hope women of Australia will contribute their full share as citizens of a world more challenging, more interesting, more promising that ever before.[63]

The programme set out to include the voices of men, which Menuhin argued was a gesture towards 'exterminating the war between man and man [by studying and stopping] the war that has been going on for centuries between man and woman', which 'all starts with his mother'. Her polemic saw not women, but men, as passive and dependent. Her introduction laid bare all that the new discourse of time management and useful leisure outlined above could not allow women to truly feel – autonomy:

> Because men never meet women on an equal basis; throughout the dark grim ages of his development, woman has always been connected with man's babying. As a baby he was helpless. As an adult she made him helpless. So throughout the whole of his life, at times hopefully, at times defiantly, he expects her to attend to marginal duties, but only in connection with his comfort. She makes his bed, rears his children, darns his socks, cuts his sandwiches and vacuums his house. In return he provides the cage with as many amenities as the love bird needs in order to have nothing to complain about. 'I want a refrigerator' or 'I want a new hat' . . . But can anyone in her right mind say 'I want freedom' or 'I want equality'? In a world of pegged prices and application forms, there is no fixed value attached to independence, and even if you find that he agrees with you, where do you buy this commodity? And how many pounds of it would you need in order to be a better housewife?[64]

Menuhin rejected the domestic role as a full-time occupation for women and as a role that should belong exclusively to women. She posed men's dependence on women as circumscribing women's agency. Hence, she challenged the way in which the discussion of women's lives was typically framed by the ABC in the 1940s, and as it continued to be framed into the 1950s despite this intervention: 'I should hate to be the wife of my house, although that is my profession according to my passport.'[65]

But her script was more equivocal than her opening and closing remarks. Introducing the discussion with the first speaker, Mrs 'Contented Homemaker', she warned the listener to turn off if she 'was the kind of woman who gets the most fun out of having no fun'; 'then you are very happy and very lucky, and you won't be interested in the rest of this session':

> But my friends and I who are here today, want to find out why men work and come home to eat and sleep. Also why women keep house and gossip and drink tea for relaxation. Between these life partners there should be a constructive, stimulating relationship. Yet there is surprisingly little fun. Women long for diversion because they are bored. Men long for silence because they are tired. Wedlock should not be padlock. What's wrong?[66]

Mrs 'Contented Homemaker', a schoolteacher before her marriage, brought her concern for childhood education to her role as a mother. She argued that by adapting the child 'to the home setup' as a mother, she would help him adapt to the 'community he lives in and to Society': 'This all sounds a bit stuffy I'm afraid, but it is an inspiration to me.'[67] She was happy because she invested her humble job with the responsibility for not just good national citizenship, but global peace:

> It isn't an easy job or a small one, it's the biggest job a woman can be called on to do. I would go as far as to say I believe Peace on earth can only come when home-makers realise that it must begin with the individual in the home. . . . If there is harmony in the home there will be order in the nation, and when there is order in the nation there will be peace in the world.[68]

The pursuit of interests outside the home was constructed as much a woman's responsibility as her right, and would be achieved by the husband taking occasional care of the children, and other families cooperating to share the care of their children during the week and on holidays:

> I would be the last person to say a homemaker must have no ideas or interests outside the home, or that she should be completely tied to the home. If she is to keep the vision splendid, she must, I feel, have opportunities to be free of the home.[69]

But she continued to operate within the parameters of the discussion typical of the ABC *Women's Session* with its focus on the need for women to have outside interests, to be connected to but not in the public world.

Nor did Mrs 'Discontented Homemaker' step outside this frame. She felt that training would make the difference between an unsatisfying and a fulfilling life as a home-maker:

> As a young girl, I received absolutely no training along domestic lines at all. . . . To know your job, and I suppose that home making is the ordinary woman's job, would fill you with contentment and confidence right from the start . . . you would look forward to your homelife and find in it perhaps more than most of us do.[70]

However, she also described her sense of frustration in terms of domesticity's exclusion from the flow of public time and its containment as a place besieged by repetition:

> Today, with distance reduced to nothing, the family has broken down; we don't need to live under the one roof permanently, and make that our world. Today, the whole world is our home, everything that goes on in its most distant parts is our business sooner or later, and so the average homemaker, like me, feels dreadfully left out of things, if all

she can do besides her housework, is to attend bridge evenings and listen to the same gossip over and over again.[71]

'Mr Husband 2' in Menuhin's script declared that the women he most admired were those who

run a home, look after a family and still retain their interests. I really believe it is the retaining of her interest that helps most to give women that sparkle that men look for. It certainly is not the shopping, the cleaning, the cooking etc. This is routine, and like all routine becomes dull.[72]

Menuhin summed up as she began by describing women's selfhood as potentially thwarted by domesticity and 'caged' in the home. In doing so she went that one step further than her scripted discussion, seeking to ensure that women at least stayed connected to the world but asking why if their abilities lie elsewhere they should not express them there:

Well, it looks like this . . . it would seem that some men are mad on home, garden and family. It is ludicrous that they should feel socially obliged to work at jobs that kill their gentle talents merely because it is said that woman's place is in the home and man must provide for this weakling, even is she is shrewd and robust. What if she can make a living? What if she longs to get out and sharpen her wits in professional competition? Such a woman caged makes a dreary lovebird that sings no songs. And it is only by fulfilling her natural desires that she can bring happiness to the home, which is the cornerstone of society. But don't let Home shut out the great stimulating and wonderful world that knocks at everybody's front doors![73]

These discussions indicate yet another site in which female subjectivity was under negotiation in the 1940s and 1950s. As a context in which the public broadcaster was feeling its way to determine what it meant to have a nation-building role, it was not surprising that this discussion should be framed by a concern with what it might mean to be bringing the modern world into the home. If radio was a modernising force in which the home was to be connected to the public world of local and international politics, then women as representatives of domesticity would need to open the world of the home – and themselves – to that other world. But how much did this mean fundamental change to the lives of women and to how home might be conceptualised in the modern world? As Patrice Petro has pointed out, the writings of Walter Benjamin and Siegfried Kracauer during the early twentieth century suggested that boredom in the modern world has a radical edge. They both argued that boredom is about the modern experience of time as being both empty and full. In waiting without aim or purpose, the subjects of boredom in the modern world might catch sight of the possibility of change.[74] By recognising and giving voice to women's experience of the home as potentially one of boredom, radio sought to fill that emptiness by bringing the outside world into the home. But by this very recognition radio intimated that it may be appropriate to consider other ways of organising and thinking about everyday life and the separation of the public and private worlds.

Declining Audiences: An Afterword on the Housewife

From the early 1950s, the session had dropped its focus on women's activism around issues of the home and began increasingly to broadcast talks on travel and fashion (usually from wealthy women who travelled to Las Vegas or Killarney in their holidays). A survey of the programme during the weeks of the royal tour of 1954 demonstrates how far the topics had strayed from the proto-feminist debates that energised it in the 1940s. During February and March, when the Queen visited Melbourne, the session featured items and interviews on 'Shopping Overseas', 'Lady's Day at the Races', 'Flowers for Special Occasions', 'Making Curry' and 'Building a House with Mud Bricks'.[75] During the following years the session seemed wilfully ignorant of contemporary culture, although, like women's magazines during the 1950s, it attempted to address social and cultural change and the 'generation gap'. The failure of the programme to take up the challenge of the 'gunpowder women' and to contribute to public life became more apparent towards the end of the decade. A talk by Arthur Young during August 1956 on the Season's Dance Tunes shows how the session had abandoned its concerns regarding issues of national relevance: 'It seems the most popular music for teenagers is still the quickstep (though the modern waltz has many devotees) and one of the favourite tunes of that tempo is "Sweet Georgia Brown".'[76] Young's talk was part of a feature series of on dancing, described by the producers in a letter to participants as an investigation of

> the current ideas about debutantes, their dressing, the etiquette, do they wear gloves, how much do they pay for their dresses, do they have formal debuts or do they just 'slip out'. We will draw our material from all grades of society, from Princes, as it were, to debutantes at functions in an industrial suburb. One talk is to about city and suburbs, and the other, by a woman from the country, about similar etiquette etc. in the country and the country towns.[77]

Despite the efforts of the National Women's Advisory Committee – who described themselves as 'not made up of recipe-hounds, but of intelligent people of wide interests'[78] – the session's timeslot was under increasing threat from other programmes. The *Women's Session*'s national audience began to decline sharply during the early 1960s, with the exception of the West Australian *Women's Session*, which held its own until the departure of its long-term host Catherine King in

1965. Without King at its controls, it too declined in audience share – although audience numbers remained constant – and was eventually replaced with a programme presented by a male announcer, called *Here Now*, that broadcast 'trendy' music.[79] When the incoming Federal Labor government instigated a review of the whole notion of the session and its audience in the early 1970s, its winding up was justified in terms of a fragmentation of its primary female audience. Women were argued to no longer recognise themselves as an audience for programming identified as 'women's only', according to submissions to the ABC State advising committee in March 1973 from Mr R.T. Newell, then the ABC's Head of Audience. Newell presented the findings of a survey conducted in Adelaide in 1968 that 'the sessions attracting the largest number of women have MALE announcers [while] they are not called "women's sessions" and it seems that women do not make this distinction between themselves and the rest of the community'.[80]

Other submissions pointed to the loss of a unifying figure of woman at home, signified by intergenerational conflict over open discussion of previously transgressive topics such as abortion.[81] Professor Geoffrey Bolton downplayed both the idea of housewives and women in general, as defining the potential audience for daytime radio with an argument for addressing the programme to a new audience of 'people at home':

> . . . I have fairly strong views about policy for women's sessions. Briefly, I think that the best results are gained by bringing informed but informal conversations about a wide variety of issues of interest to people generally who happen to be at home rather than the 'housewife'.
>
> I agree that the day has gone past when home listeners could be satisfied with chats about cake-making. . . . The issues covered can span a very wide variety ranging from social problems such as old people's housing and aboriginal wants, to practical issues such as recent nutritional advances and development of household gadgets. But the essential point is that the programmes should not really be beamed to women as a separate species of animal.[82]

But just at the moment that 'women' appeared to be fragmenting as a social category in this context of radio programming, they were being hailed anew as a general category by feminism. Second wave feminists of the late 1960s and 1970s sought to speak in the name of 'all women' at the same time as they represented the housewife as an arrested or incomplete identity to be rescued and spoken for. 'All women' were no longer to be represented by the housewife or the woman at home; as we have argued in this book, she was to become rather a personality fragment to be sloughed off by the modern woman or a shameful 'other' to be rescued or abandoned. In 1975 a very different 'women's' programme was inaugurated by the ABC, *The Coming Out Show*, which canvassed the issues of contemporary women and how they wished to lead their lives in a far more political form than had ever been contemplated by the earlier generation of women's programmes. Conceptualised as a forum to expose the 'contradictions and myths that define women's everyday lives', issues of how women could combine mothering and paid work were revisited as were new issues of rape and sexual violence, sexism and inequality in the workplace and sexuality. Very occasionally the working conditions of housewives were discussed, mostly in relation to the possibility of wages for housework.[83]

The end of the ABC *Women's Session* can be seen to mark the end of the figure of the housewife as representing a coherent set of interests subsumed under a gendered cultural form. But as the analysis of these programmes has shown, the housewife was a figure through whom various cultural technologies articulated the problem of the modern individual's relationship to home. Radio constituted itself through such programmes as a means of bringing 'the world home' to the space of domesticity, but it was uneasy about in what form and to what extent this activity could be a serious disruption to the separation of the spheres of the public and the private. The housewife's boredom in her emotional slum implied a sense of futurity that had not existed in previous imaginaries of the home, which had seen the home as not only a place apart but also as a *time* apart from the public sphere. The *Women's Session*'s uneasy negotiations around these issues demonstrated that the gendered melancholy of the housewife, provoked by the perceived futility of her lot, could not entirely be solved through the better use of domestic time. The boredom of the housewife signified her as awaiting a revolution, even though the form of it was not yet clear.

Notes

1. Ferdinand Lundberg and Marynia F. Farnham, *Modern Woman: The Lost Sex*, New York and London, Harper & Brothers, 1947, p. v.
2. Ibid.
3. Ibid.
4. Ibid., pp. 91–2.
5. Ibid., p. 20
6. Ibid., p. 21.
7. Ibid., p. 10.
8. Ibid., p. 11.
9. Ibid., p. 21.
10. Ibid., p. 117.
11. Betty Friedan, *The Feminine Mystique*, Harmondsworth, Penguin, 1983 [1956], p. 107. Friedan writes in a chapter titled 'The Happy Housewife Heroine': 'In 1949, the *Ladies' Home Journal* also ran Margaret Mead's *Male and Female*. All the magazines were echoing Farnham and Lundberg's *Modern Woman: The Lost Sex*, which came out in 1942 [*sic*], with its warning

that careers and higher education were leading to the "masculinisation of women with enormously dangerous consequences to the home, the children dependent on it and to the ability of the woman, as well as her husband, to obtain sexual gratification". And so the feminine mystique began to spread through the land, grafted on to old prejudices and comfortable conventions which so easily give the past a stranglehold on the future' (p. 37).

12. Ruth Feldstein, *Motherhood in Black and White: Race and Sex in American Liberalism, 1930–1965*, Ithaca, Cornell University Press, 2000, pp. 42–3.
13. Friedan, *The Feminine Mystique*, p. 328.
14. Ibid.
15. For a discussion on the history of women and melancholy, see Judith Shklar, 'Introduction', in Wolf Lepenies, *Melancholy and Society*, Jeremy Gaines and Doris L. Jones (trans.) Cambridge, MA, Harvard University Press, 1992, pp. vii–xvi.
16. *Australian Women's Weekly*, 2 February 1958, p. 13 (the plan was on p. 40).
17. *Australian Women's Weekly*, 15 April 1953, p. 2.
18. *Australian Women's Weekly*, 2 July 1958, p. 12.
19. *Australian Women's Weekly*, 16 September 1953, pp. 20–1; 4 May 1960, p. 55.
20. *Australian Women's Weekly*, 29 May 1957, pp. 27–36.
21. For example, *Australian Women's Weekly*, 10 October 1956, p. 2; 29 August 1951, pp. 24–5; 15 May 1957, p. 7.
22. *Australian Women's Weekly*, 18 March 1959, p. 4.
23. The Talks Department, which was responsible for the 'women's broadcasts', was the first Federal Department in the Australian Broadcasting Commission (ABC) and was established in 1936. In 1939 a Talks Assistant was appointed to specifically organise 'women's talks'. By 1935, however, Gladys Moore had joined the ABC staff and was already broadcasting on this theme. By 27 June 1969 the abolition of the Talks Department had been effected, and the new Spoken Word Department came into operation. The *Women's Session* broadcasts themselves were abolished in 1971. Source: Australian Archives (AA) website entry on *Women's Session* records, *www.naa.gov.au*.
24. Julie Lewis, *On Air: The Story of Catherine King and the ABC Women's Session*, Fremantle, Fremantle Arts Centre Press, 1979, p. 148.
25. May Couchman quoted in K.S. Inglis, *This is the ABC: The Australian Broadcasting Commission, 1932–1983*, Melbourne, Melbourne University Press, 1983, p. 32.
26. Quoted in Lewis, *On Air*, p. 150.
27. Ibid., p. 147.
28. Julie Lewis, Papers 1944–1978, Canberra, National Library of Australia, MS 9507, Box 7, Series 5/3, 'The Woman's Session, WA: 1942 to Present day', p. 1.

29. A script for a talk by Vera Wellings in October 1941 on 'Women in the Post-war World' originally contained the following typewritten notes: 'If she doesn't like her own thoughts, she's only got to start up the radio . . . and listen to a lecture . . . Did I hear an indignant snort?' The word 'lecture' was crossed out by hand and replaced with 'talk' and the last sentence was deleted and replaced by 'That's if she wants to, of course.' AA SP300/1, 'V. Wellings Talks', Box 6, 28 October 1941, p. 2.

30. 'Speaking broadly, practically all women who are not wage earners are in their homes in the mornings. Almost everyone of these women has morning tea, and I think it is undoubted that they arrange this to fit in with their favourite session on air . . . it would offer a brief respite when a woman takes her morning tea, having finished her early morning work, and before preparing the midday dinner or lunch.' Memo from Mrs Moore to Mr Horner, AA SP341/1/1, File II, 1938–1943, File No. 15.5, 5 May 1937, pp. 1–2.

31. See Lesley Johnson, *The Unseen Voice: A Cultural Study of Early Australian Radio*, London, Routledge, 1988, pp. 100ff, for a discussion particularly of women's radio programmes on commercial stations and how they set out to organise women's daily lives to ensure they could guarantee audiences for their programmes.

32. Memo from B.W. Kirke to the Federal Director of Talks and the Federal Controller of Programmes, 27 May 1943. AA SP341/1/1 File II, 1938–1943, File 15.5.

33. Miss K. Goulton and Mr A. L. Baker, 'In My Opinion – Women and War Work', AA SP300/1, Box 8, 31 October 1942, p. 4.

34. Benedict Anderson, *Imagined Communities: Reflections on the Origin and Spread of Nationalism*, London, Verso, 1983.

35. 'Women Talking – No More Private Worlds for Women' – part of the *Women's Session* of 18 November 1941. AA SP300/1, 'W's General', Box 6, p. 1.

36. Ibid.

37. Ibid.

38. Ibid., p. 2.

39. Janet Mitchell, 'This Changing Australia – Part 1', AA SP300/1, 16 August 1942, pp. 4–5.

40. Ibid., p. 4.

41. Ibid.

42. Ruth Schwartz Cowan, *More Work for Mother: The Ironies of Household Technology from the Open Hearth to the Microwave*, New York, Basic Books, 1983.

43. Kathleen Anne McHugh, *American Domesticity: From How-to Manual to Hollywood Melodrama*, New York, Oxford University Press, 1999.

44. Vera Wellings, 'Women in the Post-War World – Part 2 – The Value of Time', AA SP300/1, 'V. Wellings Talks', Box 6, 28 October 1941, p. 2.

45. Ibid., p. 3.
46. Ibid., p. 4.
47. Ibid., p. 6.
48. Ibid., p. 7.
49. Ibid., p. 9.
50. Maude Farr, 'On Being a Housewife', *Women's Session*, AA C3224/1, 12 November 1951, p. 3.
51. Ibid.
52. Ibid., p. 4.
53. Ida Elizabeth Jenkins, *Women's Session*, AA C3224/1, 12 November 1951, p. 5.
54. Nancy Donkin, 'Come Out of the Kitchen – 1 – How About Some Spare Time?', *Women's Session*, Box 15, 15 May 1952, p. 2.
55. Nancy Donkin, 'Come Out of the Kitchen – 2 – Anybody Can Do Anything', *Women's Session*, Box 15, 15 May 1952, p. 2.
56. Nancy Donkin, 'Come Out of the Kitchen – 3 – Taking the Irk Out of Housework', *Women's Session*, Box 15, 29 May 1952, p. 1.
57. Ibid.
58. Mrs Bruce Mayne, 'Marriage as a Career', C3224/1, *Women's Session*, Box 3, 14 October 1947, p. 4.
59. 'Marriage as a full-time Career' debate, C3224/1, *Women's Session*, Box 3, 28 October 1947, p. 4.
60. Listener's letter (Cranston, Campaine, Tasmania), AA SP3224/1, *Women's Session*, Box 3, 21 October 1947, pp. 7–8.
61. Listener's letter (Weethall, NSW), AA SP3224/1, *Women's Session*, Box 3, 21 October 1947, p. 8.
62. Listener's Letter (Kalourouse, Victoria), AA SP3224/1, *Women's Session*, Box 3, 21 October 1947, p. 10.
63. Script by Hepzibah Menuhin, C3224/1, *Women's Session*, Box 5, 25 February 1948, p. 2.
64. Ibid., p. 3.
65. Ibid.
66. Ibid., pp. 4–5.
67. Contented Housewife (Mrs Gerrard), C3224/1, *Women's Session*, Box 5, 25 February 1948, p. 5.
68. Script by guest editor: Hepzibah Menuhin (Mrs Nicholas): 'Woman's Place in Society, with Contented Housewife (Mrs Gerrard), Discontented Homemaker (Mrs Calvert), Mr Husbands (Mr Taylor) & (Lindsay Biggins)', C3224/1, *Women's Session*, Box 5, 25 February 1948, p. 5.
69. Contented Housewife (Mrs Gerrard), C3224/1, *Women's Session*, Box 5, 25 February 1948, p. 6.

70. Discontented Housewife (Mrs Calvert), C3224/1, *Women's Session*, Box 5, 25 February 1948, p. 7.
71. Ibid., p. 6.
72. Mr Husband 2 (Lindsay Biggins), C3224/1, *Women's Session*, Box 5, 25 February 1948, p. 10.
73. Ibid.
74. Patrice Petro, 'After Shock/Between Boredom and History', in Patrice Petro (ed.), *Fugitive Images: From Photography to Video*, Bloomington, Indiana University Press, 1995, pp. 274–5.
75. Memos from E. Chapple, 15 February and 12 March 1954, 'Talks – Sessions – Women's Session', AA B2144, 13/3/18, Part 4.
76. Script broadcast 14 August 1956; 'Talks – Sessions – Women's Session', AA B2114/6, 13/3/18, Part 6.
77. Memo, 27 July 1956, 'Talks – Sessions – Women's Session', AA B2114/6, 13/3/18, Part 6.
78. Memo from Alan Carmichael, 'Re: Proposal to Cut National Women's Session from half-hour to Quarter-hour', AA SP727/1/1, 12/2/1 PART 2, 9 July 1964.
79. Lewis, Papers 1944–1978 (as note 28), p. 2.
80. Ibid.
81. Ibid.
82. Ibid., Addendum to Agenda Item – Women's Sessions, 12 March 1973.
83. Liz Fell and Carolin Wenzel (eds), *The Coming Out Show: Twenty Years of Feminist ABC Radio*, Sydney, ABC Books, 1995.

–6–

Conclusion

Zygmunt Baumann characterises the contemporary social world as 'the individu-
alised society'. Individuals in this world are persuaded to take responsibility for
themselves, for their achievements and for their failures, without reference to the
social structures and processes that shape their lives. In these terms, Baumann's
arguments have some similarities to those of Anthony Giddens that we looked at
in Chapter 1. But Giddens focuses more on the arguments about the self-reflexivity required of modern individuals whereas Baumann takes us further into questions of critique of the society that supports and is supported by this requirement.
It is not ideological domination or any longer the workings of panopticon institutions that ensure we understand our lives and selves in particular ways, it is the
fact that we are left to ourselves. 'We are all individuals now;' says Baumann, 'not
by choice, though but by necessity.'[1] Disengagement, he argues, is the most effective form of power in the twenty-first century in a world in which people are con-
tinually confronted with the vulnerability and precariousness of their lives.
Exhorted as modern individuals to make sense of the contradictions and conflicts
that surround us, we manage a compulsive and obligatory concern with self-
determination by developing biographical solutions to what are systemic contradictions.[2]

> The point is, though, that the game of life we all play, with our self-reflexions and
> story-telling as its most prominent parts, is conducted in such a way that the rules of
> the game, the contents of the pack of cards and the fashion in which the cards are shuf-
> fled and dealt seldom come under scrutiny and even less frequently become a matter of
> reflection, let alone of serious discussion.[3]

In this book we have been looking at a period in history in which there were significant developments in this dissociation of individuals from their wider social
context, at the same time as we can see evidence of moves to re-embed individuals
in forms of social identity as a 'fact of nature'. Historical periods are complex phenomena in which it is impossible to identify clear, unified shifts in consciousness.
Instead we can only talk of tendencies, emerging ideas, contradictions as well as
convergences in the structure of feeling of the time. This book has been tracing
these uneven developments in the 1940s and 1950s in Australia to understand the
emergence of a particular feminist subject position in the following two decades.

Our argument has been that while the production of this subjectivity obviously had a huge impact in enabling a major social revolution, it also created a form of social agency which feminists have found difficult to let go. In this final chapter, we seek to bring together the various arguments of this book about the developments in the 1940s and 1950s that opened up the possibility of the emergence of this feminist subject. We use this discussion to further explore the problems that confront such an understanding of feminism in contemporary debates about home and work.

A wide range of cultural, social and political institutions in the 1940s and 1950s spoke to and of women as if their membership of this social group determined their identity and their life projects. What united them as a social group in all the stories told by these institutions about women's lives was their responsibility for and attachment to home. While some of these stories acknowledged other features of women's lives, all endorsed the gendering of the space of the home in the form that had emerged as a feature of the modern world in the eighteenth and nineteenth centuries. Women were said to be responsible, 'by nature', for domestic life and, as such, for the management of the physical and emotional requirements of their families that had been relegated to this sphere. Seemingly banished to the edges of modernity, women were to attend to the tasks of sustaining everyday life.

Western critical thought since the Enlightenment period has developed an ambivalent attitude to the realms of home and everyday life. Writers like Henri Lefebvre, for example, have acknowledged that everyday life is a distinctively modern phenomenon, at the same time as he criticised it as the realm of repetition and stasis in contrast to the movement, change and dynamism characteristic of what he saw as authentic modernity. Everyday life weighs heaviest on women, he claimed; they are 'sentenced to everyday life'.[4] Repetition is seen as a threat to the modern project of self-determination with its sense of an imposed pattern of life and the absence of change. The modern individual needs to leave this world behind in order to transcend its mundanity and the limitations of human bodily existence. Lefebvre, as Rita Felski points out, placed some value on women's connections to the ordinary rhythms of biology, emotion and sensuality, but believed them nevertheless to be the victims and quintessential representatives of the quotidian because of their responsibilities for sustaining the everyday life of the home.[5]

At the same time as the identities of women were being prescribed in the 1940s and 1950s as determined by their gender, they were being addressed as modern individuals with the responsibility and opportunity to determine their own lives and identities. Popular magazines presented consumption as a means through which women could undertake this task of self-determination. The home remained the site of their agency, but it involved powers, responsibility and expertise. Similarly, radio programmes directed specifically at a female audience exhorted them to develop life plans in which they connected themselves to the public world of local and international politics and ensured their broader education or self-development. Yet the stories told in such contexts could be quite contradictory, as demonstrated by the claims by Robert Gordon Menzies, the conservative Prime Minister of Australia in the 1950s, to be addressing women as active political agents in his call on them to take responsibility for 'the real life of the nation' to be found in the home. Women, in the name of their individuality, were to relinquish that individuality and remain confined to the gendered world of the home.

But popular films of the period demonstrate that there was no straightforward ideology of domesticity dominating the messages conveyed to women by various means at this time about what a meaningful life should involve. The films analysed in this book reveal complex negotiations taking place around feminine subjectivities, particularly as they sought to work through women's relationship to the home. Although they did not dispute that women should have primary responsibility for the home, these films were less certain about how they should care about the home and how much of a role it should play in defining their identities. Similarly, discussion of the housewife's boredom in a number of settings indicated an ambivalence about confining women to the realm of the home and everyday life. Boredom, as Patrice Petro argues, has a history. Once an experience exclusive to a particular class, boredom became a way of articulating a sense of entitlement as well as frustration in the modern world. By the twentieth century this affect had become gendered, associated with waiting but with an anticipation too 'that something (different) might occur'.[6] As modern subjects-in-waiting, bored housewives in the debates of the 1940s and 1950s were about to be drawn into public recognition. Boredom was seen as articulating a dissatisfaction with their lives and hence a desire to do something more with their time. In providing public expression to this private experience, popular culture in the period articulated a sense of victimhood that would later take on a quite different, politicised form.

In a study of Foucault's ethics, titled *Genealogies of Morals*, Jeffrey Minson discusses how Jacques Donzelot's *The Policing of Families* 'sees the formation of the housewife role as constituting the springboard for women's emancipation from patriarchy':

> To begin with, the mother/housewife is not merely constructed as a term of exclusion or isolation from the public world of men. The privatised character of domestic existence does not mean it is closed off from public scrutiny, but that its privacy is the particular terms of description of its organisation, of the supervised liberty of family life. The housewife is not in purdah but is a 'social' agent in the full glare of discourses on the domestic unit. Nor is she merely constructed as her husband's obedient helpmate. Rather, the construction of the figure of the mother on the hitherto subordinate wife primarily involved, not a stripping away of women's rights and responsibilities, but on the contrary, legal, administrative and pedagogical displacements of paternal rights and the creation of an agent, the housewife, whose 'career' and newfound rights, powers and responsibilities are created by the valorisations of tasks in respect to a domain of the domestic.[7]

Minson's reading of Donzelot is important here because he asks a question about the contradictions of such a politics of the home, and sets out its limitations:

> To what extent can we speak of this typecast role as continuing to constitute a repository of personal powers? Power does not cease to be power when it becomes a burden. Conceiving of powers as differential advantages and disadvantages . . . enables us to comprehend the possibility of there being powers which women might both no longer want for themselves, such as the prerogative of homemaking, and caring for children, but also want to hold onto, pending other changes . . . .[8]

If the requirement for the experience of boredom is a sense of historical time and a desire for change, then the translation of what Minson describes as a 'power women no longer want' into a discourse of boredom during the 1950s demonstrates that the act of being bored, while not necessarily an active state, was a source of discourses of emancipation and liberation.

Far from being something which the feminist subject had to reject in order to achieve a proper subjecthood, we are suggesting then that the figure of the housewife made the feminist subject *possible*. She made it possible, in the first instance, to think about all women as having something in common. She gave women a means of being present to themselves as a social group, even though the basis of that sense of commonality would rapidly change. She had powers, responsibilities, expertise and a sense of futurity. As a form of social agency too, the housewife enabled women to insist on their right and need to represent themselves, to speak in their own name. While this condition had been previously in existence, when women argued for a form of maternal citizenship, as well as in arguments for the right to vote, it was the range of ways in which the housewife figure intersected with such public and private concerns which made her so unique. She engendered a more complex understanding of a social agency as well as sense of entitlement and grievance. Taken together, these factors made her critical to the conditions surrounding the emergence of second wave feminism.

As Erica Carter documents in her study of the German housewife in the immediate post-war period, new feminine consumer identities emerged in the 1960s: the fashionable woman and the teenage girl.[9] These new gendered identities commenced a process which fractured the images of women to be found in women's magazines and other similar popular culture forms. No longer could such cultural forms claim to speak to and for all women, because magazines appeared such as those directed specifically at teenage girls, thus creating highly differentiated female markets. Such changes also made it difficult for the term 'housewife' to be used by women to represent themselves as a unified social group, as did the more material changes to women's lives with, in particular, the increasing number of women joining the labour market.[10] Some of the discussion of the housewife's boredom seems to have been as much about an anxiety regarding these new feminine identities and the way in which they represented a quite different modernity, one in which consumerism concerned pleasure and self-indulgence rather than the rational consumerism of the housewife. The representation of Eve Black in the movie *The Three Faces of Eve*, discussed in Chapter 4, exemplifies such a fear of a rampant and sexualised femininity. The dissatisfied housewife in this context initially reverted to such a self, rejecting the socially responsible role of home-maker and mother and finding it lacking in fulfilment. Yet this novel experience of boredom, and its association with the domestic sphere, intimated that women were modern subjects-in-waiting. The question was in what form would that subjecthood emerge. In *Three Faces of Eve*, she eventually emerges as the character 'Jane' who integrates all aspects of her sexual, maternal and economic identities as a wife, mother *and* worker. In popular magazines she emerges either as the new woman who can successfully manage the demands of working and home life or as the satisfied consumer of an increasingly attentive market who demonstrates her subjecthood by exercising her individuality through her powers of discrimination.

Second wave feminism, on the other hand, gave a particular shape to this sense of subjecthood by insisting on the need for women to leave the captivity of their homes and to reject the home-maker role. In her history of Australian feminism, Marilyn Lake documents the impact of Germaine Greer's *The Female Eunuch*. Calling on women to follow the example of Nora in Ibsen's *A Doll's House*, Greer urged them to leave home and commence the journey to awareness, to become independent, autonomous beings.[11] 'Hundreds of women', Lake claims, 'took the advice and walked out on their marriages, changed their names, formed new households and began their lives anew.'[12] But as we have discussed in Chapter 1, what Greer was providing here was a life story for women that drew on a familiar trope of modernist discourse in which the individual needed to 'leave home' in order to become autonomous, self-defining. This linear narrative provided for a number of women, for a time at least, a means of resolving a set of tensions and uncertainties about how modern women should live their lives – how they should think about work and family life. These women would claim that they were no longer 'sentenced to everyday life' and make new lives for themselves in which work would become the site of their self-actualisation.

Helen Trinca, an Australian journalist, talks of how 'work has won out' in recent decades. We define ourselves as human by the way we work and 'Western societies now take for granted that the involvement and engagement of their citizens will be through *work*, that in a sense we negotiate our role in the society through work, not through other institutions.'[13] Second wave feminism has both been shaped by and contributed to this process. Tom Lutz, as we discussed in Chapter 2, traces its beginnings to the 1920s as the professional and managerial classes resurrected and refurbished the work ethic not only to distinguish themselves as a class from the working classes, but also as an answer to boredom. Work began to be viewed as central to a person's mental and emotional health, something which professionals undertook for the fulfilment to be gained there rather than simply for material gain: 'The pleasure that professionals could find in their work constituted its difference from the work of the common laborers.'[14] In exhorting women to 'leave home' and find their fulfilment in the world of work, early second wave feminists provided a life story through which women could understand themselves as modern individuals and find the means for their self-actualisation in the world of work. But in doing so feminism confirmed the very way in which home and everyday life had been understood in modernist thought and hence the way it had banished women to the edges of modernity. This contradiction was solved by disavowing the housewife, casting her out, and positioning her in relation to the feminist as symptomatic of a failure to engage with the project of modern individuality. She was an 'other' self which needed to be expelled psychically by 'consciousness raising' or cut off literally and spatially by walking out the door of the suburban home.

In contemporary debates about work and family life, we have seen the return of this abject self of feminism. The figure of the housewife haunts contemporary feminism precisely because the feminist subject has been constituted at various times over the last forty years through the repudiation of such a figure. The problem lies in the failure of contemporary feminism to insist that the separation of home and work and the way the home remains a gendered space must always be central to its concerns and critique. These issues have been raised by feminists at various times. Arguments for 'wages for housework' in the 1970s, for example, sought to put these issues on the agenda even though they did not always challenge sufficiently why it was that women should be the ones to undertake such work. Classic texts such as *The Politics of Housework* (1980), edited by Ellen Malos, were clear that 'There will be no true liberation of women until we get rid of the assumption that it will always be women who do housework and look after children – and mostly in their own homes.'[15] But the arguments that we examined in Chapter 1 over the extent of choice available to women today and about the adequacy of child care and maternity-leave provisions suggest that these issues are not clearly enough on the agenda today. These debates do not challenge the status quo because they do not question the separation of work and home life, the continuing predominance of gendered arrangements in the home, or the importance placed on work in our society.

One of the reasons for this might lie in the continuing invisibility of housework. As Barbara Ehrenreich has argued, the use of a hired cleaner or corporate cleaning service has risen dramatically over the last decade. The extent of this change is difficult to determine because of the underground character of these arrangements in many instances. The politics of housework today is 'not only of gender but of race and class', with migrant women being the largest group of workers in this area. When feminists had put the politics of housework on the agenda in the 1970s,

Ehrenreich suggests, they made it clear that the issue was not the type of work involved but the relationships entailed:

> So the insight that distinguished the more radical, post-Friedan cohort of feminists was that when we talk about housework, we are really talking, yet again, about power. Housework was not degrading because it was manual labor, as Friedan thought, but because it was embedded in degrading relationships and inevitably served to reinforce them. To make a mess that another person will have to deal with – the dropped socks, the toothpaste sprayed on the bathroom mirror, the dirty dishes left from a late-night snack – is to exert domination in one of its more silent and intimate forms. One person's arrogance – or indifference, or hurry – becomes another person's occasion for toil. And when the person who is cleaned up after is consistently male, while the person who cleans up is consistently female, you have a formula for reproducing male domination from one generation to the next.[16]

Ehrenreich insists that the problem today is two-fold as people lose the capacity and will to look after their own human needs as well as rely on the power that comes with their economic resources to exploit the disadvantage of others. Ensuring that the work of home-making becomes more visible would challenge the long-held separation of home and work just as it would unsettle the solipsism that can arise from a lack of connectedness with one's own and others' human physical needs.

In the arguments of a number of feminists in the 1990s we can find suggestions as to how this rendering visible work of the home would contribute to a quite different project of self-actualisation than the one which assumes that such a task can only be fulfilled by leaving home behind. Such a making of the self would connect us to addressing our own and others' human needs. But it would ensure too that our search for individuality does not cut us off from the broader and necessarily complementary project of contributing to a society that is itself more reflexive, more questioning of the social structures and practices in which we operate. Seyla Benhabib, for example, interrogates the gendered subtext that underlies the modernist concept of the self-defining individual and the story of a meaningful life it tells. The individual, unrestrained by private or domestic responsibilities, and possessing a rational mind freed from the distorting effects of the emotions and the needs of the body, represents values and characteristics historically associated with the masculine. These characteristics have achieved their meaning and status, she points out, by establishing a series of negations identified with the feminine. But this dis-embedded, dis-embodied subject is an illusion, says Benhabib, that has long ceased to convince. She argues for the recognition of a situated self, a self that is not closed off, separate from the social relations that shape it. This self does not have to imagine itself as 'leaving home' to become a self; selfhood is formed precisely by a robust engagement with the social relationships of everyday existence, including those of domestic life.[17]

Iris Marion Young, as we saw in Chapter 2, argues more explicitly for home-making as the site for 'a self-conscious, *constructed* identity'. Recognising and nurturing one's own and others' humanity should be understood as the bedrock from which the individual can then seek to develop the capacity for self-reflexivity, for the continual scrutiny of one's self and one's social conditions that is the responsibility and burden of the modern individual. Arguing against both early second wave feminists, such as Simone de Beauvoir, and more contemporary feminists, such as Luce Irigaray, Young criticises the way they have been dismissive of women's own voices. The endless repetition of cleaning bathrooms, Young insists, cannot be said to characterise all the activities of home-making. De Beauvoir criticised domestic work as simply being about perpetuating the present, about immanence. But this negative valuation denies 'the experience of many women, who devote themselves to care for house and children as a meaningful human project'.[18]

Young identifies this project in the work women do in 'preserving the meaningful identity of a household or family by means of the loving care of its mementos'.[19] We would want to put a slightly different emphasis on this work. We suggest that rather than talking of 'preserving meaningful identity', we need to talk of the work of creating meaning. In the making of the home, developing its rituals and daily practices – including how and when the dishes are washed, the house is tidied and belongings are arranged – individuals and families are creating meaningful lives for themselves. And where this would seem to work best in terms of creating a robust sense of one's own individuality is when the home is open to the world rather than closed in upon itself: the home as a source of values and strength to enable us to engage with and reflect upon the world, its social practices and structures. Housewives in the 1940s and 1950s were reaching out towards such a possibility in their efforts to articulate domestic time with a form of political agency in their activism around the issues of daily life, firstly through housewives' organisations and secondly in their call for their own self-development with the assistance of radio programmes or other educational activities.

This book has examined how these struggles played out in a wide variety of cultural forms during the 1940s and 1950s. Contemporary cultural memory seems to have forgotten their struggles and negotiations, as well as their successes: the ways in which women did appropriate the housewife as a powerful agency at times of social change, and even spoke back when they found the term 'housewife' inadequate. Even at the time it was most prevalent, the figure of the housewife was not seamless with women's subjectivity, and was related to significant changes in masculinity, in what it mean to be a modern man. This book has sought to unsettle our received memories, and has shown how the housewife role, far from silencing women, actually gave women as a group a speaking position, and a political voice that is still relevant to current debates about paid maternity leave and child-care policy. By asking the state to take account of domesticity and support the home as a workplace, the housewives' organisations of the 1940s asked for public recognition of their contribution on equal terms with the male breadwinner. As activists, they based their demands for better organisation of the domestic sphere in the mould of labour politics in the public sphere; in this aspect of the debate over post-war life, the housewife was paralleled with the heroic figure of the worker. The disappearance of the figure of the housewife is therefore linked to the decline of the male-headed household.[20] Just as the housewife was an unreal figure of desire and excess, as well as distaste and lack, so too was the 'Man in the Grey Flannel Suit'.[21] While the housewife's gendered labour organised and contained the private time of the home, so did the figure of the 'family man' who found a refuge from the workplace in 'his' rest and leisure in the suburban home. Yet as we showed in Chapter 3, women's roles in the home were reshaped by post-war consumerism, which in turn contributed to a questioning of the working conditions of the housewife, and eventually brought the role itself into dispute. As shown by the women's accounts of their existence in the 1940s and 1950s home in Chapter 5 showed, women's 'drudgery' was believed to be a physical experience. It was lessened through labour-saving devices and better home designs, and the discourse on drudgery gave way to a sense of the housewife's boredom, which in contrast was psychological and spiritual and could not be so easily dispersed.

The question remains of how to continue this understanding of past changes to the domestic sphere in a way that takes account of the wide networks in which we operate, and the global circuits of exchange that now constitute our homes. The growth in migration, economic globalisation and new modes of work have now reconfigured the boundaries between public and private to such an extent that domesticity is no longer contained within the four walls of the home. As Ehrenreich and Hochschild in their recent collection *Global Woman* argue, women of the third world increasingly move in 'global survival circuits' in which 'care and love [is imported] from poor countries' to rich ones, via the bodies of the nanny and sex worker.[22] Women in the industrialised world may wish to leave the housewife role behind as they close the door on the 'modern' home and head out to work, but unless domesticity is seen as irresolutely public, the problem will simply move along and become 'somebody else's'. The now-marginal figure of the white middle-class housewife has split, on the one hand, into a racialised domestic worker from the 'third world' and, on the other, into the working wife as part of a first-world double-income family. As Ehrenreich and Hochschild show, the space and time of the home in the Western world is intimately connected to the work of women from poorer countries. However, these migrant women do not have access to citizenship on equal terms with the families they work for, and as they care for the homes of double-income families, their own families have to make do in their absence.

It is striking in this context how the figure of the full-time housewife, especially a middle-class and white woman, has reappeared in popular culture such as film and television cooking programmes at the very moment of these profound changes to the economy of the developed world. Former journalist Nigella Lawson, for example, has made a career from instructing women how to reclaim their powers of creative housewifery and become a 'domestic goddess'.[23] She suggests that women want to, and may, recapture a better sense of fit between their gender and their self in creative domesticity.

> The trouble with much modern cooking is not that the food it produces is not good, but that the mood it induces in the cook is one of skin-of-the-teeth efficiency, all briskness and little pleasure. Sometimes that's the best we can manage, but to others we want to feel not like a postmodern, post-feminist, overstretched modern woman but, rather, a domestic goddess, trailing nutmeggy fumes of baking pie in our languorous wake. So what I'm talking about is not being a domestic goddess, exactly, but feeling like one.[24]

The expenditure of the middle-class working woman's precious time on domestic tasks such as baking roast dinners and cupcakes is hardly necessary given the availability of prepared and restaurant meals, but it is an appealing vision of time to spare and the ability to feel 'languour' rather than exhaustion at the end of a working week. While Lawson's attitude is undoubtedly playful and self-aware, such a re-gendering of domestic skills (but notably restricted to the more creative and cheery aspects such as cooking, rather than cleaning or child care), and her aim to return to women the 'feeling' of being able to provide the care and love required in their families ('trailing nutmeggy fumes of baking pie in our langorous wake') underlines that the time to care and be cared for may be lacking. If feelings are 'distributable resources', as Hochschild so poignantly illustrates, and 'they behave somewhat differently from either scarce or renewable material resources', the scarcity of emotional labour in the home provoked by the first world demands of work and lifestyle has contributed to a redistribution of feeling which is playing out in such contemporary cultural forms as books and television programmes on cooking and home-renovation. While Hochschild is describing the phenomenon of a 'care drain' from the third world, her description of how new structures of feeling are made is worth considering here: 'According to Freud, we don't "withdraw" and "invest" feeling but rather *displace* or redirect it. The process is an unconscious one, whereby we don't actually give up a feeling of, say, love or hate, so much as we find a new object for it . . . .'[25]

In this movement of care about the world, Hochschild argues that we should pay attention to ethics implied in this transformation of the domestic economy: we should notice where care 'comes from and where it ends up'.[26] As the 'society of individuals' discussed at the beginning of this chapter intensifies, the figure of the housewife out of 'time' and out of 'place' has become a marker of how far this process has extended. In a set of films such as *Pleasantville, The Deep End, The Hours* and *Far from Heaven*, the housewife has recently reappeared in contemporary popular culture in a knowing way, as a figure of a certain kind of constrained and proscribed emotionality.[27] This recent reappearance of the housewife figure in the cultural imaginary points to how 'leftover' tensions about the gendering of home have not disappeared, but, as long as they remain, will return in fantasy.

Far From Heaven, a loving parody of the melodramas of the 1950s, directed by Todd Haynes, was released world-wide during 2002. It has been critically well received and was feted in the 2003 Academy Awards.[28] The film is set in 1957 in small-town East Coast USA, and Julianne Moore portrays an archetypal housewife, Cathy Whitaker. Her husband Frank (Dennis Quaid) is employed by an electronics company called Magnatech, and they have two children – a son and a daughter. So complete and beautiful is the Whitakers' home life – it looks like it has been lifted from a page of a 1950s home magazine – that the couple appear in the firm's publicity materials as 'Mr And Mrs Magnatech'. Their house is the 'dream home' of 1950s modernism and the Whitakers employ a black maid and gardener to keep it in perfect order. Describing her role in *Far from Heaven*, the actress Julianne Moore speaks of her character as 'oppressed' and 'silenced'. The housewife as a social type is no longer a desired figure – she has been made 'abject' in the terms described above, but her conspicuous consumption and subservient gender evokes a kitsch, outdated form of femininity in cultural memory.

The main character of the housewife in contemporary culture often signals such a limited emotional world, a shorthand for a barely containable repression that has to be 'broken through' for narrative closure and resolution. *Pleasantville*, for example, very cleverly uses visual shifts between black and white and colour to depict the 'monochromatic' boredom of its 1950s characters and signal their self-discovery and transcendence of conformity. *The Deep End*, a remake of 1940s B-film *The Reckless Moment*, revisits a plot centred on a mother–daughter relationship to show the actress Tilda Swinton as Margaret Hall, an upper-middle class housewife protecting her gay son from a blackmailer. In all these films the persona of the housewife operates an anchoring figure of conformism and normality allowing the film makers to introduce issues of sexuality and racism into the domestic sphere. All of the films to some extent acknowledge their dependence on representations of the fifties via the visual styles of post-war film, television and advertising, rather than any reference to historical events. *Far From Heaven*, in particular, is so excessive that it pushes the limits of a nostalgic, inauthentic relation to history into a camp emphasis on style and setting over characterisation. The entire film addresses an audience who know that this representation of the 1950s, with its themes of gay liberation and racial emancipation, would not have been possible at the time. Its art direction and cinematography provoke us to recognise that its setting is 'authentically' re-created from magazines and films, and its dialogue becomes all the more mimetic because it references the consumption of 1950s Hollywood film, rather than any intransigent details of the 1950s as an historical era. This aesthetic position toward 1950s gender roles and racial politics is currently available because of an ambivalence towards history that marks contemporary cultural studies and visual culture alike: we are both close and distant, attracted to and repelled by the signs of the past. But not all history is transformed into nostalgia: in these texts it is the privatised domestic sphere, suffocatingly cut off from public time, rather than the politicised housewife of the 1940s and 1950s that has returned in contemporary culture. Betty Friedan's mythical representation of popular images of the housewife is recaptured in these contemporary cultural references rather than the rather more complex negotiations that were going on in the media and elsewhere at the time.

Contemporary feminism – when it insists on work as the site of individual self-actualisation and when it reacts too vehemently against suggestions that a significant number of women want to stay home and look after their children – is also in danger of refusing to listen to the multiplicity of women's voices and taking for granted such representations as the 'kitsch' housewife. It is also in danger of failing to recognise the important values that home can represent. These values reside in the potential for the home to function in the way we have outlined above in the formation of the self-reflexive individual. They are also to be found in the history of domesticity, in Joan Williams' terms, as a 'dangerous supplement of liberalism'. Drawing on Jacques Derrida, she argues that 'Domesticity is "dangerous" [to dominant discourses of society] because its enshrinement of humane and communal values articulates a challenge to the legitimacy of self-interest as the guiding principle of social life.'[29] Feminism has a responsibility to reassert the importance of these values in the public world in a way that challenges the separation of home and work life and the relegation of humane values to the home and to femininity. Rather than the housewife being victim or failed self, she needs to be recognised as central to the history of the feminist subject and a useful reminder of how the project of feminism has itself been built on this tradition of domesticity as source of critique of the contemporary social world.

Notes

1. Zygmunt Baumann, *The Individualized Society*, Cambridge, Polity Press, 2001, p. 105.
2. Ibid., p. 16. Baumann draws here on Ulrick Beck's work on the Risk Society.
3. Ibid., pp. 9–10.
4. Henri Lefebvre, 'The Everyday and Everydayness', *Yale French Studies*, 73, 1987, p. 10. Translated by Christine Levich with Alice Kaplan and Kristin Ross.

5. Rita Felski, *Doing Time: Feminist Theory and Postmodern Culture*, New York, New York University Press, 2000, pp. 82–5.

6. Patrice Petro, 'After Shock/Between Boredom and History', in Patrice Petro (ed.), *Fugitive Images: From Photography to Video*, Bloomington, Indiana University Press, 1995, p. 275.

7. Jeffrey Minson, *Genealogies of Morals: Nietzsche, Foucault, Donzelot, and the Eccentricity of Ethics*, London, Macmillan Press, 1985, p. 208.

8. Ibid., p. 215.

9. Erica Carter, *How German is She? Postwar West German Reconstruction and the Consuming Woman*, Ann Arbor, University of Michigan Press, 1997, pp. 205f.

10. By 1954, the participation of married women in the workforce had more than doubled over the 1947 rate: 5 per cent, 6 per cent and 12½ per cent of married women were in the workforce in 1933, 1947 and 1954, respectively. Non-British migrant women showed the highest participation rates in the 1954 census, with nearly one-third (29.2 per cent) of women born outside Australia and the UK participating in the workforce. (Commonwealth Bureau of Census and Statistics, *Census of the Commonwealth of Australia*, Canberra, AGPS, 1954, pp. 215, 334. See also 'Australian Social Trends 1998: Work – Paid Work: Trends in Women's Employment', Australian Bureau of Statistics, 1998: *www.abs.gov.au/ausstats*.)

11. Marilyn Lake, *Getting Equal: The History of Australian Feminism*, Sydney, Allen and Unwin, 1999, p. 228

12. Ibid., p. 229.

13. Helen Trinca, speech to launch the Centre at the University of Technology, Sydney, Organisational, Vocational and Adult Learning (OVAL Research), 18 November 2002, typescript, p. 2. Helen Trinca is the editor of the *AFR*'s (*Australian Financial Review*) *BOSS* magazine.

14. Tom Lutz, '"Sweat or Die": The Hedonization of the Work Ethic in the 1920s', *American Literary History*, 8 (2), 1996, p. 278.

15. Ellen Malos, 'Introduction', in Ellen Malos (ed.), *The Politics of Housework*, London, Allison and Busby Ltd, 1980, p. 7

16. Barbara Ehrenreich, 'Maid to Order: The Politics of Other Women's Work', *Harper's Magazine*, April 2000, p. 61.

17. Seyla Benhabib, *Situating the Self: Gender, Community and Postmodernism in Contemporary Ethics*, Cambridge, Polity Press, 1992, p. 5. See also Lesley Johnson, '"As Housewives We Are Worms": Women, Modernity, and the Home Question', in Morag Shiach (ed.), *Feminism and Cultural Studies*, Oxford University Press, 1999, pp. 475–91.

18. Iris Marion Young, *Intersecting Voices: Dilemmas of Gender, Political Philosophy and Policy*, Princeton, NJ, Princeton University Press, 1997, p. 149.

162 • *Sentenced to Everyday Life*

According to Australian Bureau of Statistics (ABS) figures, the most common
    employment arrangement for Australian families is for both parents to be
    working. In 2000, almost two-thirds (63 per cent) of couple families with
    dependent children had both partners employed. In the remaining third (37
    per cent) of couple families with dependent children, the father was employed
    and the mother was not in the labour force. 'Most men were working full-time
    and their employment rate was less affected by the presence of children than
    women's, indicating that for most families, men were still the primary finan-
    cial provider.' 'Australian Social Trends 2001: Work – Paid Work: Trends in
    Employment Population Ratios', Australian Bureau of Statistics, 2002:
    www.abs.gov.au/ausstats.

See Chapter 14, 'The Housewife and the Man in the Grey Flannel Suit', in
    John Murphy, *Imagining the Fifties: Private Sentiment and Political Culture
    in Menzies' Australia*, Sydney, University of New South Wales Press and Pluto
    Press, 2000, pp. 199–222.

Barbara Ehrenreich and Arlie Russell Hochschild, 'Introduction', in Barbara
    Ehrenreich and Arlie Russell Hochschild (eds), *Global Woman: Nannies,
    Maids, and Sex Workers in the New Economy*, New York, Metropolitan Books,
    2003, p. 17.

Nigella Lawson, *How to be a Domestic Goddess*, London, Chatto & Windus,
    2000.

Nigella Lawson, 'Philosophy' from 'Nigella Lawson – the Official Site for the
    Domestic Goddess', Channel 4, 2003: *www.channel4.com/life/microsites/
    N/nigella/philosophy.shtml*.

Arlie Russell Hochschild, 'Love and Gold', in Ehrenreich and Hochschild
    (eds), *Global Woman*, p. 23.

Pleasantville, Director, Gary Ross, Script by Gary Ross, New Line Cinema,
    1998; *The Deep End*, Directors, Scott McGhee and David Siegel, Fox
    Searchlight Pictures, 2001; *The Hours*, Director, Stephen Daldry, Script by
    David Hare, Paramount Pictures, 2002; *Far from Heaven*, Director, Todd
    Haynes, Script by Todd Haynes, USA Films, 2002.

The film *Far from Heaven* was nominated for awards for Cinematography,
    Music (Score) and Writing (Original Screenplay), and Moore was nominated
    as Best Actress in a Leading Role.

Joan Williams, 'Domesticity as the Dangerous Supplement of Liberalism',
    Journal of Women's History, 2 (3), Winter 1991, p. 69.

Bibliography

General

Allan, Graham and Graham Crow (eds), *Home and Family: Creating the Domestic Sphere*, London, Macmillan, 1989.

Allport, Carolyn, 'The Princess in the Castle: Women and the New Order Housing', in Women and Labour Publications Collective (ed.), *All Her Labours: Embroidering the Framework*, Sydney, Hale and Iremonger, 1984.

Allport, Carolyn, *Women and Public Housing in Sydney, 1930–1961*', unpublished PhD thesis, Sydney, Maquarie University, 1990.

Altman, Rick, 'Rebirth of a Phantom Genre' in Film/Genre, London, BFI, 1999.

Anderson, Benedict, *Imagined Communities: Reflections on the Origin and Spread of Nationalism*, London, Verso, 1983.

Armstrong, Nancy, *Desire and Domestic Fiction: A Political History of the Novel*, New York Oxford University Press, 1987.

Army Education Service, *Home Life*, Discussion Pamphlet 9, Melbourne, Ramsay Ware Publishing, 1945.

Army Education Service, *Our Population Problem*, Discussion Pamphlet 7, Melbourne, Ramsay Ware Publishing, 1945.

Baumann, Zygmunt, *The Individualized Society*, Cambridge, Polity Press, 2001.

Baumgardner, Jennifer and Amy Richards, *Manifesta: Young Women, Feminism and the Future*, New York, Farrar, Straus and Giroux, 2000.

Beaumont, Catriona, 'Citizens Not Feminists: The Boundary Negotiated between Citizenship and Feminism by Mainstream Women's Organisations in England, 1928–39', *Women's History Review*, 9 (2), 2000.

Bell-Smith, Eric, 'Lack of Homes is Driving Them Insane', *Sunday Telegraph*, 8 January 1950.

Benhabib, Seyla, *Situating the Self: Gender, Community and Postmodernism in Contemporary Ethics*, Cambridge, Polity Press, 1992.

Biskind, Peter, *Seeing Is Believing: How Hollywood Taught Us to Stop Worrying and Love the Fifties*, New York, Pantheon Books, 1983.

Bissett, Winifred, 'Shirley – Hurdler to Housewife: Olympic Champion is Happy as She Knits October Layette', *Australian Women's Weekly*, 1 May 1957.

Blackburn, Jean and Ted Jackson, *Australian Wives Today*, NSW Fabian Society Pamphlet, 1963.

Bratton, Jacky, Jim Cook and Christine Gledhill (eds), *Melodrama: Stage, Picture, Screen*, London, BFI, 1994.

Brett, Judith, *Robert Menzies' Forgotten People*, Sydney, Pan Macmillan, 1992.

Bronfen, Elisabeth and Misha Kavka (eds), *Feminist Consequences: Theory for the New Century*, New York, Columbia University Press, 2001.

Brooks, Peter, *The Melodramatic Imagination: Balzac, Henry James, Melodrama, and the Mode of Excess*, New Haven, Yale University Press, 1976.

Brown, Nicholas, *'A Cliff of White Cleanliness': Decorating the Home, Defining the Self*, Urban Research Program Working Paper No. 48 (ed. R. Coles), Canberra, Urban Research Program, Australian National University, Canberra, 1995.

Brunsdon, Charlotte, *The Feminist, the Housewife, and the Soap Opera*, Oxford, Clarendon Press, 2000.

Bunning, Walter, 'Your Home . . . After the War', *Australian Women's Weekly*, 1 January 1944.

Byars, Jackie, *All That Hollywood Allows: Re-reading Gender in 1950s Melodrama*, London, Routledge, 1991.

Cain, James M., *The Five Great Novels of James M. Cain*, London, Pan, 1985.

Carter, Erica, *How German is She? Postwar West German Reconstruction and the Consuming Woman*, Ann Arbor, University of Michigan Press, 1997.

Colomina, Beatriz, 'The Split Wall: Domestic Voyeurism', in Beatriz Colomina (ed.), *Sexuality and Space*, New York, Princeton Architectural Press.

Cook, Pam, 'Duplicity in *Mildred Pierce*', in E. Ann Kaplan (ed.), *Women in Film Noir*, London, BFI, 1980.

Copjec, Joan, 'More! From Melodrama to Magnitude', in Janet Bergstrom (ed.), *Endless Night: Cinema and Psychoanalysis, Parallel Histories*, Berkeley, University of California Press, 1998.

Cowan, Ruth Schwartz, *More Work for Mother: The Ironies of Household Technology from the Open Hearth to the Microwave*, New York, Basic Books, 1983.

Craik, Jennifer, 'The Cultural Politics of the Queensland House', *Continuum*, 3 (1), 1990.

Curthoys, Barbara and Audrey McDonald, *More than a Hat and Glove Brigade: The Story of the Union of Australian Women*, Sydney, Union of Australian Women, 1996.

Cuffley, Peter, *Australian Houses of the Forties and Fifties*, Knoxfield, Five Mile Press, 1993.

Darian-Smith, Kate, *On the Home Front: Melbourne in Wartime, 1939–1945*, Oxford, Oxford University Press, 1990.

Davidoff, Leonore and Catherine Hall, *Family Fortunes: Men and Women of the English Middle Class 1780–1850*, London, Hutchinson, 1987.

Davis, Angela Y., *Women, Race and Class*, New York, Vintage Books, 1983.

de Beauvoir, Simone, *The Second Sex*, H.M. Parshley (trans.), Harmondsworth, Penguin, 1981.

de Certeau, Michel, *The Practice of Everyday Life*, S.F. Rendall (trans.), Berkeley, University of California Press, 1984.

Dent, Rachel, 'I'd Like to Blow Up My Kitchen!' *Australian House and Garden*, 4 (3), March 1950.

Doane, Mary Ann, *The Desire to Desire: The Woman's Film of the 1940s*, Bloomington, Indiana University Press, 1987.

Ehrenreich, Barbara, 'Maid to Order: The Politics of Other Women's Work', *Harper's Magazine*, April 2000.

Ehrenreich, Barbara, *Nickel and Dimed: On (Not) Getting By in America*, New York, Metropolitan Books, 2001.

Ehrenreich, Barbara and Arlie Russell Hochschild (eds), *Global Woman: Nannies, Maids, and Sex Workers in the New Economy*, New York, Metropolitan Books, 2003.

Feldstein, Ruth, *Motherhood in Black and White: Race and Sex in American Liberalism, 1930–1965*, Ithaca, Cornell University Press, 2000.

Fell, Liz and Carolin Wenzel (eds), *The Coming Out Show: Twenty Years of Feminist ABC Radio*, Sydney, ABC Books, 1995.

Felski, Rita, *Doing Time: Feminist Theory and Postmodern Culture*, New York, New York University Press, 2000.

Finch, Lynette, 'Could "Winnie the War Winner" Organise Women?' *Hecate*, 10 (1), 1984.

Fisher, Lucy, 'Two-Faced Women: The "Double" in Women's Melodrama of the 1940s', *Cinema Journal*, 23 (1), 1983.

Fordham, Mrs Elsie, 'Home Shortage a Cause of Marriage Troubles', *Australian Women's Weekly*, 22 April 1944.

Forte, Margaret, 'What We Need is a Pressure Group', *Woman's Day and Home*, 7 July 1952.

Friedan, Betty, *The Feminine Mystique*, Harmondsworth, Penguin, 1983.

Freud, Sigmund, *Case Histories, I. 'Dora' and 'Little Hans'*, James Strachey (trans.), Harmondsworth, Penguin, 1977.

Gawler, J.S., *A Roof over My Head*, Melbourne, Lothian, 1963.

Garton, Stephen, 'The War-Damaged Citizen', in Paul Patton and Diane Austin-Broos (eds), *Transformations in Australian Society*, Sydney, University of Sydney, Research Institute for Humanities and Social Sciences, 1997.

Giddens, Anthony, *Modernity and Self-identity: Self and Society in the Late Modern Age*, Cambridge, Polity Press, 1991.

Gilligan, Carol, *In a Different Voice*, Cambridge, MA, Harvard University Press, 1982.

Gledhill, Christine, (ed.), *Home is Where the Heart Is: Studies in Melodrama and the Woman's Film*, London, BFI, 1987.

Greer, Germaine, *The Female Eunuch*, London, Granada, 1970.

Greig, Alastair Whyte, *The Stuff Dreams Are Made Of: Housing Provision in Australia 1945–1960*, Carlton, Vic., Melbourne University Press, 1995.

Hacking, Ian, *Rewriting the Soul: Multiple Personality and the Sciences of Memory*, Princeton, Princeton University Press, 1995.

Hakim, Catherine, 'Five Feminist Myths about Women's Employment', *British Journal of Sociology*, 46 (3), 1995.

Hakim, Catherine, 'The Sexual Division of Labour and Women's Heterogeneity', *British Journal of Sociology*, 47 (1), 1996.

Haralovich, Mary Beth, 'All That Heaven Allows: Color, Narrative Space, and Melodrama', in Peter Lehman (ed.), *Close Viewings: An Anthology of New Film Criticism*, Gainesville, University Presses of Florida, 1990.

Hareven, Tamara, *Family Time and Industrial Time: The Relationship between the Family and Work in a New England Industrial Community*, Cambridge, Cambridge University Press, 1982.

Harland, Margaret, *Women's Place in Society*, Melbourne, F.W. Cheshire, 1947.

Harvey, David, *The Condition of Postmodernity*, Oxford, Basil Blackwell, 1989.

Haskell, Molly, *From Reverence to Rape: The Treatment of Women in the Movies*, Penguin, New York, 1979.

Hausseger, Virginia, 'The Sins of Our Feminist Mothers', *The Age*, 23 July 2002.

Henry, Kristen and Marlene Derlet, *Talking Up a Storm: Nine Women and Consciousness Raising*, Sydney, Hale and Iremonger, 1993.

Hewett, Dorothy, *Bobbin Up*, Melbourne, Australian Book Society, 1959.

Hochschild, Arlie Russell, 'Love and Gold', in Barbara Ehrenreich and Arlie Russell Hochschild (eds), *Global Woman: Nannies, Maids, and Sex Workers in the New Economy*, New York, Metropolitan Books, 2003.

hooks, bel, *Yearning: Race, Gender and Cultural Politics*, Boston, Southland Press, 1990.

Horowitz, Daniel, 'Rethinking Betty Friedan and *The Feminine Mystique*: Labor Union Radicalism and Feminism in Cold War America', *American Quarterly*, 48 (1), 1996.

Hutton, Nan, '"Housewife" Is Not an Apt Description', *Woman's Day and Home*, 12 December 1955.

Inglis, K.S., *This is the ABC: The Australian Broadcasting Commission, 1932–1983*, Melbourne, Melbourne University Press, 1983.

Jaggar, Alison M., 'Love and Knowledge: Emotion in Feminist Epistemology', in Alison M. Jaggar (ed.), *Gender/Body/Knowledge*, New Brunswick, Rutgers

University Press, 1989.

Johnson, Lesley, '"As Housewives We Are Worms": Women, Modernity, and the Home Question', in Morag Shiach (ed.), *Feminism and Cultural Studies*, Oxford University Press, 1999.

Johnson, Lesley, *The Modern Girl: Girlhood and Growing Up*, Buckingham, Open University Press, 1993.

Johnson, Lesley, *The Unseen Voice: A Cultural Study of Early Australian Radio*, London, Routledge, 1988.

Kaplan, E. Ann, 'Individual Response: The Spectatrix', *Camera Obscura*, 20–1, 1989.

Kaplan, E. Ann, 'Mothering, Feminism and Representation: The Maternal Melodrama and the Woman's Film 1910–1940', in Christine Gledhill (ed.), *Home is Where the Heart is: Studies in Melodrama and Women's Kilm*, London, BFI, 1987.

Kaplan, Gisela, *The Meagre Harvest: The Australian Women's Movement, 1950s–1990s*, Sydney, Allen and Unwin, 1996.

Klinger, Barbara, *Melodrama and Meaning: History, Culture, and the Films of Douglas Sirk*, Bloomington, Indiana University Press, 1994.

Lake, Marilyn, *Getting Equal: The History of Australian Feminism*, Sydney, Allen and Unwin, 1999.

Lake, Marilyn, 'Jessie Street and "Feminist Chauvinism"', in Heather Radi (ed.), *Jessie Street: Documents and Essays*, Sydney, Women's Redress Press, 1990.

LaValley, Albert J. (ed.), *Mildred Pierce*, Madison, University of Wisconsin Press, 1980.

Lawson, Nigella, *How to be a Domestic Goddess*, London, Chatto & Windus, 2000.

Lefebvre, Henri, 'The Everyday and Everydayness', *Yale French Studies*, 73, 1987.

Lewis, Julie, *On Air: The Story of Catherine King and the ABC Women's Session*, Fremantle, Fremantle Arts Centre Press, 1979.

Lord, Margaret Florence, *Interior Decoration: A Guide to Furnishing the Australian Home*, Sydney, Ure Smith, 1942.

Lundberg, Ferdinand and Marynia F. Farnham, *Modern Woman: The Lost Sex*, New York and London, Harper & Brothers, 1947.

Lutz, Tom, '"Sweat or Die": The Hedonization of the Work Ethic in the 1920s', *American Literary History*, 8 (2), 1996.

Malos, Ellen, 'Introduction', in Ellen Malos (ed.), *The Politics of Housework*, London, Allison and Busby Ltd, 1980.

Marling, Karal Ann, *As Seen on TV: The Visual Culture of Everyday Life in the 1950s*, Cambridge, Mass., Harvard University Press, 1994.

McClintock, Anne, *Imperial Leather: Race and Gender in the Colonial Conquest*, New York, Routledge, 1995.

McHugh, Kathleen Anne, *American Domesticity: From How-to Manual to Hollywood Melodrama*, New York, Oxford University Press, 1999.

McLeod, Zelie, 'Life Today is One Big Frustration for the Housewife', *Daily Telegraph*, 30 January 1947.

Meyerowitz, Joanne, 'Beyond *The Feminine Mystique*: A Reassessment of Postwar Mass Culture, 1946–1958', in Joanne Meyerowitz (ed.), *Not June Cleaver: Women and Gender in Postwar America, 1945–1960*, Philadelphia, Temple University Press, 1994.

Mills, Damon, 'Of Harpies Like Mildred', *Monthly Film Guide*, August–September 1950.

Minson, Jeffrey, *Genealogies of Morals: Nietzsche, Foucault, Donzelot, and the Eccentricity of Ethics*, London, Macmillan Press, 1985.

Mort, Frank, 'Social and Symbolic Fathers and Sons: A Cultural History', paper delivered at the University of Technology, Sydney, Ultimo Series, 2 April 1997.

Mulvey, Laura, '"It Will Be a Magnificent Obsession": The Melodrama's Role in the Developement of Contemporary Film Theory', in Jacky Bratton, Jim Cook and Christine Gledhill (eds), *Melodrama: Stage, Picture, Screen*, London, BFI, 1994.

Murphy, John, *Imagining the Fifties: Private sentiment and political culture in Menzies' Australia*, Sydney, University of New South Wales Press and Pluto Press, 2000.

Myrdal, Alva and Viola Klein, *Women's Two Roles*, London, Routledge and Kegan Paul, 1956/1968.

Nava, Mica and Alan O'Shea, 'Introduction', in Mica Nava and Alan Shea (eds), to *Modern Time: Reflections on a Century of English Modernity*, London, Routledge, 1996.

Nowell-Smith, Geoffrey, 'Minelli & Melodrama', in Christine Gledhill (ed.) *Home is Where the Heart is: Studies in Melodrama and the Woman's Film*, London BFI, 1987.

Oakley, Ann, *Housewife*, London, Penguin, 1974.

Oliver, Julie, *The Australian Home Beautiful: From Hills Hoist to High Rise*, Sydney: Pacific Publications, 1999.

Parker, Margot, 'We All Hate Housework!', *Woman's Day with Woman*, 28 July 1958.

Petro, Patrice, 'After Shock/Between Boredom and History', in Patrice Petro (ed.), *Fugitive Images: From Photography to Video*, Bloomington, Indiana University Press, 1995.

Probert, Belinda, '"Grateful Slaves" or "Self-made Women": A Matter of Choice or Policy?', Clare Burton Memorial Lecture 2001.

Radi, Heather (ed.), *Jessie Street: Documents and Essays*, Sydney, Women's Redress Press, 1990.

Ranald, Pat, 'Women's Organisations and the Issue of Communism', in Ann Curthoys and John Merrit (eds), *Better Dead Than Red: Australia's First Cold War, 1945–1959*, Sydney, Allen and Unwin, vol. 2, 1986.

Riley, Denise, *War in the Nursery: Theories of the Child and Mother*, London, Virago, 1983.

Rose, Nikolas, *Governing the Soul: The Shaping of the Private Self*, London, Routledge, 1989.

Russo, Mary, *The Female Grotesque: Risk, Excess and Modernity*, New York and London, Routledge, 1994.

Said, Edward, 'Reflections on Exile', *Granta, After the Revolution*, 13, 1984.

Sanders, Joel, 'Curtain Wars: Architects, Decorators, and the 20th-Century Domestic Interior', *Harvard Review of Design Magazine*, 16, Winter/Spring 2002.

Saunders, Kay and Raymond Evans, 'No Place Like Home: The Evolution of the Australian housewife', in Kay Saunders and Raymond Evans (eds), *Gender Relations in Australia: Domination and Negotiation*, Sydney, Harcourt, Brace & Jovanovich, 1992.

Scutt, Jocelynne (ed.), *Different, Reflections on the Women's Movement and Visions for Its future*, Ringwood, Penguin, 1987.

Seymour, Mary Jane, 'Joanna Plans a Home: 1 – The Dream', *Australian Home Beautiful*, March 1945.

Seymour, Mary Jane, 'Joanna Plans a Home: 4 – She Visualises an Ideal Kitchen', *Australian Home Beautiful*, October 1945.

Seymour, Mary Jane, 'Joanna Plans a Home: She Finds Out There Are Still Some Things to Learn About Furniture', *Australian Home Beautiful*, April 1946.

Shklar, Judith, 'Introduction', in Wolf Lepenies, *Melancholy and Society*, Jeremy Gaines and Doris L. Jones (trans.), Cambridge, MA, Harvard University Press, 1992.

Sizemore, Chris Costner and Elen Sain Pitillo, *Eve*, London, Victor Gollancz, 1978.

Smart, Judith, '"For the Good That We Can Do": Cecilia Downing and Feminist Christian citizenship', *Australian Feminist Studies*, 19, Autumn 1994.

Smart, Judith, 'Private, Public and Political: the Efflorescence of the Housewives' Associations in Eastern Australia, 1915–1960', unpublished conference paper, presented at the Australian Historical Studies Association Conference, Melbourne, 1994.

Smith, Alex, 'Carpentry in the Kitchen – Suggested Improvements', *Australian Home Beautiful*, January 1945.

Sobchack, Vivian, 'Lounge Time: Postwar Crises and the Chronotope of Film Noir', in Nick Browne (ed.), *Refiguring American Film Genres: Theory and History*, Berkeley, University of California Press, 1998.

Sobey, Pat, 'Family First for Margo Lee – She Turned Down a Hollywood Career', *Australian Women's Weekly*, 25 April 1956.

Somerset, W.A., 'Kitchens of Yesterday and Tomorrow', *Australian Home Beautiful*, January 1946.

Spacks, Patricia Meyer, *Boredom: The Literary History of a State of Mind*, Chicago, University of Chicago Press, 1995.

Spearritt, Peter, *Sydney Since the Twenties*, Sydney, Hale and Iremonger, 1978.

Sprod, George, 'If Mum Worked a 40–hour Week', *Daily Telegraph*, 17 July 1947.

Steedman, Carolyn, *Landscape for a Good Woman*, London, Virago, 1986.

Stewart, Kathleen, *A Space on the Side of the Road: Cultural Poetics in an 'Other' America*, Princeton, Princeton University Press, 1996.

Studdert, Helena, '"You're 100% Feminine if . . .": Gender Constructions in Australian Women's Magazines, 1920–1969', unpublished PhD thesis, Kensington, University of New South Wales, 1997.

Summers, Anne, *Damned Whores and God's Police: The Colonization of Women in Australia*, Harmondsworth, Penguin, 1983.

Taylor, Jenny Bourne, 'Re-locations – from Bradford to Brighton', *New Formations*, 17, 1992.

Thigpen, Corbett H. and Hervey M. Cleckley, *The Three Faces of Eve*, New York, McGraw-Hill, 1957.

Tooley, James, *The Miseducation of Women*, London, Continuum International Publishing Group, 2002.

Trinca, Helen, speech to launch the Centre at the University of Technology, Sydney, Organisational, Vocational and Adult Learning (OVAL Research), 18 November 2002.

Turney, Catharine, 'Interview with Catharine Turney', in Lee Server (ed.), *Screenwriter: Words Become Pictures*, Pittstown, Main Street Press, 1987.

Victorian Fabian Society, *The Housing Crisis in Australia*, Melbourne, Spotlight Press, 1958.

Vivioni, Christian, 'Who is Without Sin: The Maternal Melodrama in American Film, 1930–1939', in Christine Gledhill (ed.), *Home is Where the Heart is: Studies in Melodrama and Women's Film*, London, BFI, 1987.

Walkerdine, Valerie and Helen Lucey, *Democracy in the Kitchen: Regulating Mothers and Socialising Daughters*, London, Virago, 1989.

Walling, Paula, 'Film Star Happy in Housewife Role', *Australian Women's Weekly*, 11 July 1956.

Weiss, Julie, 'Feminist Film Theory and Women's History: *Mildred Pierce* and the Twentieth Century', *Film & History*, 22 (3), 1992.

Wigley, Mark, 'The Housing of Gender', in Beatriz Colomina (ed.), *Sexuality and Space*, New York, Princeton Architectural Press.

Wilkie, Douglas, 'Be Politically Active or Remain Animals', *Woman's Day and*

Home, 7 July 1952.

Williams, Joan, *Unbending Gender: Why Family and Work Conflict and What to Do About It*, Oxford University Press, 2000.

Williams, Joan, 'Domesticity as the Dangerous Supplement of Liberalism', *Journal of Women's History*, 2 (3), Winter 1991.

Williams, Linda, 'Feminist Film Theory: *Mildred Pierce* and the Second World War', in Deidre Pribram (ed.), *Female Spectators: Looking at Film and Television*, London, Verso, 1989

Williams, Raymond, *Marxism and Literature*, Oxford, Oxford University Press, 1977.

Wright, Andrée, *Brilliant Careers: Women in Australian Cinema*, Sydney, Pan Books, 1988.

Wylie, Phillip, *Generation of Vipers*, Holt, Rinehart & Winston, New York & Chicago, 1955.

X., Mr. 'Considering the Plan', *Australian Home Beautiful*, August 1945.

Young, Iris Marion, *Intersecting Voices: Dilemmas of Gender, Political Philosophy, and Policy*, Princeton, NJ, Princeton University Press, 1997.

Government and Official Sources

'Australian Social Trends 1998: Work – Paid Work: Trends in Women's Employment', Australian Bureau of Statistics, 1998.

'Australian Social Trends 2001: Work – Paid Work: Trends in Employment Population Ratios', Australian Bureau of Statistics, 2002.

British Parliamentary debates, 14 March 2002, Column 1107.

Commonwealth Bureau of Census and Statistics, *Census of the Commonwealth of Australia*, Canberra, AGPS, 1954.

Department of Post-war Reconstruction, *The Housewife Speaks*, Sydney, Associated Newspapers, c.1945.

New South Wales Parliamentary Debates, House of Assembly, 22 November 1944.

Research Council on the Decline Interim Report of the National Health and Medical in the Birth Rate, 1944.

Ryde Municipal Council, Town Clerk's report, 10 February 1947, Ryde Municipal Council records.

Newspapers and Journals

Age, 2002.
American Literary History, 1996.
Australian, 1997.
Australian Feminist Studies, 1994, 1997.

Australian Home Beautiful, various issues of the 1940s/1950s and 1999.

Australian House and Garden, various issues of the 1940s/1950s.

Australian Women's Weekly, various issues of the 1940s/1950s.

British Journal of Sociology, 1996.

Camera Obscura, 1989.

Cinema Journal, 1983.

Continuum, 1990.

Daily Telegraph, 1947.

Harper Magazine, 2000.

Harvard Review of Design Magazine, 2002.

Hecate, 1984.

Housewife, 1954.

Journal of Women's History, 1991.

Monthly Film Guide, 1950.

New Formations, 1992.

New Housewife, 1949.

Sunday Telegraph, 1950.

Sun-Herald, 2003.

Sydney Morning Herald, 1945, 1996, 2000, 2002, 2003.

Woman's Day and Home, 1952, 1955.

Woman's Day with Woman, 1958.

Women's History Review, 2000.

Websites

www.abs.gov.au/ausstats, Australian Bureau of Statistics.

www.channel4.com/life/microsites/N/nigella/philosophy.shtml, Nigella Lawson, 'Philosophy' from 'Nigella Lawson – the Official Site for the Domestic Goddess', Channel 4, 2003.

www.io.com/~wave, The 3rd WWWave.

www.naa.gov.au, *Women's Session* records, Australian Archives

www.tenuk.com, TimeEnergyNetwork.

Films

Cobra Woman, Director, Robert Siodmak, Script by Scott Darling, Gene Lewis and Richard Brooks, MCA/Universal, 1944.

Come Back Little Sheba, Director, Daniel Mann, Script by William Inge and Kettie Frings, Paramount, 1952.

The Dark Mirror, Director, Robert Siodmak, Script by Nunally Johnson and Vladimir Pozner, Universal International, 1946.

The Deep End, Director, Scott McGehee and David Siegel, Fox Searchlight Pictures, 2001.

Double Indemnity, Director, Billy Wilder, Script by Billy Wilder and Raymond Chandler, Paramount, 1944.

Far from Heaven, Director, Todd Haynes, Script by Todd Haynes, USA Films, 2002

Giant, Director, George Stevens, Script by Fred Guiol and Ivan Moffat, Warner Bros, 1956.

The Hours, Director, Stephen Daldry, Script by David Hare, Paramount Pictures, 2002.

I Remember Mama, Director, George Stevens, Script by DeWitt Bodeen, Kathyrn Forbes and John Van Druten, RKO Radio Pictures,1948.

Mildred Pierce, Director, Michael Curtiz Script by Ranald MacDougall, Catharine Turney (uncredited) and James M. Cain, Warner Bros, 1945.

Mr Chedworth Steps Out, Director, Ken G. Hall, Script by Frank Harvey, Cinesound, 1939.

Mrs Miniver, Director, William Wyler, Script by George Froeschel, James Hilton, Jan Struther, Claudine West and Arthur Wimperis, MGM, 1942.

Pillow Talk, Director, Michael Gordon, Script by Stanley Shapiro and Maurice Richlin, Universal, 1959.

Pleasantville, Directed by Gary Ross, Script by Gary Ross, New Line Cinema, 1998.

The Postman Always Rings Twice, Director, Tay Garnett, Script by Harry Ruskin, Niven Busch and James M. Cain, MGM, 1946.

A Son is Born, Director, Eric Porter, Script by Gloria Bourner, Eric Porter Studios, 1946.

A Stolen Life, Director, Paul Czinner, Script by George Barraud, Karel J. Benes and Margaret Kennedy, 1939, Orion/Paramount; *A Stolen Life*, Director, Curtis Bernhardt, Script by Karel J. Benes, Catharine Turney and Margaret Buell Wilder, Warner Bros, 1946.

The Three Faces of Eve, Director, Nunally Johnson, Script by Nunally Johnson, Twentieth Century Fox, 1957.

Archive/Library Collections

Mitchell Library/State Library of New South Wales:

'Ban the Bomb and Banish High Prices', leaflet, Janie Overton papers, File on Women's Day, Women's Movement and Union of Australian Women 1940–71, Mitchell Library, MLMSS 6968/1, Sydney.

Bill of Rights for the Home, as presented to the Premier of Victoria (Mr Holloway) on 4 February 1948, Federated Housewives' Association, Records 1945–53,

Mitchell Library, MLMSS 4155/H 3896, Sydney.

Hudson, George, Pty Ltd, *How to Build Well and Save Money with a George Hudson Pty Ltd 'Ready Cut' Home*, Sydney, George Hudson Pty Ltd, c. 1950, n.p. Pamplet held at Mitchell Library, ref. no.643.209944/1, Sydney.

New Housewives' Association, 'Report of Canberra Delegation, 5 April 1948', Chatswood Branch, Correspondence and Reports, Mitchell Library, MLMSS 6229, Sydney, 1947–48.

'New Housewives' Association Constitution 1948/1949', Janie Overton papers, File on Women's Day, Women's Movement and Union of Australian Women 1940–71, Mitchell Library, MLMSS 6968/1, Sydney.

New South Wales State Archives:

Purcell, J.T., 'Home Sweet? (a Study of the Housing Problem)', unpublished manuscript, 1 March 1954, semi-personal file of J.T. Purcell, 1953,1969, File No. 7/7580, Sydney, New South Wales State Archives.

National Library of Australia:

Lewis, Julie, Papers 1944–78, National Library of Australia, MS 9507, Canberra, Box 7, Series 5/3, 'The Women's Session, WA: 1942 to Present Day'.

Ryan, Mary, *Homes of the Future*, Typescript, JAFp SOC 18SS, Canberra, National Library of Australia, 1944.

National Archives of Australia:

Carmichael, Alan, Memo, 'Re: Proposal to Cut National Women's Session for Half-hour to Quarter-hour', AA SP727/1/1, 12/2/1 PART 2, 9 July 1964.

Chapple, E., Memos, 15 February and 12 March 1954, 'Talks – Sessions – Women's Session', AA B2144, 13/3/18, Part 4.

Donkin, Nancy, 'Come Out of the Kitchen – 1 – How About Some Spare Time?', *Women's Session*, Box 15, 15 May 1952.

Donkin, Nancy, 'Come Out of the Kitchen – 2 – Anybody Can Do Anything', *Women's Session*, Box 15, 15 May 1952.

Donkin, Nancy, 'Come Out of the Kitchen – 3 – Taking the Irk Out of Housework', *Women's Session*, Box 15, 29 May 1952.

Downing, (Cecilia) John and Bill Newnham (interviewer), 'The Housewives' Association and a Bill of Rights for the Home', *Women's Session*, presented by Sheila Hunt, AA SP 300/1 Box 7, 28 September 1949.

Farr, Maude, 'On Being a Housewife', *Women's Session*, AA C3224/1, 12 November 1951.

Goulton, Miss K. and Mr A.L. Baker, 'In My Opinion – Women and War Work', AA SP300/1, Box 8, 31 October 1942.

Jenkins, Ida Elizabeth, *Women's Session*, AA C3224/1, 12 November 1951.

Kirke, B.W., Memo to the Federal Director of Talks and the Federal Controller of Programmes, 27 May 1943. AA SP341/1/1 File II, 1938–1943, File 15.5.

Listener's letter (Cranston, Campaine, Tasmania), AA SP3224/1, *Women's Session*, Box 3, 21 October 1947.

Listener's letter (Weethall, NSW), AA SP3224/1, *Women's Session*, Box 3, 21 October 1947.

Listener's letter (Kalourouse, Victoria), AA SP3224/1, *Women's Session*, Box 3, 21 October 1947.

'Marriage as a Full-time Career' debate, C3224/1, *Women's Session*, Box 3, 28 October 1947.

Mayne, Mrs Bruce, 'Marriage as a Career', C3224/1, *Women's Session*, Box 3, 14 October 1947.

Hepzibah, Menuhin, Script by, C3224/1, *Women's Session*, Box 5, 25 February 1948.

Contented Housewife (Mrs Gerrard), C3224/1, *Women's Session*, Box 5, 25 February 1948; Script by guest editor: Hepzibah Menuhin (Mrs Nicholas): 'Woman's Place in Society, with Contented Housewife (Mrs Gerrard), Discontented Homemaker (Mrs Calvert), Mr Husbands (Mr Taylor) & (Lindsay Biggins)', C3224/1, *Women's Session*, Box 5, 25 February 1948; Contented Housewife (Mrs Gerrard), C3224/1, *Women's Session*, Box 5, 25 February 1948; Discontented Housewife (Mrs Calvert), C3224/1, *Women's Session*, Box 5, 25 February 1948; Mr Husband 2 (Lindsay Biggins), C3224/1, *Women's Session*, Box 5, 25 February 1948.

Mitchell, Janet, 'This Changing Australia – Part 1', AA SP300/1, 16 August 1942.

Progressive Housewives' Association, 'Objectives 1946', Records, A6122/45 Item 1291.

'Talks – Sessions – Women's Session', AA B2114/6, 13/3/18, Part 6, Script broadcast 14 August 1956; 'Memo, 27 July 1956, 'Talks – Sessions – Women's Session', AA B2114/6, 13/3/18, Part 6.

Wellings, V., AA SP300/1, 'V. Wellings Talks', Box 6, 28 October 1941.

'Women Talking – No More Private Worlds for Women' – part of the *Women's Session* of 18 November 1941. AA SP300/1, 'W's General', Box 6.

'A Woman's World', *Women's Session*, presented by Clare Mitchell, AA SP300/1 Box 5, 13 June 1947.

Index